Unstuck and On Target!

AGES 11–15

Unstuck and On Target!

AGES 11–15

An Executive Function Curriculum to Support Flexibility, Planning, and Organization

by

John F. Strang, Psy.D.
Children's National Hospital
Washington, D.C.

Lauren Kenworthy, Ph.D.
George Washington University
Washington, D.C.

Lynn Cannon, M.Ed.
The Ivymount School
The Maddux School
Rockville, Maryland

Katie C. Alexander, OTD, M.S., OTR/L
The Occupational Therapy Institute
La Mesa, California

Monica Adler Werner, M.A.
Monica Werner Counseling
Chevy Chase, Maryland

Cara E. Pugliese, Ph.D.
George Washington University
Washington, D.C.

and

Laura Gutermuth Anthony, Ph.D.
The University of Colorado
Aurora, Colorado

Baltimore • London • Sydney

Paul H. Brookes Publishing Co.
Post Office Box 10624
Baltimore, Maryland 21285-0624
USA

www.brookespublishing.com

Copyright © 2024 by Paul H. Brookes Publishing Co., Inc.
All rights reserved.

"Paul H. Brookes Publishing Co." is a registered trademark of
Paul H. Brookes Publishing Co., Inc.

Typeset by Progressive Publishing Services, York, Pennsylvania.
Manufactured in the United States of America by Sheridan Books, Inc.

Purchasers of *Unstuck and On Target! Ages 11–15: An Executive Function Curriculum to Support Flexibility, Planning, and Organization* are granted permission to download, print, and photocopy the worksheets in the text for educational purposes. These forms may not be reproduced to generate revenue for any program or individual. Photocopies may only be made from an original book. *Unauthorized use beyond this privilege may be prosecutable under federal law.* You will see the copyright protection notice at the bottom of each reproducible page.

Cover image © Adobe Stock/Paul Bradbury/Caia Image.
Clip art © iStock.com and stock.adobe.com.

Library of Congress Cataloging-in-Publication Data

Names: Strang, John F., author.
Title: Unstuck and on target! Ages 11–15: An executive function curriculum to support flexibility, planning, and organization / John F. Strang, Lauren Kenworthy, Lynn Cannon, Katie C. Alexander, Monica Adler Werner, Cara E. Pugliese, Laura Gutermuth Anthony.
Description: Baltimore: Paul H. Brookes Publishing Co., 2023. | Includes index.
Identifiers: LCCN 2023000779 (print) | LCCN 2023000780 (ebook) | ISBN 9781681254876 (paperback) | ISBN 9781681254883 (epub) | ISBN 9781681254890 (pdf)
Subjects: LCSH: Children with mental disabilities—Education. | Youth with mental disabilities—Education. | Executive functions (Neuropsychology) | Critical thinking—Study and teaching
Classification: LCC LC4601 .S76 2023 (print) | LCC LC4601 (ebook) | DDC 370.15/2—dc23/eng/20230111
LC record available at https://lccn.loc.gov/2023000779
LC ebook record available at https://lccn.loc.gov/2023000780

British Library Cataloguing in Publication data are available from the British Library.

2027   2026   2025   2024

10   9   8   7   6   5   4   3   2

Contents

About the Online Materials vii
About the Authors viii
Acknowledgments x
Introduction xi

Unit 1	**Flexibility, Power, and Planning**	1
Topic 1.1	Flexible Thinking	2
Topic 1.2	Plan A/Plan B = More Power	15
Topic 1.3	How to Increase Your Power to Help Yourself and the World	29
Topic 1.4	Coping Strategies to Feel Better and Get Unstuck When Overwhelmed, Stressed, Frustrated, or Disappointed	40
Topic 1.5	Flexible Thinking—Accepting and Letting Go of Frustration and Disappointment	54
Topic 1.6	Putting a Plan on Trial (Checking Your Plan Before Trying It Out)	65
Topic 1.7	Celebration Day! The Plan B Party	77
Unit 2	**Compromise**	83
Topic 2.1	Compromising Is a Win-Win	84
Topic 2.2	Should I Compromise?	96
Topic 2.3	Try Out Your Compromise Skills	105
Topic 2.4	Plan Another Special Event Together Using Compromise Skills (Two Sessions)	113
Topic 2.5	The Special Event	121
Topic 2.6	Reviewing the Special Event	126
Unit 3	**Efficient Planning**	131
Topic 3.1	Getting (and Staying) Excited About a Future Goal	132
Topic 3.2	Efficient Planning—Staying Focused on the Big Picture Goal	142
Topic 3.3	Efficient Planning—Watching the Clock	150
Topic 3.4	Pulling It All Together—Using All the Key Vocabulary/ Skills to Finalize the Plan	158
Topic 3.5	The Longer-Term Event/Project—Efficient Planning = Power!	165
Topic 3.6	Reviewing the Longer-Term Event/Project: Learning from Our Successes and Challenges	171

Unit 4	**Making Executive Function Skills Work in Your Life**	177
Topic 4.1	Developing a Personal Goal: Using Executive Function Skills in Our Real Lives	178
Topic 4.2	Using Executive Function Skills for Personal Goals	189
Topic 4.3	Putting Personal Plans on Trial	196
Topic 4.4	Preparing for Graduation: Celebrating Our Executive Function Skills	204
Topic 4.5	Graduation	211
Appendix A	Questions for Reflection	219
Appendix B	Troubleshooting FAQs: When Challenges Come Up	221
	I'm having a hard time keeping my students engaged. What should I do?	221
	I feel like I am constantly nagging and redirecting the students. What should I do?	221
	How can I help my students use the Key Vocabulary and skills in their everyday lives, both in and out of school?	222
	Some of the Key Vocabulary terms and phrases seem to greatly annoy one of my students. How important is it for me to stick to the Key Vocabulary?	223
	What do I do if my students don't like an activity?	223
	My students are finding some of the concepts in these lessons too hard. How do I help them understand?	223
	How do I avoid power struggles?	224
	Sometimes I can't tell what is willful misbehavior and what is an executive function difficulty. How can I make that distinction?	224
Index		227

About the Online Materials

Unstuck and On Target! Ages 11–15: An Executive Function Curriculum to Improve Flexibility, Planning, and Organization offers online companion materials to supplement and expand the knowledge and strategies provided in this text. In addition to the Worksheets and Home Extensions in this text, purchasers of the book may access, download, photocopy, and print the workbooks, posters, and PowerPoint files for educational purposes. The online materials include:

- One digital Student Workbook, available as a fillable PDF
- One digital Parent Workbook
- Two digital posters, available as print-ready PDFs and PowerPoint files
- 21 Lesson PowerPoint files

To access the materials that come with this book:

1. Go to the Brookes Publishing Download Hub: http://downloads.brookespublishing.com
2. Register to create an account (or log in with an existing account)
3. Redeem the code **mvcLaduiC** to access any locked materials.

PRINTED MATERIALS SOLD SEPARATELY

Printed copies of the Student Workbook (sold in packs of 5) and a printed copy of the Power Equation Poster can be purchased separately at www.brookespublishing.com.

About the Authors

John F. Strang, Psy.D., is Associate Professor of Neurology, Psychiatry, Behavioral Sciences, and Pediatrics at the George Washington University School of Medicine and a neuropsychologist and Director of the Gender and Autism Program at Children's National Hospital in Washington, D.C. Dr. Strang completed his bachelor and master's degrees at the University of Michigan and his doctoral degree in clinical psychology at George Washington University. His research focuses on adolescent development, including the impact of executive functioning differences on a young person's ability to effectively advocate for their needs. Dr. Strang is an expert in autism and gender development, including the common intersection of autism and gender diversity. Community-based participatory research methods, partnering with autistic community members to drive research priorities, is a focus of Dr. Strang's work. Dr. Strang identifies as neurodivergent and celebrates that multiple members of his family are autistic.

Lauren Kenworthy, Ph.D., is Professor of Neurology, Pediatrics, and Psychiatry at the George Washington University School of Medicine, Chief of the Neuropsychology Division, and Director of the Center for Autism Spectrum Disorders at Children's National Hospital. Dr. Kenworthy received her Bachelor of Arts degree from Yale University and her doctoral degree from the University of Maryland. Her research interests are in describing, supporting, and treating neuropsychological phenotypes in autism. She is the author of more than 85 peer-reviewed publications and three treatment manuals, and a coauthor of the Behavior Rating Inventory of Executive Function. She has participated in more than 25 funded research projects related to executive function, treatment evaluation, and child development.

Lynn Cannon, M.Ed., is a social learning specialist at The Ivymount School and The Maddux School. Ms. Cannon received her master's degree in special education from the University of Virginia. For more than 15 years, she has worked as an educator, administrator, and program director, serving students with neurodevelopmental disabilities. Ms. Cannon is also a coauthor of *Solving Executive Function Challenges: Simple Ways to Get Kids with Autism Unstuck and on Target* (Paul H. Brookes Publishing Co., 2014), a resource guide for educators and parents; *The Conversation Club* (Autism Asperger Publishing Company, 2018), an instructional manual for teaching conversation skills to students with neurodevelopmental disabilities; and IvySCIP, an assessment, individualized education program development tool, and curricular resource for children with neurodevelopmental disabilities. Her research and teaching interests are in developing interventions and support materials for students with neurodevelopmental disabilities and their families, therapists, and educators.

Katie C. Alexander, OTD, M.S., OTR/L, is an occupational therapist and clinician-researcher. Dr. Alexander received her Bachelor of Science and postprofessional graduate degrees from the University of Kansas Medical Center. For almost two decades, she has specialized in community and school-based intervention for individuals with neurodevelopmental disabilities, and she served as the founding program director for the Model Asperger Program at The Ivymount School. Her research and clinical interests are in developing interventions and supports that improve the daily lives of neurodivergent individuals and their families. Through her work as an author and national presenter, Dr. Alexander remains committed to enhancing evidence-based and collaborative practices across professional disciplines.

About the Authors

Monica Adler Werner, M.A., is a counselor working in private practice in the Washington, D.C., area. Prior to that she was the director of the Model Asperger Program (MAP) at The Ivymount School. In that capacity, she spearheaded the development of a social learning curriculum that emphasizes problem solving, self-advocacy, and self-regulation while keeping students on track academically. She is a coauthor of the first edition of *Unstuck and On Target!* (Paul H. Brookes Publishing Co., 2011) and *Solving Executive Function Challenges: Simple Ways to Get Kids with Autism Unstuck and on Target* (Paul H. Brookes Publishing Co., 2014). She is the coauthor of numerous papers and posters about working with children with Asperger syndrome/high-functioning autism. Prior to joining The Ivymount School staff, Ms. Werner co-founded Take2 Summer Camp, a program designed to pilot the application of evidence-based social skills programs. Ms. Werner has an undergraduate degree from the University of Pennsylvania and a master's degree from Johns Hopkins University. She has completed the coursework for her Board Certified Behavior Analyst certification.

Cara E. Pugliese, Ph.D., is Associate Professor of Psychiatry, Behavioral Sciences, and Pediatrics at the George Washington University School of Medicine and a clinical psychologist at the Center for Autism Spectrum Disorders at Children's National Hospital. Dr. Pugliese received her Bachelor of Arts degree from the University of Richmond and her doctoral degree from Virginia Polytechnic Institute and State University. Dr. Pugliese specializes in the assessment and treatment of children and adolescents with autism spectrum disorders, with an emphasis on transition to adulthood. Her research interests include the development, evaluation, implementation, and dissemination of evidence-based interventions into community settings to reduce disparities in access to care and improve quality of life for autistic individuals. In this context, she values community-based participatory research methods and stakeholder partnerships to ensure that interventions are relevant, strengths-based, and engaging. Dr. Pugliese has authored or coauthored more than 20 publications and received or participated in 10 externally funded research grants.

Laura Gutermuth Anthony, Ph.D., is Professor in the Division of Child and Adolescent Psychiatry, Department of Psychiatry, University of Colorado School of Medicine, and a psychologist at the Children's Hospital of Colorado. Dr. Anthony completed a dual degree doctoral program in clinical and developmental psychology at the University of Illinois, Chicago, in 1997. She has focused most of her research and clinical work on children with neurodevelopmental disabilities and authored or coauthored more than 75 publications. She has also received or participated in 32 externally funded research grants. She has specialized training and research experience using Community Based Participatory Research methods and partnerships to develop interventions, contextualize and disseminate results, and implement findings in the community. In 2021, she was appointed the inaugural Director of Research for Child and Adolescent Mental Health at the University of Colorado.

Acknowledgments

Special thanks to the following, who provided significant contributions to the development of *Unstuck and On Target! Ages 11–15: An Executive Function Curriculum to Support Flexibility, Planning, and Organization*

Alexis Khuu (Children's National Hospital)

Reid Caplan (Accessible Academia)

Bonnie Beers (The Ivymount School)

Bryan Keith Lester (The Ivymount School)

Jamie Rina Park (The Ivymount School)

Naomi Baum-Skorija (The Ivymount School)

Marquis Clements (The Ivymount School)

Katerina Dudley (Children's National Hospital)

Sydney Seese (Children's National Hospital)

Mary Troxel (University of Colorado Denver)

Sara Cooner (Fairfax County Public Schools)

Jonathan Hopkins

The Organization for Autism Research

Gudelsky Family Foundation

Fairfax County Public Schools

Children's National Hospital Division of Pediatric Neuropsychology and Center for Autism Spectrum Disorders

The many students, educators, and families who have helped to shape this intervention

This project would not be possible without the insight, creativity, and patience of our incredible editor, Sharon Larkin (Senior Acquisitions Editor, Brookes Publishing). We are deeply grateful to have such a terrific partner whose talents help bring our ideas to such beautiful life. Thank you, Sharon.

Introduction

GOAL OF THIS MANUAL

Unstuck and On Target! Ages 11–15: An Executive Function Curriculum to Support Flexibility, Planning, and Organization is a plan of action for teaching students how to develop their executive function skills in key areas, including flexibility, big picture thinking, planning, compromising, and self-monitoring.

WHO WILL BENEFIT FROM THIS INTERVENTION?

Unstuck and On Target! Ages 11–15 is designed for students ages 11 through 15 years who struggle with executive function skills, including flexibility, organization, and planning. It may be especially helpful for autistic students as well as students with attention-deficit/hyperactivity disorder (ADHD), anxiety, or other related diagnoses.

WHO SHOULD TEACH THIS CURRICULUM?

Unstuck and On Target! Ages 11–15 is designed for use in small classes or groups, with 10–12 students max. *Unstuck* is suitable for school-, clinic-, or community-based settings and can be taught in daily to weekly sessions led by a professional (e.g., a teacher, psychologist, social worker, speech-language therapist, occupational therapist, counselor, or highly trained teaching assistant). Those teaching this curriculum should read the entire manual beforehand and have experience working with students with a range of learning needs, as well as an understanding of positive reinforcement techniques.

WHAT IS EXECUTIVE FUNCTION?

Executive function is a set of brain-based abilities that help people control their behavior (e.g., staying seated at a desk) and reach their goals (e.g., finishing something with multiple steps, like getting ready for school). There are many different skills that make up executive function, including the following:

- **Initiation:** Getting started on something quickly and easily.
- **Inhibition:** Showing impulse control and thinking before acting.
- **Flexibility:** Shifting easily from one activity or idea to another and being able to accept a different way of seeing or doing things.
- **Working memory:** Keeping information in mind while performing a task, like remembering directions while driving to your destination.
- **Organization:** Keeping track of materials, understanding what the main point is, seeing the big picture, and knowing what the top priority is at any given time.

- **Planning:** Developing, carrying out, and modifying a plan of action for a multistep assignment, such as a science fair project.
- **Self-monitoring.** Tracking your performance by asking questions like "How am I doing?" and "Am I doing what I am supposed to be doing?"

WHY TEACH EXECUTIVE FUNCTION?

Executive function skills underlie all aspects of our lives and are particularly relevant for school and learning settings. As children get older, demands on their executive function skills increase, as they are tasked with increasing amounts of independent work while also being expected to successfully collaborate with their peers. The number of abstract and flexible thinking tasks also increases, and by middle school, students are expected to independently generate organizational strategies, such as structuring a paper or presentation, taking notes, and developing approaches for independent learning and studying. Fortunately, executive function skills can be taught using fairly simple techniques. *Unstuck and On Target! Ages 11–15* makes use of simple, research-based educational methods to improve executive function skills in young teens.

HOW THIS CURRICULUM HELPS YOU TEACH EXECUTIVE FUNCTION SKILLS

Although executive function skills provide a foundation for some of the most complex human behaviors (e.g., planning our futures and flexibly responding to a changing world), the skills are themselves fairly easy to teach.

The *Unstuck and On Target! Ages 11–15* curriculum is composed of 24 topics, which should occur over the course of a school year (or part of a school year). We intentionally use the word topics instead of lessons so that, as necessary, educators can extend a topic beyond a single class period. We encouraged educators to think of the topics as "chapters," each of which may take some time to unpack with the class. Some of the topics will clearly require multiple sessions, which is indicated at the beginning of the lesson. We recommend taking sufficient time to get through the material in the first unit of the curriculum so that students feel comfortable with the basic concepts, Key Vocabulary, and techniques. The time the educator spends reading and preparing the seven Unit 1 topics is also critical and will allow for smooth implementation of the *Unstuck* curriculum. This is not the type of curriculum that can be conducted effectively without having first read through and prepared the topic prior to class.

>   Note: Some topics may require you to gather additional materials not typically found in a classroom or school.

Here are the key techniques used in the *Unstuck* curriculum to support students' executive function skills:

- **The curriculum should be offered in small classes.** The curriculum should be taught in small classes with 10–12 students at the most. Classes should meet at least once a week or more often if necessary. The plans and activities in each topic are important, though you have the flexibility to adapt each topic to best reach your students. For example, educators are encouraged to simplify any language that might be too complex for their students. The educator is also encouraged to share techniques taught in the *Unstuck* classes (particularly the Key Vocabulary and visuals) with the students' other educators and team members so that the skills can be reinforced (see the "encourage generalization" guidelines below).
- **Incorporate the Key Vocabulary.** The most critical component of this curriculum is the use of Key Vocabulary. The Key Vocabulary is a set of words or short, catchy phrases that communicate the basic skills taught in the curriculum. Key Vocabulary is designed to be easily incorporated into instruction, conversation, problem solving, and everyday life. Educators should aim to use the Key Vocabulary as much as possible, ideally employing one of the words or phrases in every other sentence spoken to the students. Students should be encouraged to

use the Key Vocabulary and related skills on their own and in all settings at school and home. Praise and reward your students when they use the Key Vocabulary and keep a list of the words and phrases present and visible at all times as a reminder for everyone to use them. New Key Vocabulary is introduced as the curriculum progresses but be sure to continue using the vocabulary introduced in previous sessions whenever you can, so by the end of the curriculum all of the key words and phrases are employed regularly.

- **Use visuals to highlight key points.** People who struggle with executive function often benefit from the use of visuals to help them remember to use the skills. *Unstuck and On Target! Ages 11–15* is a richly visual curriculum with accompanying PowerPoints for each topic and a central poster meant to be displayed and referred to by the educator throughout each class. The poster and worksheets can also be shared as visual reminders in the student's general education classrooms and at home.

- **Encourage generalization.** People with executive function challenges often have difficulty remembering to use their skills in different settings. For example, they may remember to use their new skills in their *Unstuck* class but may struggle to use them in their other classes and at home without reminders to do so. Because the Key Vocabulary in this curriculum is easily used in many settings, the students' academic educators may incorporate these words and phrases into their own classroom routine. Other educators are also encouraged to post key *Unstuck* visuals in their classrooms. Additionally, at the end of each topic, parents and caregivers are given home extension worksheets that encourage use of the Key Vocabulary, skills, and visuals during their daily routines at home.

- **Keep it positive and fun.** A key component to improving executive function is the students' ability and motivation to use the skills spontaneously in different parts of their lives. The job of educators and interventionists is to help students fall in love with the Key Vocabulary and skills by presenting them in positive and fun ways.

- **Avoid using Key Vocabulary in negative, critical, or punitive ways;** otherwise, your students may come to dislike these words and skills. Research shows that when educators model flexibility and positivity, that attitude is mirrored by their students. A simple formula for nurturing classroom positivity is to use at least four specific praise statements (or gestures, or other ways of communicating praise) for every correction or command. Praising statements should clearly identify what the student has done well. Here are a few examples:

"David, I really like how you use Plan A/Plan B. Awesome work!"

(praise #1)

"I'm proud of this class—you all came up with a great compromise."

(praise #2)

"Nice work, David, that was flexible thinking."

(praise #3)

"Good work." (followed by a thumbs up)

(praise #4)

"David, can you help us come up with a Plan B? It seems our group is a little stuck."

(a correction, presented in a simple and positive way)

Next, offer a praising statement to maintain a 4:1 praise-to-correction ratio.

- **Target students' motivation.** The *Unstuck and On Target! Ages 11–15* curriculum was developed with the help of young teens, and the activities are designed to be meaningful and appealing to this age range. Modifications and additions to the curriculum are encouraged if they will increase student motivation and engagement. Here are a few motivational techniques that may be helpful:

- **Focus on the "why."** A central part of each topic is giving the students a chance to think about and discuss why the skills presented are important. By bringing these skills to a personal level, students are able to consider how they are relevant to their lives now and in the future. In examining why a skill is important, the adolescent is building motivation for using the skill.

- **Use humor and playfulness.** Humor can be an effective way to connect with your students and to engage them in using their new executive function skills. Because your students will have different ideas of what's funny, you may need to tailor your humor to each individual student.

- **Model the Key Vocabulary and skills.** Focus on yourself to start, rather than on the problems and challenges of your students. Later, as your students become more comfortable with the Key Vocabulary and related skills, you can begin to use them to address their challenges. Focusing on your own problems to start takes pressure off the students and allows them to begin to learn the Key Vocabulary and skills without feeling criticized. If students can help fix your challenges (either real or invented), they get a great opportunity to practice the skills and appreciate how powerful they can be. For example, if your Plan A was to watch a video with the class but the Internet went down, you could mention that you feel stuck and ask the class to help you come up with a Plan B (e.g., watching the video during the next class).

- **Use materials, visuals, activities, and examples that connect with your students' interests.** For example, if a student has particular interest in computers, they may respond well if Key Vocabulary is translated into the world of computers. You could say, *"When I'm stuck it's like when my computer gets frozen. Then I need to be flexible and reset."*

- **Link the Key Vocabulary, skills, and activities to real, motivating power in your students' lives.** For example, if your students are motivated by social justice, they may be inspired by a goal of raising money for refugees. If a student has a passion for astronomy, link the Power Equation to their dream of being an astronomer: *"Your goal is to become an astronomer. Science is one skill you will need. You will also need flexibility, big picture thinking, and planning,"* or *"Nice work using a Plan B, Kim; you are one step closer to becoming an astronomer."*

- **Reduce complexity of language.** The use of simple visuals helps support young people with executive function challenges. Long periods of talking and using more complex language don't stick with students as well as the use of Key Vocabulary and visuals. **Note:** Since overly complex visuals can be overloading and confusing to some students, keep visuals simple and straightforward. If there's enough interest from the class, students can also help design and create their own visuals.

- **Use the Power Plan.** Each lesson starts and ends with a Power Plan. This visual is the essence of the unstuck approach: Goal-Why-Plan-Check. The Power Plan sets out the Goal and Plan at the beginning of each class. At the end of the class, students can Check if they followed their plan, as well as discuss Why the Goal was important. Last, the Power Plan helps students notice if they are getting off track, or stuck.

- **Focus on doing over knowing.** Although there are many key concepts to be taught, the most important part of the curriculum is the doing (i.e., practicing) of the skills in many different settings. If students feel that they already know the skills (e.g., "I know what compromise is" or "I know how to plan"), change the focus to the goal of making these skills habits by saying something like: *"I know you know about planning, and you've done some great planning already. This class is about getting into the habit of planning in lots of different parts of your life so that you can get more power. Let's use this skill to help plan your English paper."*

- **Think Can't, Not Won't.** Key to the success of *Unstuck* is the concept of can't, not won't. Tragically, students struggling with executive function challenges are often labeled in many negative ways (e.g., lazy, inconsiderate, rigid) when in fact their real brain-based differences are the issue. If we acknowledge that a student can't, or can't *yet*, do something, we teach the skills and strategies in *Unstuck*, turning can'ts into cans. The key idea is to move away from explanations of student behavior as willful or disobedient and instead focus on students' neurodiversity and individual patterns of strengths and weaknesses.

Table A.1. Reasons for Unexpected Behaviors

What looks like *won't* . . .	May actually be *can't yet*
"Oppositional, stubborn"	• Cognitive inflexibility • Protective effort to avoid overload
"Can do it when they want to"	• Difficulty shifting from one thing to another • Trouble paying attention to what other people think is important • Subtle changes in demands can drastically impact performance
"Self-centered"; "Doesn't care what others think"	• Impaired social problem solving • Trouble understanding subtle social cues
"Doesn't try"	• Difficulty getting started (initiation) • Impaired planning and trouble generating new ideas
"Won't put good ideas on paper"	• Poor fine motor skills • Trouble organizing thoughts in a way that makes sense to a reader
"Sloppy, erratic"	• Problems monitoring/checking • Overload • Impaired impulse control
"Won't control outbursts"	• Overload • Impaired inhibition or impulse control
"Prefers to be alone"	• Impaired social understanding • Needs a break from processing complex social information • Social system just works differently (i.e., less socially motivated)
"Doesn't care about what is important"	• Natural ability to focus on details, but has a harder time relating to the big picture/main idea or other people's priorities

A final powerful idea: The developers of this curriculum, along with autistic adults, educators, parents, and therapists who have used the curriculum, have often described the *Unstuck* executive function skills and vocabulary as useful not only for the students, but also for themselves. For example, the Plan B routine is a powerful tool for a person of any age to help them manage unexpected and/or challenging situations (e.g., forgetting your wallet, getting a flat tire). With this in mind, educators are encouraged to apply these skills in their everyday lives and to model them in ways that make the skills and vocabulary come to life for their students. By sharing some of your own flexibility and planning challenges, as well as how you are working to apply the *Unstuck* executive function skills and vocabulary in your life, you're truly collaborating with your students and learning together.

UNIT 1

Flexibility, Power, and Planning

TOPIC 1.1 Flexible Thinking

BIG PICTURE SUMMARY

This topic teaches and encourages students to practice the language and skills for flexible thinking, an important part of executive functioning. In this topic, students will learn through simple experiments that being flexible helps you get more of what you want and need. The important concept of getting **stuck on a detail** instead of practicing **big picture thinking** is also introduced.

Key Things to Do (This topic will take more than one class period to complete)

Here are the two most important things to do in today's class:

1. Use the following Key Vocabulary often and in fun and playful ways:

    ★ Executive Function Skills

    ★ Flexible

    ★ Flexible Thinking

    ★ Stuck/Unstuck

    ★ Stuck on a Detail

    ★ Big Picture

    ★ Plan A/Plan B

2. **Find ways to spontaneously model flexibility *at least once* during class today.** Something going wrong during class (or in an unexpected way) is a perfect opportunity to model flexible thinking! You can also stage unexpected events to provide opportunities to demonstrate and practice flexibility with students. For example: *"My **Plan A** was to play this video for you, but it's not working. So, I need a **Plan B**! Can anyone use **flexible thinking** and help me come up with a **Plan B**?"*

Key Vocabulary

The Key Vocabulary is a critical part of the curriculum; it is more important than the actual activities in each topic! The Key Vocabulary should be spoken as often as possible and should be presented in fun and enjoyable ways. Avoid punitive uses of the Key Vocabulary because that can interfere with student buy-in and use of the words and skills. The goal is to get your students to *want* to use the Key Vocabulary and related skills in their everyday lives.

Materials

★ Unit 1 Daily Self-Awareness Rating (this worksheet can be copied for each student or found in the Student Workbook)

★ PowerPoint for Topic 1.1, projected

★ Videos demonstrating that flexible objects can be stronger (or find similar videos if these links do not work):

- Flexible Bridge: https://www.youtube.com/watch?v=N7PFAofvztw

- Flexible Trees: https://www.youtube.com/watch?v=zdkEhg_BQ74

- Flexible Japanese Building: https://www.youtube.com/watch?v=uG37gQSvrf4

- ★ Pillows, chairs, and so forth for obstacle course
- ★ Stopwatch (to time obstacle course)
- ★ How to Boost Our Power Level: Reminder List (can be reproduced for each student; located on the Brookes Download Hub and in the Student Workbook)

EDUCATOR PLAN

Goal: Introduce and practice flexibility.

Why: Flexibility is an executive function skill that helps students gain more power and choice in their lives.

Plan: Do the following before class:

- ★ Watch the "flexible objects can be stronger" videos before class to make sure that the links are still current and you know what to expect. Pull up the videos, so they're ready to show.
- ★ Project the PowerPoint for Topic 1.1.

CLASS LESSON PLAN

Slide 1: Power Plan

1a. **Review with the class the goal and plan for today, pointing to the Power Plan visual for Topic 1.1.** Explain how the Power Plan works (see the Educator Note below). Ask students to imagine why today's goal is to learn how and why to be flexible. At the end of class, students will again be asked to give thoughts about the "why" behind today's goal.

Each topic has an accompanying Power Plan visual. This visual teaches students a routine for how to set a goal, develop a plan, and check progress toward reaching the goal. It reminds students of the importance of having a Plan B if Plan A does not work out. It also reminds students of the risk of getting "stuck," which can interfere with moving forward with a goal and a plan. Finally, the visual indicates that by setting a goal, planning, and following through, students are increasing the power in their lives to get what they want and need.

1b. Introduce the purpose of the group. Get students excited about the skills and the group. Here are some key discussion points to cover:

* In this group, we'll be doing games and planning fun parties and events.
* Our goal is to practice executive function skills. These skills include being flexible, setting goals, and planning.
* These skills will help us get more power and choice in our lives.
* Why is power and choice important in your lives?

1c. Briefly brainstorm the kinds of power this group can help students gain. Ask students in what areas of their lives they want more power, freedom, and choice. Be careful to affirm your students' ideas as much as possible. The next topic will discuss the difference between realistic and unrealistic power, but for this topic we just want to build enthusiasm. Here are some examples of powers that this group can help to build:

* The power to make friends
* The power to get good grades
* The power to earn money
* The power to get more say in your life
* The power to get a car someday
* The power to succeed with your goals
* The power to have more choice in your life

Slide 2: Skills We'll Practice in This Group

2. Briefly introduce and discuss the main skills that will be practiced in this group:

   * Flexible thinking
   * Focusing on the big picture
   * Being kind to yourself and others
   * Setting goals and making plans
   * Knowing when and how to compromise

   Here are some key discussion points to cover:

   * Have your students vote on each skill—ask them if they're using the skill already.
   * Go through each skill or several of them individually and ask: How does this skill help you? How does this skill help you get more power?
   * Ask students why they think it's important to practice this skill and make it a habit.

Slide 3: How to Boost Your Power and Get More of What You Want and Need

 3. **Introduce Power Boosters—ways to increase your power and get more of what you want and need**, titled How to Boost Our Power Level: Reminder List (also included in the Student Workbook). Here are some key discussion points to cover:

* We are here to help each other get more power in our lives.

- ★ It is important to support each other—we are a team, so whenever one person is flexible, we all benefit.
- ★ Let's explore some ways that we can increase our power with each other.

"We're flexible. We share the conversation. We don't get stuck on too many details. We give everyone a chance to talk." Review these key concepts: Be flexible; don't just get stuck on your ideas; speak up and include others by giving them time to talk, too; ask questions about people's ideas; show interest in people's ideas.

"We have flexible feelings. If possible, we let go of our frustration and get unstuck." Review this key concept: We all get frustrated sometimes, and it is our job to use coping strategies to feel calmer so that we can get unstuck and meet our goals.

"We care about people. We are kind to ourselves and others." Review these key concepts: Listen to people; pay attention to people's feelings; be kind when you give feedback.

 At the end of this topic, the How to Boost Our Power Level: Reminder List offers more specific behaviors that increase and decrease power. (This list can also be found in the Student Workbook.)

Slide 4: Power Equation

4. **Introduce the Power Equation, using your finger to trace the directions of power (left to right).** You can use or adapt this script:

   "This is the Power Equation. This equation tells us how we can increase the power in our lives to get more of what we want and need and to make the world a better place. These skills that help us build our power—they're called executive function skills. And these executive function skills include being flexible, using big picture thinking, and setting goals and making plans."

   Here are some key discussion points to cover:
   - ★ We get more power and choice in our lives by being flexible, by using big picture thinking, and by setting goals and making plans.
   - ★ I know you use many of these skills already.
   - ★ We're going to practice getting really good at these executive function skills and making them a habit.
   - ★ Let's discuss the meaning of the different parts of the Power Equation.
   - ★ Can you come up with examples for different parts of the equation? For example, how did being flexible or planning help you get more power in your life?

Slide 5: Flexibility (the First Part of the Power Equation)

5. **Introduce and discuss the power of flexibility.** Here are some key discussion points to cover:
   - ★ Flexibility is one of the best ways to boost our power.
   - ★ Flexibility helps us get what we want because we don't get stuck.
   - ★ When we're stuck, we may not be able to move forward.

- ★ When we're stuck, we may not get what we want because we get off track.
- ★ Getting stuck means we might lose power. We might not get what we want.
- ★ Getting stuck can also annoy other people.
- ★ What are some ideas you have about the importance of flexibility?
- ★ Also, are there some situations when getting stuck might be the right thing to do (e.g., when standing up for civil rights and not backing down)?

Slide 6: Flexible–Rigid Table

6. **Draw a Flexible-Rigid Table on the board (or type in the PowerPoint Flexible-Rigid Table).** Ask students to provide examples under each column and write/type their examples in the table. Give ideas/hints if necessary. Continue to fill out the table during the next several activities (activities 6-8 that follow). Below is a sample Flexible-Rigid Table you can use as a model:

Flexible Things	Rigid/Stuck Things	Flexible Thinking	Stuck Thinking
1. Rubber band	1. Dry spaghetti	1. Trying Plan B when Plan A doesn't work	1. Giving up when it doesn't work the first time
2.	2.	2.	2.
3.	3.	3.	3.
4.	4.	4.	4.
5.	5.	5.	5.

Here is a sample script you can use as you fill in the table:

"There are different kinds of flexibility—physical flexibility and flexible thinking. In this group, we are going to focus on flexible thinking, but let's start by talking about flexible and rigid things. We have 60 seconds—name as many flexible and rigid things as you can!" Fill in the first two columns with student ideas.

Slide 7: Flexibility Videos: Flexibility Is Stronger

7. **Discuss how flexibility can make things stronger using the three short videos of physical objects bending but not breaking.** Begin to connect this to the idea of flexible thinking if the group is ready to do so. Add students' ideas to the Flexible Thinking and Stuck Thinking columns of the Flexible-Rigid Table. (Go back to Slide 6 if you're using the PowerPoint Flexible-Rigid Table.)

Show the following short videos, which demonstrate (through real-life scenarios) how being flexible often increases physical strength. After each video, ask students to think about how and why the object was powerful (e.g., because it was flexible and could bend, it didn't break).

Flexible Bridge: https://www.youtube.com/watch?v=N7PFAofvztw

Flexible Trees: https://www.youtube.com/watch?v=zdkEhg_BQ74

Flexible Japanese Building: https://www.youtube.com/watch?v=uG37gQSvrf4

Topic 1.1: Flexible Thinking

Here are some key discussion points to cover as you add ideas to the Flexible-Rigid Table:

★ How can being flexible make things stronger? (Flexibility allows things to bend and adapt instead of breaking.)

★ How can flexible thinking help you to be stronger?

★ How might stuck thinking make it harder to get what you want?

Slide 8: Obstacle Course: Flexible Is Faster

8. **Try this flexibility experiment with students to demonstrate how flexibility is faster.** Say to your students: *"In this flexibility experiment, I need you to make a simple obstacle course for me to walk through. I will go through it first with a **rigid** body and then a **flexible** body to see which is faster."* Make sure students understand the words rigid and flexible.

   Invite students to build a simple obstacle course using pillows, chairs, and so forth. Have them time with a stopwatch which is faster: when you go through the course with a totally rigid and stiff body (slower) or when you go through with a flexible body (faster). Make this fun and comedic.

   After the experiment, remind your students that *being flexible also helps us be faster.* Now transition to the idea of flexible thinking and ask students:

   ★ How does flexible thinking help us be faster and more efficient?

   ★ How does stuck thinking slow us down?

   Add students' ideas to the Flexible Thinking and Stuck Thinking columns of the Flexible-Rigid Table. *(Go back to Slide 6 if you're using the PowerPoint Flexible-Rigid Table.)*

Slide 9: Stuck on a Detail Versus Big Picture Thinking

9a. **Model stuck on a detail versus big picture thinking by role-playing.** Ask students to raise their hands when they notice you getting stuck on a detail. Here's a sample script you can use:

   "Flexible thinking is powerful. Getting stuck can make it hard for us to get what we want. It can also sometimes be annoying. In this experiment, my big picture idea is to describe my favorite animal, but I'm going to get stuck on a detail (maybe even a few details). Let me know when you can tell what detail I'm stuck on by raising your hand."

   Use the example below or create your own example of getting stuck (overfocused) on a detail such as your pet's feeding schedule. You can also try getting stuck on a detail at some point during the lesson and see if your students catch it. In the example below, getting stuck on the details about ostriches gets in the way of the big picture because it takes more time, and there are so many details that it gets hard for the listener to remember the main point.

   "So, I really like ostriches. They are my favorite animal. I always used to dream about having an ostrich as a pet, but then I learned that they probably wouldn't make the best pet. Actually, sometimes I even have dreams about ostriches at night—I think they are so cool. But as I said, probably not the best pet because they are way too

big for cages, and they can run faster than dogs (and people). They can be pretty aggressive, so I like to see ostriches from a distance or in shows. I don't know if you know, but ostriches can't fly—and if they could fly, that would be pretty wild because they can weigh up to 350 pounds! I can't really imagine a 350-pound bird flying around, but it sounds kind of scary. I bet you're wondering how I got interested in ostriches: I first saw ostriches at the zoo when I was a little kid, and now I like to watch shows and videos about them. I have a picture of an ostrich on my wall at home, and I was even thinking of naming my cat Ostrich. But then I decided that it would be a little weird to name a cat after a bird. I bet my cat would be scared of an ostrich, anyway, considering how big they are. I could talk about ostriches all day, and maybe I will . . . .

Now, sometimes it's useful to be stuck on a detail, but you can't be stuck on details all the time! So when we get stuck on details, we need to decide how long we want to be stuck on that interesting detail. For 1 minute or 2 minutes?"

Role-play other examples of getting stuck on a detail using student volunteers. To start, have students identify a big picture topic (e.g., discussing the best movie; answering "What's your favorite color?"). If your students show difficulty understanding the concept, you can role-play with them and continue modeling getting stuck on a detail. Or your students may be ready to playfully engage with getting stuck on a detail in improvised role-plays with each other. Introduce the question *"How long do you want to be stuck on that detail? One minute or 2 minutes?"* as a way of helping the class to manage getting stuck on details in such a way that it does not interfere with the big picture lesson goal.

Important Note

The stuck on a detail routine should be used throughout the remainder of the curriculum at any point during each class when student interest in a detail could get in the way of the lesson goal, topic, or activity (or big picture). Whenever a student (or the educator!) gets stuck on a detail, such as a specific off-topic idea, you can ask, *"How long do we want to be stuck on that interesting detail?"* The important point here is to praise the student or the class for their interesting topic and also remind them that at some point we will need to get back to the main topic or activity, which we call the big picture.

After you ask, *"How long should we be stuck on this interesting detail?"* you can present a couple of choices: *"Thirty seconds or 1 minute?"* Then use a timer to time the 30 seconds or 1 minute duration. When the time's up, you can say, *"Great! We were stuck on the detail for 1 minute, and now we can get back to the big picture."* This gentle approach to getting back on task can help students who struggle with maintaining the big picture topic and being flexible to improve their self-regulation skills.

9b. **Have students help you complete and review the Flexible Thinking/Stuck Thinking part of the Flexible-Rigid Table.** *(Go back to Slide 6 if you're using the PowerPoint Flexible-Rigid Table.)*

Say to your students: *"Now let's go back to our table. What do we know about flexible and rigid thinking?"* Have the students brainstorm different kinds of flexible and stuck thinking. Provide support and examples as needed.

- ★ **Examples of flexible thinking:** Trying a new way of doing something, listening to another person's ideas, moving on when stuck on an idea, considering a different perspective

- ★ **Examples of stuck thinking:** Getting stuck on one idea, trying only one way, ignoring other people's ideas, missing the big picture because you're stuck on a detail

Slide 10: Topic 1.1 Wrap-Up: Why Practice Flexibility?

10a. **Ask students why our goal was to learn how and why to be flexible.** Point to the Why section on the Power Plan. Students can fill in the answer, or just discuss. Gently lead discussion to focus on how flexibility can help us gain more power in our lives. Ask students to consider how they might use flexibility at school or home to help them increase their power to get more of what they want and need. Also mention the term executive function and explain that flexibility is one of the most important executive function skills. If students have heard about executive functioning, they can discuss what they know about it. Make sure to affirm the variety of thoughts and opinions the students give so all of the students feel heard and celebrated.

10b. **Ask the students to fill out the Unit 1 Daily Self-Awareness Rating worksheet by marking an X somewhere on the arrow to show how they are feeling.** Let them know that it helps you to know how they are feeling.

10c. **Send Home Extension for Topic 1.1 home with students or e-mail it to parents.** Encourage parents to read this handout and follow the suggested tips with their child at home.

10d. **Talk to other educators about generalization opportunities in other classes.** Share the Executive Function Skills List with your students' educators (this handout is found at the end of Topic 1.1 and can be copied). Ask the other educators to post the list in a highly visible location, so their students can remember to use the Key Vocabulary spontaneously during class. Explain to educators the use of the Key Vocabulary:

- ★ Educators should work to integrate the words into lessons and discussions with the entire class, not just a few students.

- ★ Educators should use the words in a positive way, not as a punishment.

- ★ For this week, educators should focus on the following Key Vocabulary words: flexible thinking, stuck/unstuck.

- ★ Help educators come up with a few examples of how they could use these words during their lessons. For example:

  - In history class: *"Benjamin Franklin was a **flexible thinker**. He wasn't **stuck** on what already was. He thought **flexibly** and came up with new inventions. For example, his **flexible thinking** helped him invent swim fins and the lightning rod. He even invented a new musical instrument."*

  - In science class: *"Okay, our first try with the experiment didn't work, but let's not be **stuck** there! Let's use **flexible thinking** and try it in a slightly different way."*

  - In any class: *"Thank you for helping me get **unstuck**. You helped me see a different way of thinking about that problem. That's **flexible thinking**!"*

> **CHECK:** How are my students doing?
> Do I need to make any adjustments for next class?

- ★ Were students engaged?
- ★ It is critical to give the students praise much more often than commands/corrections. Did I maintain a 4:1 praise-to-correction ratio? (Avoid using Key Vocabulary in negative, critical, or punitive ways; see the Introduction for more information.)
- ★ Did I reinforce the Key Vocabulary during class?
- ★ How can I help my students use the Key Vocabulary and skills in their everyday lives?
- ★ Are there specific words or activities that students do not like? If so, can I come up with alternatives?
- ★ Was this topic too hard?
- ★ Did I get into a power struggle with a student?
- ★ Am I having trouble telling the difference between executive function difficulties and willful behavior? (See the section Think Can't, Not Won't in the Introduction for more information.)

These questions also appear in Appendix A so that you may use them for reflection after each unit. If your answers to the questions above suggest that adjusting your approach could be helpful, see the Troubleshooting section (Appendix B) for guidance on how to proceed.

TOPIC 1.1: Flexible Thinking

DAILY SELF-AWARENESS RATING: UNIT 1

NAME: _____

Executive Function Skills

Flexibility + Big Picture Thinking + Goals and Planning = POWER

Mark an X on the arrow to show how you feel today:

How flexible are you today?

Stuck   Somewhat Flexible   Very Flexible

Are you stuck on details today?

Stuck on Details   Somewhat Stuck on Details   Focused on the Big Picture

TOPIC 1.1: Flexible Thinking

HOW TO BOOST OUR POWER LEVEL: REMINDER LIST

How to Get **More** of What You Want *How to increase your power*	How to Get **Less** of What You Want *How to decrease your power*
Using a calm voice	Using a loud voice
Leaving space for other people to talk	Interrupting
Asking what other people want: *"What do you want to do?"*	Not including what other people want
Using kind words: *"Cool. I'm not sure it will work, but it's a good idea."*	Using harsh words: *"No, that would never work," "That's wrong," "My idea is better."*
Flexible feeling and thinking	Stuck feeling and thinking
Making kind suggestions: *"Do you want to put that on top?"*	Telling people what to do: *"Put that on top."*
Participating	Getting distracted or distracting other people

TOPIC 1.1: Flexible Thinking

HOME EXTENSION FOR TOPIC 1.1: FLEXIBLE THINKING

In today's topic, students learned about *flexibility*. Flexibility is an important executive functioning skill. Just as students can build a flexible body, they can also build a *flexible mind*. Being flexible helps you get more of what you want, creating *more power* in your own life. They learned that getting stuck on a detail can prevent them from seeing the big picture. Getting "unstuck" can help students reach their goal, get what they want, and gain more power in their lives.

In the next topic, students will learn an important way to be flexible: When a first plan (Plan A) doesn't work, they can be flexible and choose another plan (Plan B).

Here are the Key Vocabulary words and skills your child is learning about:

Flexible	*Flexible Thinking*	*Unstuck*
Stuck	*Stuck on a Detail*	*Big Picture*
Plan A/Plan B		

Your child will be watching a Pink Panther, Minecraft Pig and Apple, or Chicken Little video during our next group session. The Pink Panther video, called "Think Before You Pink," shows the Pink Panther making many different plans to cross a busy street. He comes up with one Plan B after another. In the Minecraft Pig and Apple video, the pig tries various plans in order to get an apple that is out of reach. In the Chicken Little video, Chicken Little quickly shifts from Plan A to Plan B to Plan C to achieve his goal to save the planet from alien invasion.

See if you can find these videos by searching the Internet and watch the videos with your child (they are only a few minutes long). We found the videos here:

- Pink Panther video: https://www.youtube.com/watch?v=mPzCkajdLvE
- Pig and Apple [Minecraft Animation]: https://youtu.be/gwVlsv1n7Mo
- Chicken Little video: https://youtu.be/RicWg5H9QIM

The next time your child hits an obstacle, ask them, "What would Pink Panther (or Pig) do right now?" ("He'd come up with another plan!") or "Should we try Pink Panther's (or Pig's) way and come up with a Plan B?"

TOPIC 1.1: Flexible Thinking

EXECUTIVE FUNCTION SKILLS LIST

Flexible thinking
"Thanks for being flexible!"
"Nice job being flexible."
"You were flexible and got what you wanted even faster. Nice job!"

Plan A/Plan B
"If Plan A doesn't work, then we'll try a Plan B."
"I'm feeling stuck—my Plan A didn't work. Can you help me come up with a Plan B?"
"Do you need a Plan B?"

Stuck/Unstuck
"How can I get unstuck?"
"Nice work. You were flexible and got unstuck."
"You noticed you were stuck and then got unstuck. That's how you boost your power!"

Goal-Why-Plan-Check
"What's the goal?"
"Why is the goal important?"
"What are the steps of the plan?"
"Let's check to see if we reached our goal."

Are we focused on our big picture goal or stuck on an off-topic detail?
"What's our big picture goal?"
"Is this an off-topic detail?"
"Should we get stuck on this detail or get back to our big picture goal?"

Compromise
"Let's come up with a compromise."
"Compromising lets us both get some of what we want."
"Nice compromise! It's a win-win for both of you."
"You both let go of your Plan A so you both could get *some* of what you want. That is a winning compromise and helps you boost your power!"

Efficiency = doing a task well and fairly quickly
"Keep your eyes on the prize—stay focused and excited about your goal!"
"Keep your eyes on the clock—don't get stuck on off-topic details!"
"Great work. You were efficient. You didn't get stuck."

Managing frustration and disappointment
"Being disappointed is normal. How can we manage it?"
"When we're frustrated, there's always a Plan B!"

TOPIC 1.2   Plan A/Plan B = More Power

BIG PICTURE SUMMARY

Many teenagers want more choice. Their drive for more choice and power can motivate them to learn and use executive function skills like flexible thinking. In this topic, students will consider how being flexible can earn people more power in their lives. This isn't about having power over *every* decision; it's about learning ways to gain more power. With more power, you have more choices (as shown in the Power Equation). The Plan A/Plan B skill and the idea of gaining power through flexible thinking will be practiced in a game.

Key Things to Do (This topic may take more than one class period to complete)

Here are the two most important things to do in today's class:

1. **Use the following Key Vocabulary often and in fun and playful ways:**
    - ★ Executive Function Skills
    - ★ Power
    - ★ Flexibility
    - ★ Flexible Thinking
    - ★ Stuck/Unstuck
    - ★ Plan A/Plan B
    - ★ Stuck on a Detail
    - ★ Big Picture

2. **Find ways to spontaneously model flexibility *at least once* during class today.** Something going wrong during class (or in an unexpected way) is a perfect opportunity to model flexible thinking! You can also stage unexpected events to provide opportunities to demonstrate and practice flexibility with students. For example: *"We're all working on **flexible thinking** together. I have a **flexibility** challenge today: I forgot my lunch! I thought you all could help me come up with some possible **Plan Bs** for what to do!"*

Materials

 ★ Unit 1 Daily Self-Awareness Rating (this worksheet can be copied for each student or found in the Student Workbook)

 ★ PowerPoint for Topic 1.2, projected

 ★ Realistic-Unrealistic Power List. This list can be shown in PowerPoint, written on the board, or printed (all printables can be found at the end of each topic). The list is also in the Student Workbook.

★ Plan A/Plan B videos:
  - Pink Panther video: https://www.youtube.com/watch?v=mPzCkajdLvE
  - Pig and Apple [Minecraft Animation]: https://youtu.be/gwVlsv1n7Mo
  - Chicken Little video: https://youtu.be/RicWg5H9QIM

- ★ The Power Game supplies (pick either of these two options):
  - • The Power Game board (printable) and several game pieces (not included; e.g., red, green, and blue pieces from another board game)
  - • Five pieces of paper, each with one of the following words printed: Goal, Plan A, Plan B, Plan C, Power Zone (post each piece of paper in a different part of the classroom)
- ★ Optional: How to Boost Our Power Level: Reminder List (printed from Topic 1.1 or located in the front cover of the Student Workbook)

EDUCATOR PLAN

Goal: Students will learn how we can gain more power by using the Plan A/Plan B skill (flexible thinking).

Why: Being able to shift from a Plan A to a Plan B (or C) helps students face challenges, setbacks, and unexpected changes.

Plan: Do the following before class:

- ★ Watch the Plan A/Plan B videos prior to class and select the one that best matches your students' interests and maturity level. Pull up the link, so they're ready to show during class.
- ★ Practice leading the Power Game before class. Decide whether the class will use the game board (printable) and game pieces (not included) or use stations set up around the classroom (see the Power Game supplies above and Activity 7 below).
- ★ Project the PowerPoint for Topic 1.2.

CLASS LESSON PLAN

Slide 1: Power Plan

1. **Review with your class the goal and plan for today, pointing to the Power Plan visual for Topic 1.2.** Ask the class to think about why we are learning how to be flexible. You can ask, *"Why does it give us power? What is Plan A/Plan B?"* Following the discussion, ask the students to fill out the Unit 1 Daily Self-Awareness Rating worksheet.

Slide 2: Power Boosters: How to Boost Your Power and Get More of What You Want and Need

 2. **Review and discuss Power Boosters (from Topic 1.1)—ways to increase your power and get more of what you want and need** (also duplicated in the Student Workbook). Here are some key discussion points to cover:

- ★ We're here to help each other learn executive function skills so that we can have more power in our lives.

- ★ We're a team, so it is important to support each other.
- ★ Here are some ways that we can increase our power together:

  "We're flexible. We share the conversation. We don't get stuck on too many details. We give everyone a chance to talk." Review these key concepts: Be flexible; don't get stuck too much on your ideas; speak up and include others by giving them time to talk, too; ask questions about people's ideas; and show interest in people's ideas.

  "We have flexible feelings. If possible, we let go of our frustration and get unstuck." Review these key concepts: We all get frustrated sometimes, and it is our job to use coping strategies to feel calmer so that we can get unstuck and meet our goals.

  "We care about people. We are kind to ourselves and others." Review these key concepts: Listen to what people are saying; pay attention to people's feelings; be kind when you give feedback.

- At the end of Topic 1.1, the How to Boost Our Power Level: Reminder List offers more specific behaviors that increase and decrease power. (This list can also be found in the front cover of the Student Workbook.)

Slide 3: Realistic–Unrealistic Power List

3. **Discuss the difference between realistic and unrealistic power.** Write a Realistic–Unrealistic Power List on the board or type in the PowerPoint table. Ask the class to come up with examples of unrealistic power (e.g., the power to see the future, the power to rule the world). Then have them come up with examples of realistic power (e.g., the power to make a friend, the power to get better grades, the power to earn money).

Here are some key discussion points to cover:
- ★ In this class, we are learning how to get more realistic power in our lives now and in the future.
- ★ In what parts of your life do you want more power? In what parts of your life do you want more choice, freedom, or independence?
- ★ When we don't have power, we don't have as much choice. Why?
- ★ Examples:
  - If you have the power to study for and pass your classes, you have the ability to choose a better college and get a job you enjoy.
  - If you don't have the power to earn money, you might not have the choice to buy a new computer when your computer stops working.
  - Can you think of more examples of how power gives you more choice?

Slide 4: Power Equation

4. **Review the Power Equation, noting how flexibility is a great way to build power.** Discuss **flexibility** by briefly reflecting on the activities from the last topic: the Flexible–Rigid Table, the flexibility videos, the obstacle course (Flexible Is Faster), and the **stuck on a detail** example(s). Ask the class to consider how flexibility can increase our power.

Here are some key discussion points to cover (have the class come up with examples of these):

- ★ Flexibility can make us stronger—it often helps us adapt.
- ★ Flexibility can give us more choices, so we aren't stuck.
- ★ Flexibility helps us be faster and more efficient.
- ★ Being stuck can slow us down.
- ★ Being stuck can be annoying to other people.
- ★ When we're flexible, it helps other people be flexible.
- ★ Being flexible can give us a lot of power.
- ★ Sometimes it's important to be stuck on a detail—but we don't want to be stuck for too long.

Important Note

Stuck on a Detail Routine: As described in Topic 1.1, use the stuck on a detail routine whenever a student (or educator!) gets stuck on a detail like a specific off-topic idea (e.g., a video game, a subject of deep interest or passion). Ask one of the following questions: *"How long do we want to be stuck on that interesting detail?"* or *"Do we want to get stuck on that detail or get back to the big picture?"* If the class wants to get stuck on the detail, you can say, *"Great! Do we want to be stuck on it for 30 seconds or 1 minute?"* Then use a timer to count 30 seconds or 1 minute. When the time is up, you can say, *"Great! We were stuck on the detail for 1 minute, and now we can get back to the big picture."* This gentle approach to getting back on task can help improve the self-regulation skills of students who struggle with staying on topic and being flexible.

Slide 5: Plan A/Plan B = Power

5. **Introduce Plan A/Plan B (a routine for getting unstuck).** Here are some key discussion points to cover:
   - ★ Getting stuck can make us lose power.
   - ★ We might not get what we want when we're stuck.
   - ★ We need a way to get unstuck.
   - ★ Plan A/Plan B is a powerful way to get unstuck.
   - ★ When our Plan A doesn't work, we don't give up—we try a Plan B (Plan C, etc.).
   - ★ Plan A/Plan B is flexible thinking.

Slide 6: Plan A/Plan B Video

6. **Watch the Pink Panther, Minecraft Pig and Apple, or Chicken Little video (depending on class interest and maturity).** Introduce the video and ask students to pay attention

to how many different plans the characters use. Place a hash mark on the board each time someone notices a new plan. Here's a sample script you can use:

"Here the Pink Panther is trying to cross the street (or the pig is trying to get the apple, or the characters are trying to return the alien baby to its parents). Does he get stuck and just give up, or does he use flexible thinking? Let's count how many times he was flexible and used a Plan B. Tell me each time he uses a Plan B and I'll put a mark on the board so we can count them at the end."

The videos for this activity can be found here:

Pink Panther video: https://www.youtube.com/watch?v=mPzCkajdLvE

Pig and Apple [Minecraft Animation]: https://youtu.be/gwVIsv1n7Mo

Chicken Little video: https://youtu.be/RicWg5H9QIM

Here are some key discussion points:

- How many plans did they come up with?
- Were they flexible?
- If they had been stuck, would they ever have met their goal?
- Plan A/Plan B helps you get what you want—it helps you be flexible.
- Plan A/Plan B can be lots of fun!
- Plan A/Plan B = power.

Teaching Key Vocabulary: As you teach the Key Vocabulary throughout the topic, consider leaving out parts of a phrase and having the students complete the phrase. For example, you could say, *"Plan A . . ."* and then gesture for the students to say "Plan B." Or say, *"So when you're flexible, you get more . . ."* and let the students supply the word "power" (perhaps giving them a hint with the sound of the letter "p").

Slide 7: The Power Game

Power Game Options

For the Power Game, choose from these two options:

A. Use the game board (printable) with game pieces (not included).

B. Set up stations in the room with the following labels posted on them and have students move from station to station as the game progresses:

- Goal (e.g., on the educator's desk)
- Plan A (e.g., at the whiteboard)

- Plan B (e.g., on the door)
- Plan C (e.g., at the back of the room)
- Power Zone (e.g., on the computer)

7. **Explain the Power Game before students start playing.** Say, *"We're going to play the Power Game. The **goal** of the Power Game is to practice using the Plan A/Plan B skill to overcome obstacles. **Why** is this game useful? Because Plan A/Plan B helps us be flexible in our daily lives. And being flexible increases our power to get more of what we want and need."*

   Briefly summarize how the game works using the steps below as a guide. Don't go into too much detail—the students will learn how to play by doing it:

   1. Choose two to three teams of students.
   2. Start with Level 1 goals, then move on to Level 2 goals (see below or PowerPoint).
   3. Have one team complete Steps 4-13, followed by the next team.
   4. Start at the **goal** location (on the game board or at the educator's desk in the classroom): Read the **goal** out loud.
   5. Read the obstacle out loud. Remind students that obstacles are opportunities to be flexible and come up with another plan.
   6. Once the team comes up with a realistic **Plan A** to overcome the obstacle, they should move to the **Plan A** location on the game board or in the classroom.
   7. Make up a second obstacle or ask the students from the other team(s) to come up with a second realistic obstacle.
   8. When the playing team comes up with a realistic **Plan B** to overcome the second obstacle, they should move to the **Plan B** location on the game board or in the classroom.
   9. Make up a third obstacle or ask students from the other team(s) to come up with a third realistic obstacle.
   10. When the playing team comes up with a realistic **Plan C** to overcome the third obstacle, they should move to the **Plan C** location on the game board or in the classroom.
   11. As the final step in each round, in order to move to the **Power Zone**, ask the playing team to answer one of the following Power Questions (or make up your own). If students are really struggling, model your own flexibility by saying, *"I can be flexible and pick another question"*:

       Why is Plan A/Plan B important?

       Why is power important?

       Where do you want more power in your lives?

       What is one kind of realistic power?

What kind of flexibility are we talking about?

What does it mean to get stuck on a detail?

What is an example of an unrealistic power?

Why is flexibility important?

What is an example of using Plan A/Plan B in your life?

What does it mean to be stuck?

What is an example of getting stuck on a detail?

12. After the team answers a Power Question, they should move to the **Power Zone** location on the game board or in the classroom.

13. When a team moves into the **Power Zone**, they earn a point for the class. Keep a tally on the board and celebrate how many points the students earn!

Here is an example of an event sequence when playing the Power Game:

Goal: Go bike riding.

Obstacle 1: The bike has a flat tire.

Plan A: Get the tire fixed (move to Plan A on game board or in classroom).

Obstacle 2: The store is too far.

Plan B: Ask parents for a ride (move to Plan B).

Obstacle 3: Parents don't have time today.

Plan C: Find out when parents will have time (move to Plan C).

Power Question: Why is Plan A/Plan B important?

Answer: It helps you get unstuck, so you can reach your goals. In this example, having a Plan B helped me get my bike fixed so I could go biking (move to the **Power Zone**).

Slide 8: The Power Game Level 1 Scenarios

The Power Game scenarios are listed in PowerPoint slides 8 and 9. You can also create your own scenarios or have students create scenarios for themselves (just make sure the goals are realistic).

8. **Level 1: Basic Goals and Obstacles for the Power Game**

   ★ **Goal:** You've planned a hike.

   Obstacle: It rains.

   ★ **Goal:** You have a friend over to play a video game.

   Obstacle: One person wins every game.

   ★ **Goal:** You know you have math homework.

   Obstacle: You didn't write it down in your agenda book.

- ★ **Goal:** You want to buy a video game as soon as it is released.
  Obstacle: You can't find your wallet.
- ★ **Goal:** You want to go over to a friend's house.
  Obstacle: Your friend is sick.
- ★ **Goal:** You need to get to the store to buy something for school.
  Obstacle: Your dad gets a flat tire.
- ★ **Goal:** You need to eat breakfast before the bus comes.
  Obstacle: Your sibling ate the last of your favorite cereal.

Slide 9: The Power Game Level 2 Scenarios

9. Level 2: Advanced Goals and Obstacles for the Power Game
   - ★ **Goal:** You are 16 years old, and you want to learn how to drive.
     Obstacle: Your parents don't think you're mature enough to drive.
   - ★ **Goal:** You are in high school, and you want to be a computer programmer someday.
     Obstacle: Your grades aren't where they need to be to get into college.
   - ★ **Goal:** You want more friends.
     Obstacle: You aren't very flexible, and you just talk about your own interests all the time.
   - ★ **Goal:** You are an adult and want to live on your own.
     Obstacle: You don't have a job.
   - ★ **Goal:** You are an adult, and you need a way to get to work.
     Obstacle: You don't own a car.
   - ★ **Goal:** You want a good grade in math.
     Obstacle: You keep forgetting your homework.
   - ★ **Goal:** You want your friend to hang out with you.
     Obstacle: You always get stuck on one game, and your friend doesn't like that game.

Slide 10: Flexibility = Power

10a. **Wrap up the Power Game.** Here's a sample script you can use: *"Nice job! We're getting more and more flexible, and when we're flexible, we get more power. But what's so good about getting power? Why does it matter? Let's discuss how the Power Game is like real life."*

10b. **Discuss how the Power Game is like real life**—for example, we have goals but sometimes there are obstacles. To get past the obstacles we have to be flexible and come up with Plan Bs, which help us meet our goals. Using the Realistic-Unrealistic Power List as a starting point, review different types of realistic power that can be earned by being flexible. Discuss the different kinds of power students would like to gain in their own lives.

Here are some key discussion points to cover:

- ★ We have goals, but sometimes there are obstacles, so we have to come up with Plan Bs.
- ★ Plan Bs (Cs, etc.) help us meet our goals, so we don't get stuck.
- ★ Getting more power means that we have more choice and control in our lives.
- ★ Power = more choice (refer to the Power Equation).
- ★ We're practicing how to get more power in our lives by being flexible and making plans.
- ★ We're going to practice flexibility and planning by organizing some fun parties and events together in the next few weeks.
- ★ What kinds of power can be earned by being flexible—for example, the power to make friends, power to get better grades, power to earn money, power to get more of what we want?
- ★ What kinds of power do you want?

10c. Discuss how we are flexible with words in this group. Here's a sample script you can use: *"I know we may be using some words in a new way and with different meanings. For example, as we continue to meet, you will see that power doesn't only mean getting things immediately and exactly your way. You are doing a great job thinking flexibly."*

10d. Praise students for their flexibility, and note that by being flexible, they can increase the power in their lives to get what they want and need.

Important Note

When Students Struggle to Accept New Words and Ideas: Some students may struggle with new ideas. Affirm those who question or challenge the ideas by saying something like *"I know you may not totally believe in all of this yet, and I completely understand that. In our upcoming classes, we are going to continue to talk about this. I think you will see how this can work for you as we go along. I'm asking you to keep an open mind and let me know if you feel the same way by the end."*

Slide 11: Topic 1.2 Wrap-Up: Why Practice Coming Up With Plan Bs?

11a. Ask students why we talked about how being flexible helps us gain power. Point to the Why section of the Power Plan and ask students to fill in the answer or just discuss. Gently lead the discussion to focus on how flexibility can help us gain more power in our lives. Ask students to consider how they might use the flexibility and Plan A/Plan B skills at school or home to help them get more power. Occasionally mix in the term executive function, and explain that flexibility is one of the most important executive function skills. If students have heard about executive functioning, they can discuss what they know about it. Be sure to affirm the variety of thoughts and opinions the students give, so all of the students feel heard and celebrated.

11b. Send Home Extension for Topic 1.2 home. You can send this home with students or e-mail it to parents.

11c. Look for generalization opportunities in other classes. Keep encouraging your students' other educators to use Key Vocabulary from the Executive Function Skills List (found at the end of Topic 1.1). Have the other educators been able to post the Executive Function Skills List in their classrooms? Discuss the Plan A/Plan B skill with the educators and encourage them to use this language in their classes and lessons. For example, an educator might say, *"Our Plan A was to get through Chapter 2 today. We didn't quite make it, which is okay, so we'll try a Plan B: We'll finish Chapter 2 tomorrow."*

> **CHECK:** How are my students doing?
> Do I need to make any adjustments for the next class?

- ★ Were students engaged?
- ★ Did I maintain a 4:1 praise-to-correction ratio? (Avoid using Key Vocabulary in negative, critical, or punitive ways; see the Introduction for more information.)
- ★ Did I reinforce the Key Vocabulary during class?
- ★ How can I help my students use the Key Vocabulary and skills in their everyday lives?
- ★ Are there specific words or activities that students do not like? If so, can I come up with alternatives?
- ★ Was this topic too hard?
- ★ Did I get into a power struggle with a student?
- ★ Am I having trouble telling the difference between executive function difficulties and willful behavior? (See Think Can't, Not Won't in the Introduction for more information.)

See Appendix A for a list of questions to guide your self-reflection and refer to the Troubleshooting section (Appendix B) to address common problems or any challenges that may have arisen with the curriculum.

TOPIC 1.2: Plan A/Plan B = More Power

DAILY SELF-AWARENESS RATING: UNIT 1

NAME: _____

Executive Function Skills

Flexibility + Big Picture Thinking + Goals and Planning = POWER

Mark an X on the arrow to show how you feel today:

How flexible are you today?

Stuck   Somewhat Flexible   Very Flexible

Are you stuck on details today?

Stuck on Details   Somewhat Stuck on Details   Focused on the Big Picture

TOPIC 1.2: Plan A/Plan B = More Power

REALISTIC–UNREALISTIC POWER LIST

Realistic Powers

- ✓ Power to make more decisions
- ✓ Power to make friends
- ✓ Power to make money
- ✓ Power to get good grades

Unrealistic Powers

- ✓ Power to turn invisible
- ✓ Power to teleport

TOPIC 1.2: Plan A/Plan B = More Power

THE POWER GAME

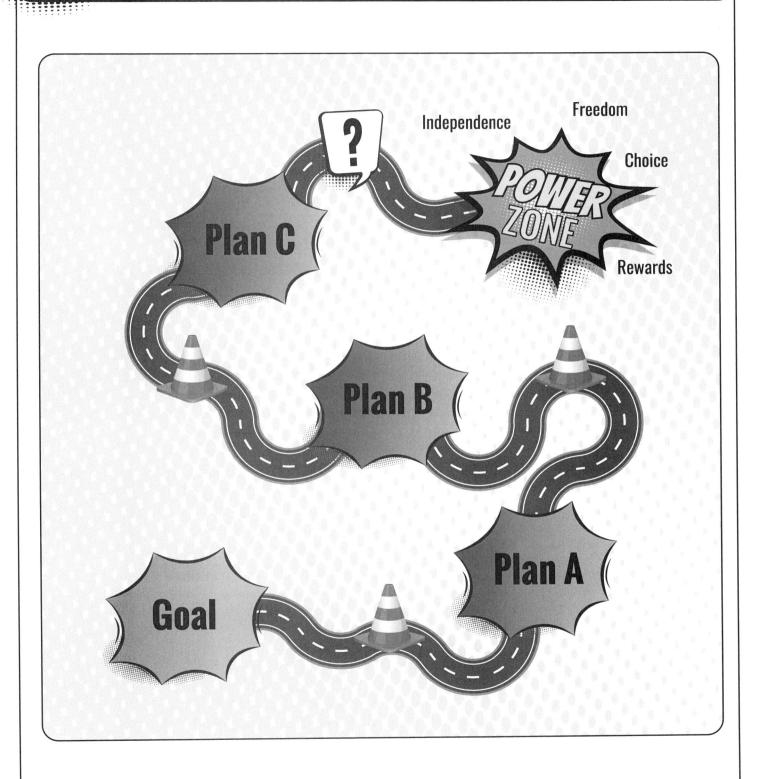

TOPIC 1.2: Plan A/Plan B = More Power

HOME EXTENSION FOR TOPIC 1.2: PLAN A/PLAN B = MORE POWER

Summary: Teenagers often want more choice. Their drive for more choice and power can help motivate them to learn and use executive function skills like flexibility. In today's topic, your child considered how being flexible earns people more power. This is not about having power over every decision but is about learning ways to get more power, so they have more choices in their lives.

Key Vocabulary/skills:

Flexible	*Flexible Thinking*	*Unstuck*
Stuck	*Stuck on a Detail*	*Big Picture*
Plan A/Plan B	*Goal*	

How to use the Key Vocabulary: Try to use the flexibility words above on a daily basis. Work to make this fun, without putting pressure on your child to be flexible. Do not criticize your child for being stuck, but instead praise them for being flexible!

1. **Practice Key Vocabulary in your daily life:** Be playful with your child in a way that they will enjoy. You can tell your child that you are confused about what the Key Vocabulary words mean and need some help to understand them. Be careful not to use these terms in a negative way and try to use them in reference to yourself rather than your child. Let your child be the teacher and you be the student. Offer lots of praise if they use any of the vocabulary on their own. Consider asking:

   "What's the big picture in this situation?"
   "Do we want to get stuck on that interesting detail, or should we get back to the big picture?"
   "Is my Plan A working? Do I need a Plan B?"
   "I've hit an obstacle. I need a Plan B."

2. **Share your experiences:** Share with your child an example from your life in which you are stuck and need a Plan B. If possible, find a real situation (something simple and easy to solve), or you can make up a situation. Gently mention that you are stuck and ask your child to help you think of a Plan B to solve your problem. For example: *"I want to make spaghetti and meatballs, but we're out of meatballs! I'm feeling stuck. I think I need a Plan B!"* During the week, continue to think out loud when you feel stuck (e.g., in a traffic jam or when something goes differently than expected), and ask your child to help you think of Plan Bs to help you get unstuck. Help your child feel powerful and helpful by using flexible thinking (and the vocabulary of flexibility) to solve your problems.

TOPIC 1.3 How to Increase Your Power to Help Yourself and the World

> **BIG PICTURE SUMMARY**

This topic teaches students to consider areas in their lives where they want and need more influence and power. Adolescents often seek freedom and control in their lives, and we have illustrated that idea in this curriculum through the word "power"—that is, wanting to gain more power over your life instead of other people controlling it.

In this topic, your students will learn that you gain more power in your life by doing things like being flexible, being kind to yourself and others, and using big picture thinking and planning. A key takeaway for students is "You gain power when you are kind to yourself and others and when you're flexible with other people because they will then be more kind, and flexible with you."

The Power Level system is introduced in this topic as a tool to help you reinforce important executive function skills such as flexibility, being kind to yourself and others, and thoughtful planning. This is a group system, and moving the Power Level card up the arrow on the Power Equation Poster shows students in a concrete way how using executive function skills (being flexible and kind and using Big Picture Thinking and Planning) increases their power and that of the group. (This Power Level system routine will be used throughout the remainder of the curriculum.) In today's class, flexibility, kindness, and big picture thinking and planning will be practiced and encouraged through the use of the Power Level system during three fun group planning tasks.

Key Things to Do (This topic may take more than one class period to complete)

Here are the two most important things to do in today's class:

1. **Use the following Key Vocabulary often and in fun and playful ways:**

   ★ Executive Function Skills
   ★ Power
   ★ Flexible
   ★ Flexible Thinking
   ★ Stuck/Unstuck
   ★ Planning
   ★ Plan A/Plan B
   ★ Stuck on a Detail
   ★ Big Picture
   ★ Be Kind to Yourself and Others

2. **Find ways to spontaneously model executive function skills (e.g., flexibility and planning) *at least once* during class today.** Make this fun and engaging! Use flexibility and planning skills with your students to solve challenges that come up naturally or

challenges that you've invented. For example, tell students you are teaching this curriculum for the first time and that there are a lot of things to remember. You've had to be flexible with your time, and instead of talking to your friend at lunch, you focused on your goal and reviewed the topic.

Materials

- Unit 1 Daily Self-Awareness Rating (this worksheet can be copied for each student or found in the Student Workbook)
- PowerPoint for Topic 1.3, projected
- Power Equation Poster, posted
- Power Level card: The Power Level card can be made using a sticky note or an index card with tape. If you have a magnetic strip mounted on the back of the Power Equation Poster, a magnet could also be used.
- 10 pieces of 8.5 × 11 paper, plus tape, straws, and string
- Optional: How to Boost Our Power Level: Reminder List (printed from Topic 1.1 or located in the front cover of the Student Workbook)

EDUCATOR PLAN

Goal: Students will learn how to increase their power to get more of what they want or need and help make the world a better place; practice working together in a group using flexibility, kindness, and big picture thinking and planning skills.

Why: People with executive function challenges often struggle to self-monitor. The activities in today's topic help students see how their use of flexibility, kindness, and big picture thinking and planning skills helps them increase their power and reach their goals.

Plan: Do the following before class:
- Post the Power Equation Poster.
- Project the PowerPoint for Topic 1.3.

CLASS LESSON PLAN

Slide 1: Power Plan

1. **Review with the class the goal and plan for today, pointing to the Power Plan visual for Topic 1.3.** Ask students to fill out the Unit 1 Daily Self-Awareness Rating worksheet.

 There is a Power Plan visual for each topic. The Power Plan visual teaches students a routine for how to set a goal, develop a plan, and check progress toward reaching the goal. It reminds students of the importance of having a Plan B if Plan A doesn't work out. It also reminds students of the risk of getting stuck, which can interfere with moving forward with a goal and plan. Finally, the visual indicates that by setting a goal, planning, and following through, students are increasing the power in their lives to get what they want and need.

Slide 2: Power Equation

2. Briefly review the different parts of the Power Equation (on the Power Equation Poster).

Stuck on a Detail Routine: As described in Topic 1.1, use the stuck on a detail routine whenever a student (or educator!) gets stuck on a detail like a specific off-topic idea (e.g., a video game, a subject of deep interest or passion). Ask one of the following questions: *"How long do we want to be stuck on that interesting detail?"* or *"Do we want to get stuck on that detail or get back to the big picture?"* If the class wants to get stuck on the detail, you can say, *"Great! Do we want to be stuck on it for 30 seconds or 1 minute?"* Then use a timer to count 30 seconds or 1 minute. When time's up you can say, *"Great! We were stuck on the detail for 1 minute, and now we can get back to the big picture."* This gentle approach to getting back on task can help improve the self-regulation skills of students who struggle with staying on topic and being flexible.

Slide 3: Power for Self and the World: Power Level

3a. **Point to the Power Arrow on the Power Equation (right side).** Discuss how increasing our power helps us 1) get more of what we want and need for ourselves (the lower box) and 2) helps us make the world a better place (the upper box). Tap into students' desires to make both their lives and the world better. Discuss the students' goals for themselves and the world and write their ideas into the two boxes above the Power Arrow on the Power Equation Poster.

Here are some key discussion points to cover:

★ Why is it important to have more power in your life to get more of what you want and need?

- ★ Why is it important to have more power to help make the world a better place?
- ★ What kind of power do you want and need for yourself and the world?
  - The power to make a positive impact on the world?
  - The power to help yourself?
  - The power to get the things you need in life?
  - The power to help people in need?
  - The power to help the environment and the planet?
  - The power to help things be more fair?
  - The power to fight racism?
  - The power to handle stress and setbacks?
  - The power to have free time for your own activities and interests?

3b. **Introduce the Power Level** as a way of showing how our power increases when we are kind to ourselves and others and use executive function skills like flexibility, big picture thinking, and planning. Explain that each person has their own Power Level in every moment of their lives. For example, *"We need power to improve our lives and the world. We have a Power Level with each person we interact with. We can boost our power and build relationships with others in different ways. We can boost our power by being kind to ourselves and others and using executive function skills like flexibility. When we're kind and flexible with others, they may be more kind and flexible with us. In this class we're going to practice increasing our power. We'll show our power going up on the Power Equation by adjusting our Power Level. And the Power Level is for all of us, including me, because we're a team. We'll use the Power Equation so we can start to see how and why our power can go up and how it can get stuck. We have a lot of control over our power, and we can use it in all parts of our lives."*

POWER LEVEL: The group's Power Level will be used in every session for the remainder of the program. In every class, the group's Power Level card will start at the bottom of the arrow on the Power Equation Poster. Students can practice flexibility, planning, and being kind during the group to help boost the group's power. Praise individual students, or the group as whole, for executive function skills they use such as being flexible, planning, or being kind to one another, while simultaneously raising the Power Level card part of the way up the arrow. Be careful to explain why the Power Level is going up, so students know that they are doing well. Find a way to praise each student at least once each class, so everyone feels connected to the group's progress and reaching the top of the arrow by the end of class.

> **Important Note**
>
> Remember, the Power Arrow and Power Level offer a way to help students learn to self-monitor and make connections between what they do and how they can boost their power to get more of what they want for themselves and the world. This is NOT an extrinsic reward-based behavior modification system like a point system. When you increase the Power Level and provide verbal feedback, your goal is to sound like a guide or coach, who's helping to build understanding and connection.

Slide 4: Power Boost and Power Loss: What Makes Our Power Go Up or Down?

4. **Discuss with the students what makes our power go up or down.** Here are some key discussion points to cover:
   - ★ **How do we make our power go up (Power Boost)?** Review the list provided on the PowerPoint slide and ask the class if they have other examples.
     - Being flexible
     - Being kind to yourself and others
     - Avoiding getting stuck on details
     - Including others and giving other people a chance to talk
   - ★ **What can make us lose power (power loss)?** Review the list provided on the PowerPoint slide and ask the class if they have other examples.
     - Getting overly stuck on a topic
     - Being unkind to yourself and others
     - Talking while others talk
     - Ignoring or excluding other people's ideas
   - ★ **How does being flexible increase our power?**
   - ★ **How does setting goals and making plans increase our power?**
   - ★ **How does being kind to yourself and others increase our power?** Here are two key ideas to cover:
     - When we are kind and flexible with other people, they may be more kind and flexible with us.
     - When we are flexible, it helps to improve our reputation and build relationships, and it makes our power go up. Why?

Slide 5: Practice Using the Power Level System: Story 1

5. **Show how the Power Level goes up or down using the story examples on this slide and the next one.** Although the Power Level card will go up and down during the story

below, remember that the Power Level should not drop when the Power Level card is being used to track the group's power.

Start with an introduction: *"So now we're going to practice to see how power can go up or down. Here is the Power Level card that will go up or down to show when power goes up or down."*

Take the Power Level card and affix it halfway up the arrow on the Power Equation Poster. Go through the story examples on this slide and the next one. Have a student read an example out loud and then have the class act out the story. This should be done in a fun and playful way—don't let things get too serious. Ask one student volunteer to move the Power Level card up or down based on whether the story is demonstrating a Power Boost or Power Loss.

Story 1: Building a Lego Tower

1. Read the following story, or ask a student to read it: *"The class is building a Lego tower together. Jack wants to make the tower using only red pieces. Jack is stuck on the idea that the tower needs to be red. Jack uses a loud voice, doesn't seem to care about what other people want, and uses harsh words to pressure the group to use red pieces only. He tells the other students what to do."*

2. Ask students to make a quick plan together and act out the story.

3. Have one student volunteer to move the Power Level card to show the Power Loss.

4. Discuss the following questions with the students: *"What happens to Jack's power? Why? Will other students want to be flexible with Jack? What could Jack do differently to increase his power? Let's try a Plan B version of the story where Jack increases his power."*

5. Have the students come up with and act out a new (Plan B) version of the story where Jack increases his power instead of loses power. Once again, a student volunteer should move the Power Level card, this time up the Power Equation Poster Arrow, to show that Jack builds power instead of losing it.

Slide 6: Practice Using the Power Level System: Story 2

6. Follow the same five-step sequence you used for Story 1, but swap in the following story.

Story 2: Building a Paper Airplane

"The class is working together on an assignment to build a paper airplane. It is due by the end of class. Erin and Jay get stuck on talking about Minecraft instead of working on the project. Then the rest of the class gets stuck on talking about Minecraft, and the project does not get finished."

Slide 7: Tracking the Power Level for Our Group

7. **Move the Power Level card to the bottom of the Power Arrow.** Explain to the students:

"Although we can't see it, each of us has a Power Level with the other people we interact with. And there's a lot we can do to increase our Power Level with other people,

like being flexible and kind, and avoiding getting stuck on our own topics too much. When any of us helps the group by being flexible or kind, we will raise the Power Level for the group—we will be working together as a team to reach our goals and gaining power!

 Optional: At the end of Topic 1.1, the How to Boost Our Power Level: Reminder List offers more specific behaviors that increase and decrease power (this list is also in the front cover of the Student Workbook).

Slide 8: Playing Group Planning Games While Keeping Track of Our Power

8. **Practice moving the Power Level card up when students show flexibility, kindness, and good planning while working together on a group activity.** Here's a sample script you can use: *"Let's have some fun. I have a few planning games for you. The trick is that we have to be flexible, be kind to ourselves and each other, and show good planning. That's what will help us be successful. While you're working together on these planning activities, I'll be moving the Power Level card up whenever you are flexible, work together as a team, show good planning skills, and are kind to yourself and to each other."*

   Start with the Power Level card at the bottom of the Power Arrow on the Power Equation Poster. While the class is doing the planning tasks below, clearly announce each time you notice a student using a skill (e.g., flexibility, kindness, planning skills) and move the Power Level card part of the way up the Power Arrow. Do not move the card down! Here are a few examples of what to say while moving the Power Level card:

   "Nice job, Jose; you were so flexible. You listened to Mesfin's idea. Our power is going way up."

   "Awesome work, group! You're giving everyone a chance to talk. Everyone's power is way up!"

   "I really like how Cindy was kind and flexible with Junaid. Power boost!"

   "Great compromise, guys! Our power is going up."

   "Wow, we are almost at the top of the Power Arrow, Tyreek—nice Plan B!"

   The following are two planning tasks that your students can work on together while you move the Power Level card based on the skills students show during the group activity. If it's helpful, the class can be split into two to three groups, with each group working with their own set of planning materials.

   ★ **Planning task 1:** Have the students work together to build the tallest structure they can using five pieces of tape, three pieces of paper, and two straws. Tell the students that their goal is to work together using power skills while you observe them and move the card up the Power Arrow. Ask them to see how high they can make the Power Level card go.

   ★ **Planning task 2:** Have the students work together to build a bridge connecting two chairs using three pieces of paper, three pieces of tape, string, and straws. Tell the students that their goal is to work together using power skills while you move the Power Level card up the Power Arrow.

Important Note

When Students Struggle to Accept Words/Ideas: Some students may struggle with new ideas. Affirm those who question or challenge the ideas by saying something like: *"I know you may not totally believe in all of this yet, and I completely understand that. In our upcoming classes, we are going to continue to talk about this. I think you will see how this can work for you as we go along. I'm asking you to keep an open mind and let me know if you feel the same way by the end."*

Slide 9: Topic 1.3 Wrap-Up: Why Are We Learning How to Gain More Power?

9a. **Ask students why our goal was to learn about gaining more power.** Point to the Why section of the Power Plan and ask students to fill in the answer or just discuss. Gently lead the discussion to focus on how flexibility, kindness, and working together to plan helps other people be more flexible with us. Also discuss with students some of the limits of flexibility and some of the situations in which flexibility may not be the most appropriate choice. Talk about how sometimes it is really important to stick to your idea, in other words, be a little stuck—for example, if people aren't listening to your requests for accommodations, or in situations where a person is being pressured to do something inappropriate or risky, it may be important to not give in. Ask students to consider how they might use flexibility and kindness at school and at home to help them get more power and success. Be sure to affirm the variety of thoughts and opinions your students give so that all your students feel heard and celebrated.

At the end of the group session today, praise the students for their flexibility and planning, and celebrate that they have increased their power by reaching the top of the Power Arrow. Remind the class that flexibility and planning skills are also known as executive function skills.

9b. **Send Home Extension for Topic 1.3 home with students or e-mail it to parents.**

9c. **Look for generalization opportunities in other classes.** Keep encouraging your students' other educators to use Key Vocabulary from the Executive Function Skills List (found at the end of Topic 1.1). Have the other educators been able to post the Executive Function Skills List in their classrooms?

Discuss with the other educators the Key Vocabulary related to setting goals and making plans. The following are examples of how educators might integrate the goal- and planning-related Key Vocabulary into their classes:

★ In any class: *"Our **goal** for today is . . . . Our **plan** for reaching this goal is . . . ."*

★ In history class: *"Dr. Martin Luther King, Jr. had **a Big Picture goal** of ending racism in the United States. His **plan** for moving toward this **goal** included nonviolent action."*

★ In math class: *"Our **goal** is to solve this problem. Our **plan** for solving the problem is to follow the order of operations: parentheses, exponents, multiplication, division, addition, and subtraction (PEMDAS)."*

> **CHECK:** How are my students doing?
> Do I need to make any adjustments for the next class?

See Appendix A for a list of questions to guide your self-reflection and refer to the Troubleshooting section (Appendix B) to address common problems or any challenges that may have arisen with the curriculum.

TOPIC 1.3: How to Increase Your Power to Help Yourself and the World

DAILY SELF-AWARENESS RATING: UNIT 1

NAME: _____

Executive Function Skills

Flexibility + Big Picture Thinking + Goals and Planning = POWER

Mark an X on the arrow to show how you feel today:

How flexible are you today?

Stuck   Somewhat Flexible   Very Flexible

Are you stuck on details today?

Stuck on Details   Somewhat Stuck on Details   Focused on the Big Picture

TOPIC 1.3: How to Increase Your Power to Help Yourself and the World

HOME EXTENSION FOR TOPIC 1.3: HOW TO INCREASE YOUR POWER TO HELP YOURSELF AND THE WORLD

In this week's topic, students learned that there are some easy ways to boost their power in the world. When we say "power," we mean the ability to get more of what you want and need. Some of the skills that increase our power and success are flexibility, kindness to yourself and others, and planning, which includes setting goals and making plans to achieve those goals.

By using these skills, your child will be better able to reach goals, increase their power, and gain more influence over their lives. When we are flexible and kind to ourselves and others, they are more likely to be flexible and collaborative with us. Your child tested this by working collaboratively on a group building project, while at the same time keeping track of their flexibility and kindness skills. We also talked about the fact that sometimes it is important to stick to your idea and not be flexible—for example, if people aren't listening to your requests for accommodations, or if someone is pressuring you to do something inappropriate or risky.

Key Vocabulary/skills:

Power (gaining more power in your life)   *Flexible*

Kindness to Yourself and Others   *Big Picture*   *Planning*

How to use the Key Vocabulary:

Praise your child when they do things to boost their power. Here are a few examples of power-building skills:

- Being flexible
- Giving others a chance to talk
- Asking questions about other's ideas
- Being kind to yourself and others
- Setting a goal and planning how to reach a goal
- Stepping back and considering the big picture (main idea)

When you see your child using any of the above skills, let them know that you like what you see. Try saying something like:

"Thanks for letting me talk. That helps me be more flexible with you."
"It's really kind and thoughtful of you to ask about my visit with Grandma. Power Boost!"
"What you said to Jon was so kind. I bet your power went up with him."
"Great to see you planning the steps for how to solve that problem."

Only point out positive behaviors. **Don't focus on the negative.**

TOPIC 1.4   Coping Strategies to Feel Better and Get Unstuck When Overwhelmed, Stressed, Frustrated, or Disappointed

BIG PICTURE SUMMARY

The purpose of this topic is to teach students that there's a scientific reason for why we experience feelings in our bodies. Students will identify bodily clues that indicate when they are feeling overwhelmed or stressed, and practice coping strategies to feel better and get back on target to reach their goals.

Key Things to Do (This topic may take more than one class period to complete)

Here are the two most important things to do in today's class:

1. **Use the following Key Vocabulary often and in fun and playful ways:**
   ★ Executive Function Skills
   ★ Coping Strategies
   ★ On/Off Target
   ★ Unstuck

2. **Find ways to spontaneously model executive function skills (flexibility and planning)** *at least once* **during class today.** Make this fun and engaging! Use flexibility and planning skills with your students to solve challenges that come up naturally or challenges that you've invented. For example, you could say, *"I can't believe I forgot my lunch at home today! I am so disappointed. I am going to need to be flexible and think of a Plan B to reach my big picture goal of not getting 'hangry'."*

Materials

 ★ Unit 1 Daily Self-Awareness Rating (this worksheet can be copied for each student or found in the Student Workbook)

 ★ PowerPoint for Topic 1.4, projected

★ Power Equation Poster, posted

★ Power Level. Affix the group's Power Level card to the bottom of the Power Arrow.

 ★ Optional: How to Boost Our Power Level: Reminder List (printed from Topic 1.1 or located in the front cover of the Student Workbook)

EDUCATOR PLAN

Goal: Learn the bodily clues that can help us know the intensity of different feelings. Identify if feelings are overwhelming and coping strategies that could be helpful. Try out different coping strategies in daily life.

Topic 1.4: Coping Strategies to Feel Better and Get Unstuck When Overwhelmed, Stressed, Frustrated, or Disappointed 41

Why: We *all* have overwhelming feelings, and we all have developed coping strategies to help us through those difficult times. People with executive function difficulties often have extra difficulty regulating their emotions and figuring out when to use coping strategies. This lesson gives students the opportunity to practice these important strategies when calm.

> **Important Note**
>
> It is very important that you do not invalidate students' feelings and do not tell students to "calm down." Students need to choose their own ways and times to use their coping strategies, and not have anything imposed on them. Sometimes students need to be stuck for a little while before they can use a coping strategy or be flexible.

Plan: Do the following before class:

★ Post the Power Equation Poster and place the group Power Level card at the bottom of the Power Arrow. (You'll move it up when students are flexible or kind to themselves or others, or when they identify and cope with their feelings.)

★ Project PowerPoint for Topic 1.4.

CLASS LESSON PLAN

Slide 1: Power Plan

1. **Review with the class the goal and plan for today, pointing to the Power Plan visual for Topic 1.4.** Ask students to fill out the Unit 1 Daily Self-Awareness Rating worksheet.

Slide 2: Power Equation Review

2. **Briefly review the Power Equation.** Remind students that they are working to have more power in their lives.

POWER LEVEL: As in all sessions, continue moving the Power Level up throughout the class. As you praise students for being flexible, planning, participating, engaging in big picture thinking, or being kind during class, raise the Power Level card part of the way up the Power Arrow. Explain why the Power Level is going up, so the group sees what they're doing well. Find a way to praise every student so it is clear that power is achieved through group effort.

Slide 3: Stress, Frustration, and Disappointment and Strategies to Feel Better

3. **Introduce and discuss the two big picture ideas for today's lesson** (pointing out the third box of the Power Equation, "Make a Plan for Reaching My Goal"):

   Big Picture Idea #1: Planning and working toward a goal is powerful, but it can sometimes make you feel stress, frustration, and disappointment. That's normal. Explain to the class:

   "Planning and working toward a goal is very powerful. Planning helps us reach our goals, and when we reach our goals, we get more of what we want and need. Part of planning is having a way of dealing with frustration and disappointment. Frustration and disappointment often come up when we are working toward a goal, so we need to be ready to cope with those feelings, especially because getting stuck by our strong feelings can also get in the way of boosting our power."

   Big Picture Idea #2: We can use coping strategies to feel better when our feelings are overwhelming or stuck so that we can get back on target, which is how we get more power.

   "If we get stuck by a strong feeling, we could also get off target and then we can't get what we want (we lose our power to get to our goal). It's important to accept that stress, frustration, and disappointment are normal and that there are strategies that we can use to cope and feel better."

   Here are some key questions to ask the class:

   ★ *"Can you tell us about a time when you felt stress, disappointment, or frustration, and what helped you feel better?"*

   ★ *"Why is it important to learn how to cope with overwhelming or stuck feelings?"*

Slide 4: Feelings Target Visual

4a. **Introduce the Feelings Target visual to students and help them connect to it with comparisons like playing darts, where the goal is to be at the center point of the Feelings Target.**

   "This is the Feelings Target. If you've ever played darts before, you know the purpose of the game is to hit the bullseye or the center point. The center point of our Feelings Target, the 1, means 'On Target.' What are some words you would use to describe how you feel when you're on target (happy, calm, good)? What are you able to do when you're at a 1 (schoolwork, hang out with friends, relax, do whatever it is you need to do)?"

4b. **Have your students practice rating different feelings.** Teach students they may benefit from using a coping strategy when they're at a level of 3 or higher. Call out, one by one, in random order, the feeling words listed below. As you say each of the feelings words, ask the students to call out what level of intensity they feel the word is on the Feelings Target (i.e., 1, 2, 3, 4, 5). Or students can raise the corresponding number of fingers on their hand. Level ratings will differ across students, and that's great. The purpose of this exercise is for students to differentiate the **intensity** of different emotions:

   ★ Level 1: calm, happy, just right, on target, feeling good

   ★ Level 2: okay, fine, pretty good, happy

- ★ Level 3: nervous, so-so, annoyed, grumpy
- ★ Level 4: mad, scared, frustrated, embarrassed, disappointed
- ★ Level 5: overwhelmed, out of control, furious, very upset, terrified, shut down

"As the numbers get higher, we get more and more off target. It's almost impossible to get what we want (we can lose our power) when we are a 4 or 5, because we feel too overwhelmed. Often, we feel stuck at this point. But the good news is that there are tools that we can use to feel better. If we can catch ourselves before we get to 5, it will be easier to use a coping strategy to get back on target."

Slide 5: Web Quest: Feelings in the World

5. **Have students search for interesting or fun videos that illustrate a variety of feelings and then share and discuss them as a class. Encourage creativity (and reminders about your school's policies related to online videos as needed for your class).**

"I bet you can think of videos you've seen that show an animal or person or character experiencing a variety of feelings. Maybe you've already thought of one that you'd like to share with the class. You can also search for one now. Can you find a short video or a picture of a person, character, or animal experiencing feelings that are a 1 or 2? or a 3? What about a 4 or a 5? Let's take 5 to 10 minutes to look for the videos now and then we'll share them with each other."

Here are some key points and questions to ask the class about the videos they share:

- ★ Highlight any videos that show escalating feelings—when feelings are rising from a low to a high number.
- ★ How do you imagine those feelings felt in their body?
- ★ What are the clues that led you to your answers?

Modifications for videos/pictures: You could pre-select videos that your students might enjoy to save time, or students can describe scenes from a movie, book, video game, or meme.

Slide 6: What's Your Clue That You're Getting Off Target?

6. **Have students figure out the first clue that they're getting off target using the What's Your Clue That You're Getting Off Target? worksheet. Share the instructions for the worksheet:** *"We all have clues that our emotions are getting more intense. Look at the list below of physical clues. Check off any of the clues that you have experienced. Then, after you have checked off all of the clues that you have experienced, give each one a rating of 1 (on target) to 5 (off target). Finally, write the clues with the lowest number into the space below. These are your first clues that you are getting Off Target."*

Share everyone's first clues as a group.

"Great job connecting the feelings with the Feelings Target and describing some of the clues you observed or felt that helped you understand those feelings. Because the brain and body communicate with each other, all of our bodies give us clues about how we're feeling, and as you move outward on the Feelings Target, your body gives off physical clues that your feelings are getting stronger and that you may be getting off target.

Everybody has different clues, and sometimes they are hard to notice. Check off any clue that applies to you, and give each one a rating, from 1 (on target) to 5 (off target). Then write your lowest number clues into the space at the bottom—these are your first clues that you are getting off target."

Important Note

The most important part of this activity is for students to catch themselves when they are getting off target early enough so that they are calm enough to use a coping strategy. The goal is for students to say "Uh-oh, my heart is beginning to race! I want to try a strategy to get back on target." Some students, however, may have a hard time noticing their body sensations and you might want to help them notice things like clenched fists, looking down more, or engaging in a repetitive motion.

Slide 7: How the Brain and Body Experience and React to Overwhelming Feelings

7a. **Teach students that our brains highly prioritize our safety.** You can do this in a playful way. You could ask, *"How would you feel and what would you do if you saw a swarm of bear-sized bees outside?"* Use your students' responses, and your own, to help students understand that your feelings and reactions to the world can help you stay safe, and your feelings of stress are biologically meant to protect you. The nervous system goes throughout your entire body, which is how feelings can be physically felt throughout your body. They can make your hands or feet sweaty or make your heart race. Remind students that feelings of stress, disappointment, and frustration are normal, but that when our feelings get too intense, we can feel stuck or get off target.

7b. **Describe how we can use the brain-body connection to help us feel better and get unstuck.**

*"The good news is that we can also use our senses and brain to help us feel less overwhelmed and to remind our body and brain that we're okay. We can use coping strategies that help us feel better so that we can get back on target. Coping strategies can help us get **unstuck**."*

7c. **Ask students what helps them feel calm and okay.** You may want to share your own most helpful coping strategies.

Slide 8: How the Brain and Body Experience and React to Overwhelming Feelings

8. **Teach students about the inner and outer brain.** Point to the inner and outer regions as you describe the higher-level functions of the outer brain compared to the more primitive, essential functions of the inner brain. Describe how as our feelings get more intense and we get overwhelmed, the outer part of our brain begins to sort of "turn off" or "shut down" as a protective mechanism and the inner brain takes over. Teach

students that we can all use coping strategies to help us feel better, turn the outer part of our brain back on, and get back on target.

"We especially need coping strategies when we're at a 4 or a 5. We need to talk a little bit about the brain to understand that better. Every human has an inner brain and an outer brain. The outer brain does really cool stuff like talking, thinking, and all of our executive functions while the inner brain manages essential stuff like breathing, keeping our heart beating, and feelings. If our feelings get too intense, they can make the outer brain turn off—it's a protective response. We can use coping strategies to help us turn the outer brain back on and get back on target."

Slide 9: Recognizing When You're Getting Off Target

9. **Have students complete the Recognizing When You're Getting Off Target worksheet.** Students rate different situations on the Feelings Target and identify whether they have Stuck or Flexible Thoughts. Don't have them brainstorm coping strategies in the last column (What's My Strategy?) yet.

   "Let's practice recognizing when we are getting **Off Target***. For each situation, give your rating, describe how you might feel or what you might be thinking, and then rate your feeling/thought as* **Stuck** *or* **Flexible***. If there's a situation that happens a lot at school that's not listed on the worksheet, write it down at the bottom."*

Slide 10: Coping Strategies to Get Unstuck

10. **Discuss coping strategies students can use at school to get back on target—the most powerful ways to get unstuck are things you can do anywhere and anytime.** All of the strategies below should be time limited within the classroom setting—allow students to use a timer or some other type of reminder, as needed. *"Now we're going to explore some* **coping strategies** *that could help you when you're feeling overwhelmed, stressed, frustrated, disappointed, or stuck. In this list are some of the most commonly helpful* **coping strategies***."*

Important Note: Some students might identify **coping strategies** that they tend to get stuck on, such as video games. In these situations, emphasize that it's not always possible to play video games (e.g., at school), and this tactic might prevent them from reaching goals if they get stuck on it. Instead, they may need to modify their strategy (e.g., singing a song from the video game inside their head) or choose a different strategy (deep breathing).

★ **Trigger a happy thought or feeling:** Look at photos saved on your phone or smartwatch, Google image search ugly puppies, watch videos of fainting goats, help someone else.

★ **Deep breathing:** Use deep breathing as a relaxation tool: Breathe in for 5 seconds, hold for 5 seconds, and breathe out for 5 seconds.

- ★ **Do a favorite thing:** If a favorite thing is a video game, sing the theme song in your head or draw the video game characters on a piece of paper. If a favorite thing is drawing, doodle rather than getting lost in a complicated drawing.
- ★ **Do a repetitive action:** Doodling, twirling a pencil, flipping a coin over your fingers, using a fidget ring, rocking, bouncing your leg, twirling your hair, picking stickers off of a notebook or pencil.
- ★ **Eat a piece of chocolate or a mint, or chew gum:** Focus on the sensation, including pressure on your teeth and jaw, smell, and taste.
- ★ **Imagine a favorite place or thing:** Set a timer for 2 minutes and imagine the scene silently (e.g., Who is there? What do I see around me? What do I hear?).
- ★ **Take a quick break:** Get a drink of water, go to the bathroom and splash water on your face, walk up and down the hall.
- ★ **Ask for help:** Ask your teacher or other trusted adult in your school for help in using a coping strategy, or ask a friend to quietly sit with you, to listen to you, or even for a hug.
- ★ **Think up your own!** You might want to choose something that is all yours!

Slide 11: What's Your Strategy?

11a. **Have students go back to their Recognizing When You're Getting Off Target worksheet and write in which coping strategy they could use to get back On Target for each situation that they rated higher than a 2.** First have students work on their own. Then you can ask for volunteers to talk about a strategy they think they could try in one of the situations.

11b. **Ask students if there were any situations they had rated at a 4 or 5.** Try talking this through with students, and ask them to imagine what their rating would be after the strategy. Ask what they'd do if the strategy didn't work the first time: Wait a while and try again? Try a different strategy?

Slide 12: Coping Strategies Experiment Log

12a. **Explain how to use the Coping Strategies Experiment Log to help students find individualized, effective strategies to cope with stress.** Using the Coping Strategies Experiment Log worksheet, pick one of the strategies and set up an "experiment" for students to gather data to determine which strategy works the best to get them back **On Target**. For example, lead students through a deep breathing exercise.

- ★ Have students rate themselves on their Feelings Target before and after using a strategy to determine whether it reduced their stress. Identify whether they liked it and where they can use it (some strategies may be more appropriate in different settings).
- ★ Emphasize that one strategy doesn't always work for everyone or in every situation, so it's important to have several tools (strategies) in their toolbox. Encourage students to take the worksheet home and practice on their own.

12b. **At the end of this activity, encourage students to experiment at home and school with different coping strategies—ask them to record data to see if the strategy works and report back the following week.**

These tools and the Coping Strategies Experiment Log can be referred to throughout the rest of the curriculum to promote generalization. If a student experiences stress during the lesson or other parts of the school day, encourage them to rate their stress on the Feelings Target, try a coping strategy, and re-rate it to see if it helped.

★ Remind students to come back to these strategies when they experience uncomfortable feelings or get stuck during group. Praise them for using these strategies to get Unstuck.

Slide 13: Topic 1.4 Wrap-Up: Why Learn Coping Strategies?

13a. **Ask students why we had a goal to figure out when your feelings are overwhelming or you feel stuck and use strategies to cope. Why is it important to understand and cope with feelings?** Point to the Why section of the Power Plan and ask students to fill in the answer or just discuss. Gently lead the discussion to focus on using coping strategies when they're feeling overwhelmed, stressed, frustrated, disappointed, or stuck. Encourage students to consider how they will use coping strategies in their classes, at home, and in the future. Remind students that coping strategies are an important part of being kind to yourself, increasing your power, and building relationships. Be sure to affirm the variety of thoughts and opinions the students give, so all of your students feel heard and celebrated. If helpful, you might say:

"It is incredibly powerful to learn how to cope with overwhelm, stress, getting stuck, disappointment, and frustration. Coping strategies help you get unstuck and reach your goals. Because you learned these skills today, your power goes way up. How will you use coping strategies in your life at school or at home?"

13b. **Send Home Extension for Topic 1.4 home.** You can send this home with students or e-mail it to parents.

13c. **Look for generalization opportunities in other classes.** Keep encouraging your students' other educators to use Key Vocabulary from the Executive Function Skills List (found at the end of Topic 1.1). Have the other educators been able to post the Executive Function Skills List in their classrooms? Discuss the Coping Strategies and Feelings Target with the educators, and encourage them to use this language in their classes and lessons. For example, a educator might say, *"Our Plan A was to get through Chapter 2 today. We didn't quite make it, which really made me frustrated, so I'm going to use a coping strategy so I can make a Plan B."*

CHECK: How are my students doing?
Do I need to make any adjustments for the next class?

See Appendix A for a list of questions to guide your self-reflection and refer to the Troubleshooting section (Appendix B) to address common problems or any challenges that may have arisen with the curriculum.

TOPIC 1.4: Coping Strategies to Feel Better and Get Unstuck When Overwhelmed, Stressed, Frustrated, or Disappointed

DAILY SELF-AWARENESS RATING: UNIT 1

NAME: _____

Executive Function Skills

Flexibility + Big Picture Thinking + Goals and Planning = POWER

Mark an X on the arrow to show how you feel today:

How flexible are you today?

Stuck   Somewhat Flexible   Very Flexible

Are you stuck on details today?

Stuck on Details   Somewhat Stuck on Details   Focused on the Big Picture

TOPIC 1.4: Coping Strategies to Feel Better and Get Unstuck When Overwhelmed, Stressed, Frustrated, or Disappointed

WHAT'S YOUR CLUE THAT YOU'RE GETTING OFF TARGET?

Instructions: We all have clues that our emotions are getting more intense. Look at the list below of physical clues. Check off any of the clues that you have experienced. Then, after you have checked off all of the clues that you have experienced, give each one a rating of 1 (On Target) to 5 (Off Target). Finally, write the clues with the lowest number into the space below. These are your first clues that you are getting Off Target.

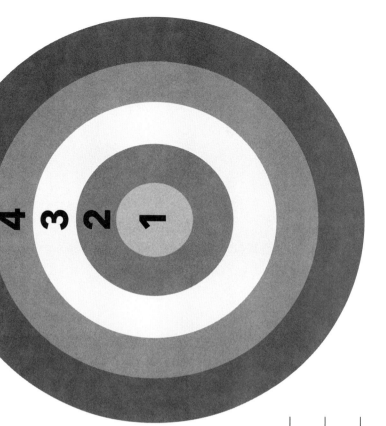

- ◯ Tears in your eyes
- ◯ Clenched teeth
- ◯ Voice quavering
- ◯ Sweaty hands
- ◯ Heart pounding
- ◯ Fluttering in stomach
- ◯ Upset stomach
- ◯ Hands shaking
- ◯ Clenched hands
- ◯ Feeling too hot or cold
- ◯ Feeling tired
- ◯ Tense muscles

- ◯ Headache
- ◯ Difficult to think
- ◯ Raised voice
- ◯ Shutting down
- ◯ Clouded thinking
- ◯ Urge to run or need to escape
- ◯ Other: _____

My first clues that I'm getting Off Target: _____

TOPIC 1.4: Coping Strategies to Feel Better and Get Unstuck When Overwhelmed, Stressed, Frustrated, or Disappointed

RECOGNIZING WHEN YOU'RE GETTING OFF TARGET

5
4
3
2
1

For each situation, give your rating, rate your feeling as stuck or flexible, identify if you need a strategy, and add a coping strategy you could try to the last column.

Situation	Target Rating	Stuck or Flexible?	Do I Need a Strategy?	What's My Strategy?
We have to add a day to the school year because of the weather.				
My friend cancelled our plans.				
My teacher gave three bonus points to everyone on our quiz.				
My family is in my space. All. Of. The. Time.				
I just found out there will be a sequel to my favorite video game.				
My friend is coming over to hang out this weekend.				
I just found out we have to run one mile in gym tomorrow.				
My cell phone/screen device is not working.				
I got a D on my math test, and I thought I had done really well.				
I forgot to turn in my homework for class.				
My example:				

TOPIC 1.4: Coping Strategies to Feel Better and Get Unstuck When Overwhelmed, Stressed, Frustrated, or Disappointed

COPING STRATEGIES EXPERIMENT LOG

During the week, record which coping strategies you use and when you use them. Give Feelings Target ratings before and after to see how that strategy worked.

Strategy	Rating: Before	Rating: After	When Did I Use It?	How Will I Remember to Use It Later?
Trigger a happy thought or feeling				
Deep breathing				
Do a favorite thing				
Do a repetitive action				
Eat a mint/chew gum				
Imagine a favorite place or thing				
Take a quick break				
Ask for help				
Something else:				

TOPIC 1.4: Coping Strategies to Feel Better and Get Unstuck When Overwhelmed, Stressed, Frustrated, or Disappointed

HOME EXTENSION FOR TOPIC 1.4: COPING STRATEGIES

Planning and working toward a goal can sometimes make you feel stress, frustration, and disappointment. That's normal. We can use coping strategies to feel better when our feelings are overwhelming so that we can get back on target. Your child has been practicing identifying the intensity of their feelings on the Feelings Target (the next page of this handout). The first step is to recognize just how stressed or overwhelmed you are. When we are at a 5, our only coping strategy is to run or shut down. But when we can catch ourselves at a 3, we can try different coping strategies to get ourselves back to 1.

Key Words to Use at Home: *Coping Strategies, How Do I Get Back on Target?*

There are several things you can do at home to help your child:

Post a Feelings Target at home. Use the Feelings Target to rate your <u>own</u> emotions, both positive and negative, this week. Encourage your child to rate themselves, first in positive situations and, when they become more skilled, in negative ones. At first, your child may need to rate negative emotions after the fact, during a debrief, to prevent conflict when emotions are high. Before long, you can just use words without the target, such as: *"I am really disappointed that's closed today, I'm at a 3. I'm going to take a few deep breaths and then I'll get back on target and figure out what to do."*

Practice coping strategies together.

- **Trigger a happy feeling:** Look at photos, watch funny animal videos, help someone else.
- **Deep breathing:** Use deep breathing as a relaxation tool: Breathe in for 5 seconds, hold for 5 seconds, and breathe out for 5 seconds.
- **Do a favorite thing:** Read, draw or paint, play a game.
- **Do a repetitive action:** Doodling, twirling a pencil, using a fidget ring, bouncing your leg, twirling your hair, picking stickers off of a notebook or pencil.
- **Eat a piece of chocolate or a mint, or chew gum:** Focus on the sensation, including pressure on your teeth and jaw, smell, and taste.
- **Imagine a favorite place or thing:** Set a timer for 2 minutes and imagine the scene silently (e.g., Who is there? What do I see around me? What do I hear?).
- **Take a quick break:** Get a drink of water, splash water on your face, take a walk.
- **Ask for help:** Ask a family member for help in using a coping strategy or solving a problem, or ask a friend to quietly sit with you, to listen to you, or even for a hug.
- **Think up your own!** You might want to choose something that is all yours!

TOPIC 1.4: Coping Strategies to Feel Better and Get Unstuck When Overwhelmed, Stressed, Frustrated, or Disappointed (continued)

FEELINGS TARGET

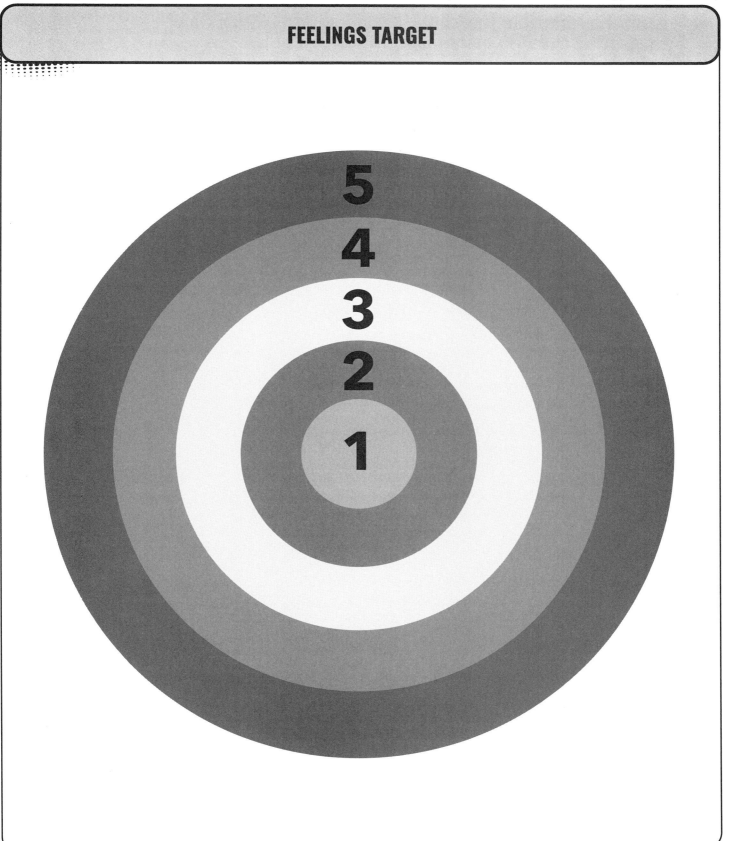

TOPIC 1.5   Flexible Thinking—Accepting and Letting Go of Frustration and Disappointment

BIG PICTURE SUMMARY

The purpose of this topic is to expand the number of coping skills students have and to teach students that challenges and setbacks are normal. For students to increase their power and reach their goals, they must manage their frustration and disappointment. Sometimes students will need to use **coping strategies** discussed in the last lesson to manage some of those feelings. Sometimes they can use a set of cognitive coping strategies called **flexible thinking strategies.** Sometimes they might need both. Using three flexible thinking strategies (or tricks), students will explore how to regulate strong feelings by asking themselves:

★   How long they should be stuck on a feeling

★   How they can refocus on their big picture goals

★   How they can remind themselves that there's always a Plan B if Plan A doesn't work

Key Things to Do (This topic may take more than one class period to complete)

Here are the two most important things to do in today's class:

1. **Use the following Key Vocabulary often and in fun and playful ways:**

    ★   Executive Function Skills

    ★   Can I Use Coping Strategies and Flexible Thinking If I Need To?

    ★   How Long Should I Be Stuck on That Strong Feeling?

    ★   Managing Frustration and Disappointment

    ★   How Can I Refocus on My Big Picture Goal?

    ★   Plan B

2. **Find ways to spontaneously model executive function skills (flexibility and planning)** *at least once during class today.* Make this fun and engaging! Use flexibility and planning skills with your students to solve challenges that come up naturally or challenges that you've invented. For example, you could say, *"I can't believe my favorite team lost last night! I am so disappointed. I need a coping strategy to get refocused on my big picture goal of having a good group today."*

Reminder About Key Vocabulary

Using the Key Vocabulary is a critical part of the curriculum. Integrate the Key Vocabulary as much as possible and keep it positive. Use the Key Vocabulary listed for the topic and all the other Key Vocabulary introduced in previous topics (the Key Vocabulary is cumulative).

Topic 1.5: Flexible Thinking—Accepting and Letting Go of Frustration and Disappointment

Materials

- Unit 1 Daily Self-Awareness Rating (this worksheet can be copied for each student or found in the Student Workbook)

- PowerPoint for Topic 1.5, projected
- Videos from Topic 1.2:
  - Pink Panther video: https://www.youtube.com/watch?v=mPzCkajdLvE
  - Pig and Apple [Minecraft Animation]: https://youtu.be/gwVlsv1n7Mo
  - Chicken Little video: https://youtu.be/RicWg5H9QIM
- Power Equation Poster, posted
- Power Level card. Affix the card to the bottom of the Power Arrow.

- Optional: How to Boost Our Power Level: Reminder List (printed from Topic 1.1 or located in the front cover of the Student Workbook)

EDUCATOR PLAN

Goal: Learn to accept that disappointment and frustration are part of planning and accomplishing goals. Practice three **flexible thinking** tricks for managing strong feelings and getting back on target.

Why: People with executive function challenges may be at risk for getting stuck on negative details and bad feelings, which can lead them to feel overwhelmed and shut down. Practicing flexible thinking as a coping strategy can help them normalize and better tolerate frustration and disappointment.

Important note about today's topic on handling disappointment: Today's session introduces a variation on the "How long should we be stuck on this detail?" routine from Topic 1.1. In today's topic, the following questions are introduced: "How long should I be stuck on that strong feeling?", "How long should I be frustrated?", and "How long should I be disappointed?" As with the stuck on a detail routine from Topic 1.1, it is essential to use these prompts in an affirming way, *not* as criticism of a student's disappointment. Convey empathy during this routine by saying something like *"That seems really frustrating and disappointing. It's normal to get frustrated—how long should we allow ourselves to be upset? When should we get back to the big picture? Do we want to use a coping strategy first?"* Some educators find it useful to offer 1 or 2 minutes to be "stuck on the feeling," before the students shift back to the big picture.

Some students may need additional support to use a coping strategy from the last lesson to manage overwhelm and feel calmer before they can be available for flexible thinking.

Plan: Do the following before class:

- ★ Post the Power Equation Poster and place the Power Level card at the bottom part of the Power Arrow on the poster. (You'll move it up when students are flexible or kind, work together, or manage their frustration and disappointment.)
- ★ Pull up the link for the Pink Panther video (or the Minecraft Pig and Apple or Chicken Little video) so it's ready to show.
- ★ Project the PowerPoint for Topic 1.5.

CLASS LESSON PLAN

Slide 1: Power Plan

1. **Review with the class the goal and plan for today, pointing to the Power Plan visual for Topic 1.5.** Ask students to fill out the Unit 1 Daily Self-Awareness Rating worksheet.

Slide 2: Power Equation Review

2. **Briefly review the Power Equation.** Remind students that they are working to have more power in their lives.

POWER LEVEL: As in all sessions, continue moving the Power Level card up throughout the remainder of today's class. As you praise students for being flexible, planning, participating, engaging in big picture thinking, or being kind during class, raise the Power Level card part of the way up the Power Arrow. Explain why the card is going up, so the group knows what they are doing well. Find a way to praise every student so it is clear that power is achieved through group effort.

Slide 3: Dealing With Frustration and Disappointment

3. **Introduce and discuss the two big picture ideas for today's lesson** (pointing out the third box of the Power Equation, "Do I have a plan?" and "Can I use coping strategies and flexible thinking if I need to?"):

Big Picture Idea 1: Planning and working toward a goal is powerful, but it sometimes involves some frustration and disappointment. That's normal. Explain to the class:

"Planning and working toward a goal is very powerful. Planning helps us reach our goals, and when we reach our goals, we get more of what we want and need. Part of planning is having a way of dealing with frustration and disappointment. Frustration and disappointment often come up when we are working toward a goal, so we need to be ready to deal with those feelings. Last time we talked about some coping strategies as a

way to make those feelings less intense. Today we're going add a few thinking strategies that can help us too."

Big Picture Idea 2: Being flexible helps us overcome frustration and disappointment. Explain to the class:

"If we get stuck on a strong feeling and give up when there is a challenge, then we don't get what we want (we lose our power). It's important to be flexible and accept that frustration, challenges, and disappointment are normal and okay. When those feelings are at a 3 or higher, we might try our favorite coping strategy. Once that helps us feel better, what do we do next? Flexible thinking skills can help us to get back on target."

Here are some key questions to ask the class:

★ Did any of you try out the **coping strategies** on your Coping Strategies Experiment Log worksheet from last session? Did any of you find them really helpful? Does anyone need help identifying some new strategies?

★ Can you tell us about a time when you overcame frustration?

★ Can you tell us about a time when you overcame disappointment?

★ Why is it important to learn how to deal with frustration and disappointment?

Slide 4: How the Brain Handles Frustration and Disappointment

4. **Explain how the prefrontal cortex of the human brain helps to regulate the emotional (limbic) system of the brain:**

"Great job practicing your coping strategies and coming up with examples of times when you managed frustration and disappointment. Now we are going to learn a little more about the specific outer parts of our brain that help us manage strong feelings, like frustration and disappointment. Frustration and disappointment are normal and often come up when we are working toward a goal. The outer part of our brain behind our forehead has a part called the prefrontal cortex that uses executive functions to regulate and manage the emotional, inner part of our brain."

Point to the prefrontal cortex in the PowerPoint and explain that the arrow going back to the limbic system (the inner, emotional system of the brain) show the prefrontal cortex regulating and managing strong emotions so they don't control us. Tell your class that when we manage and control our strong feelings, it helps us plan better and achieve our goals.

Slide 5: Three Flexible Thinking Tricks to Deal With Frustration and Disappointment

5. **Briefly introduce that we will be learning three flexible thinking tricks that our prefrontal cortex can use to manage the emotional (limbic) system of our brains:**

"We've learned about how the prefrontal cortex, or frontal lobes, of our outer brain help to manage the inner emotional parts of our brain. Now we're going to learn three flexible thinking tricks that our frontal lobes can use to manage strong feelings, like frustration and disappointment."

★ **Trick 1:** When I'm frustrated or disappointed, how long I should be stuck on those feelings? A short time or a longer time? (It depends on the situation.)

- **Trick 2:** When I'm frustrated or disappointed, how can I get unstuck and refocus on my big picture goal? Should I try a coping strategy?
- **Trick 3:** When I'm frustrated or disappointed, I need to remember that there's always a Plan B (a way to get unstuck).

Slide 6: Flexible Thinking Trick 1: How Long Should I Be Stuck on Being Frustrated or Disappointed?

6a. **Introduce the idea that we have some control over how long we are stuck on a feeling:**

"We have some control over how long we will be stuck on a strong feeling. If something is a big deal, sometimes we need to be stuck for longer. But if we stay stuck too long, there is a cost. Staying stuck on a strong feeling can interfere with our lives. So our first flexible thinking trick for dealing with frustration and disappointment is to use our prefrontal cortex to think about and decide how long we should be stuck on a certain feeling. It depends on the situation."

6b. **Refer to the PowerPoint scale and ask the students' opinions about the different lengths of time:**

"This scale shows different lengths of time that someone might be stuck on a strong feeling. What do you think about this? Are there certain times when you might be stuck on a strong feeling for a shorter time or longer time? What happens if you are stuck on a strong feeling for too long?"

6c. **Review and discuss these examples with students (or come up with your own):**

"Let's consider some situations that lead to strong feelings. Think about how long the person might be stuck on a certain feeling."

Example 1: My friend is sick and can't hang out. I'm disappointed. Ask the students to consider, *"How long should I be stuck on being disappointed?"* Refer to the PowerPoint scale (1 minute, 5 minutes, half an hour, 1 day, etc.). Discuss the following points with students:

- What are the consequences for staying stuck for a whole day?
- If you stay stuck forever, will you ever see the friend again?

 Every time a student offers an idea that is even somewhat on target, raise the group's Power Level card and verbally praise them for their flexible thinking or big picture thinking.

Example 2: I really wanted to go on a hike to celebrate the first day of summer break, but then my brother broke his leg so we couldn't go. Ask the students to consider how long they should be stuck on being disappointed. Here are a few key ideas to cover with the class:

- What if you're stuck on being disappointed all summer? What would that do to your life and your power?
- Even though disappointment may last for a while in some situations, you can still move on even while you are feeling disappointed or frustrated. That's a positive way of dealing with disappointment and frustration and building power in our lives.

Topic 1.5: Flexible Thinking—Accepting and Letting Go of Frustration and Disappointment 59

- ★ Can you share examples from your own life of things that have frustrated or disappointed you? How long did you stay stuck on the strong feeling? What did you do to get unstuck and move on?

 When a student gives an example, raise the Power Level card with a praising statement, such as *"That was a great example of flexible thinking—your power is going up!"*

Slide 7: Flexible Thinking Trick 2: How Can I Refocus on My Big Picture Goal?

7a. **Introduce the idea that when we are frustrated or disappointed—when we hit obstacles—it helps us if we get refocused on our big picture goal:**

"It's completely normal to feel disappointed and frustrated. Obstacles often come up! But the important thing is not to lose track of our big picture goal. Our second flexible thinking trick for today is figuring out how we can refocus on our big picture goal and not stay stuck in disappointment."

7b. **Refer to the PowerPoint, showing how you forget about your big picture goal if you stay frustrated or disappointed when you hit an obstacle. Emphasize the importance of refocusing on your big picture goal:**

"This person is trying to reach his goal of climbing to the top of the mountain. He's heard there is a great view of the other mountains when you get to the top. You can see here that he's hit an obstacle in his path. It is frustrating to him, and he's tempted to give up and go back down the mountain. But the powerful choice for him is to refocus on his big picture goal of getting to the top. Instead of giving up, he can focus on his goal and deal with the obstacle and his frustration."

7c. **Review and discuss these examples with students (or come up with your own):**

"Let's consider some more situations that lead to strong feelings. Think about how the person can refocus on their big picture goal instead of being stuck."

Example 1: I really wanted to get a good grade in a computer coding class I'm taking, but I bombed my test. Now I'm frustrated and disappointed, and it's making it hard to do my homework. Ask the students to consider, "How can I refocus on my big picture goal?" Use the following questions to lead a class discussion:

- ★ What is my big picture goal: getting a good grade on one test or in the whole class?
- ★ What if I stay stuck on being disappointed? Will I reach my big picture goal?
- ★ How can I refocus on my goal of getting a good grade?

 Every time a student offers an idea that is even somewhat on target, raise the Power Level card and verbally praise the flexible thinking or big picture thinking.

Example 2: I really wanted my best friend to come to my birthday party, but she wouldn't cancel her plans with her family. Now I'm feeling disappointed, and I haven't returned any of her text messages. Ask the students to consider, "How can I refocus on my big picture goal?" Here are a few ideas to cover with the class:

- ★ What is my big picture goal: having my friend come to my birthday party or maintaining my friendship with my friend?

- ★ What if I stay disappointed and keep ignoring my friend? Will that help me reach my goal of staying friends?
- ★ How can I refocus on my goal of keeping my friend?

7d. Ask the students to give examples from their lives of things that have disappointed them and how they refocused on their big picture goal.

 When a student gives an example, raise the Power Level card with a praising statement, such as *"That was a good example of flexible thinking—our power is going up!"*

Slide 8: Flexible Thinking Trick 3: There's Always a Plan B

8a. Introduce the idea that when we hit an obstacle and get frustrated or disappointed, there is always a Plan B available to us (a way to get unstuck). We just have to give it some thought, or ask for advice, and we can come up with a Plan B to overcome or work around the obstacle:

"When we hit a roadblock and feel frustrated or disappointed, a great way to feel better fast is to try a Plan B. Plan A didn't work out, so we try a Plan B. This is how we get unstuck. This is flexible thinking!"

8b. Refer to the PowerPoint, showing how obstacles are normal and expected, and that what matters is how we react to the obstacles:

"Okay, so we've seen that this person is trying to reach his goal of climbing to the top of the mountain. He ran into an obstacle, which often happens when we are working toward a goal. Instead of getting stuck on being frustrated and disappointed, he used his flexible thinking to come up with a Plan B. He found a trail around the lake that led him close to the top of the mountain. And his Plan B was even better than his Plan A because he got to see exciting views of the lake <u>and</u> the mountain."

8c. Review and discuss these examples with students (or come up with your own):

"Let's consider some more situations that lead to strong feelings. Think about how the person can come up with a Plan B to get unstuck and make progress toward their goal."

Example 1: I love roller coasters, so I went to the theme park to ride the new coaster. The line was 3 hours long and I was really mad and disappointed. Remind the students, *"There's always a Plan B."* Here are a few prompts for class discussion:

- ★ What if I stay stuck on being disappointed about the new roller coaster and leave the amusement park?
- ★ What are some Plan Bs?
- ★ If I can get unstuck and ride other great roller coasters, what happens to my power and happiness?

 Every time a student offers an idea that is even somewhat on target, raise the Power Level card and verbally praise flexible thinking or big picture thinking.

Example 2: I was supposed to make cookies for the class end-of-year party. I started to make chocolate chip cookies but discovered I was almost out of

chocolate chips. I was really frustrated because it was getting late. Remind the students, *"There's always a Plan B."* Here are a few ideas to cover with the class:

- ★ What if I stay frustrated and disappointed?
- ★ What are some Plan Bs?
- ★ If I can get unstuck and come up with a Plan B, how will I feel?

8d. **Ask the students to give examples from their lives of things that frustrated or disappointed them and how they used a Plan B to move on.**

 When a student gives an example, raise the Power Level card with a praising statement, such as *"That was a great example of Plan A/Plan B thinking—the group's power is going up!"*

Slide 9: Revisiting the Pink Panther: How Does He Deal With Frustration and Disappointment?

9a. **Inform the students that they'll be re-watching the Pink Panther video, now looking for how the Pink Panther deals with frustration and disappointment.** If the class watched the Minecraft Pig and Apple or Chicken Little video in Topic 1.2 instead, either the class can watch the Pink Panther video now (https://www.youtube.com/watch?v=mPzCkajdLvE), or you can adjust the following ideas and language for one of the other videos. Here's a sample script you can use:

"Remember, in order for us to have more power, we have to learn how to manage frustration and disappointment. We've learned three flexible thinking tricks to help us manage disappointment:

- ★ *Flexible Thinking Trick 1: Consider how long you should be stuck on being frustrated or disappointed. It depends on the situation.*
- ★ *Flexible Thinking Trick 2: Think about how to refocus on the big picture goal.*
- ★ *Flexible Thinking Trick 3. There's always a Plan B (a way to get unstuck). Come up with a Plan B and move on.*

We're going watch the Pink Panther video again, but this time let's focus on how the Pink Panther gains power by managing his disappointment and frustration. Which of the three flexible thinking tricks does he use? I'll pause it in the middle and we'll discuss the first half of the video. Then we'll watch the rest of it, and we'll discuss the skills he uses to manage disappointment and frustration."

9b. **Start the video and then pause it midway through.** Ask students which of the flexible thinking tricks the Pink Panther used to deal with frustration and disappointment. Ask for examples, and link the discussion to the three flexible thinking tricks as much as possible.

9c. **Restart the video and finish watching it.** Now ask the students:

- ★ *"How long is the Pink Panther staying stuck when he fails?"*
- ★ *"He is getting frustrated each time, but how long is he frustrated?"*
- ★ *"If he stays stuck being frustrated, will he be able to move forward? Why shouldn't he just give up?"*
- ★ *"If he gives up on his big picture goal of crossing the street, who is he hurting?"*

Important Note

When Students Struggle to Accept Words/Ideas: Some students may struggle with new ideas. Affirm those who question or challenge the ideas by saying something like: *"I know you may not totally believe in all of this yet, and I completely understand that. In our upcoming classes, we are going to continue to talk about this. I think you will see how this can work for you to help you get more of what you want and need as we go along. I'm asking you to keep an open mind and let me know if you feel the same way by the end."*

Slide 10: Topic 1.5 Wrap-Up: Why Practice Managing Frustration and Disappointment?

10a. Ask students why we had a goal to learn about managing frustration and disappointment. **Why is it important to accept that you might need a Plan B?** Point to the Why section of the Power Plan and ask students to fill in the answer or just discuss. Gently lead the discussion to focus on using coping strategies and flexible thinking tricks to deal with frustration and disappointment when things aren't perfect. Encourage students to consider how they will use these strategies and skills in their classes, at home, and in the future. Remind the students that flexible thinking is an important executive function skill. Be sure to affirm the variety of thoughts and opinions the students give, so all of your students feel heard and celebrated. If helpful, you might say: *"One of the most powerful skills is learning to deal with disappointment and frustration. This skill lets you overcome more obstacles in life and have more joy in life. Because you learned these skills today, our power goes way up. How will you use the skill of managing frustration in your life at school or at home?"*

10b. Send Home Extension for Topic 1.5 home with students or e-mail it to parents.

10c. Look for generalization opportunities in other classes. Check in with educators to see how they're doing with the Key Vocabulary on the Executive Function Skills List (found at the end of Topic 1.1). If it's helpful, provide an additional copy of the Executive Function Skills List and encourage educators to use the flexibility words in a positive manner. Remind them to use the vocabulary with the entire class and not to focus on the specific students who are in this program. Educators might benefit from learning that over the course of several research projects related to *Unstuck and On Target*, educators have shared that the Key Vocabulary and related skills have helped many of their students improve, whether or not those students had identified needs.

CHECK: How are my students doing?
Do I need to make any adjustments for the next class?

See Appendix A for a list of questions to guide your self-reflection and refer to the Troubleshooting section (Appendix B) to address common problems or any challenges that may have arisen with the curriculum.

TOPIC 1.5: Flexible Thinking—Accepting and Letting Go of Frustration and Disappointment

DAILY SELF-AWARENESS RATING: UNIT 1

NAME: _____

Executive Function Skills

Flexibility + Big Picture Thinking + Goals and Planning = POWER

Mark an X on the arrow to show how you feel today:

How flexible are you today?

Stuck   Somewhat Flexible   Very Flexible

Are you stuck on details today?

Stuck on Details   Somewhat Stuck on Details   Focused on the Big Picture

TOPIC 1.5: Flexible Thinking—Accepting and Letting Go of Frustration and Disappointment

HOME EXTENSION FOR TOPIC 1.5: FLEXIBLE FEELINGS—ACCEPTING AND LETTING GO OF FRUSTRATION AND DISAPPOINTMENT

In this week's topic, your child's class learned that frustration and disappointment are normal parts of life. The key is knowing how to let go of frustration and disappointment, so you don't get stuck on it for too long. Most things aren't perfect, and that's okay.

Key Vocabulary/skills:

Plan A/Plan B
There's Always a Plan B
Frustration and Disappointment Are Normal
How to Deal With Frustration and Disappointment

How to use the Key Vocabulary:

When your child is frustrated or disappointed, you can gently help them use a coping skill or strategy like the ones listed below. Demonstrate the coping skill and see if your child will consider joining you. Even if your child doesn't join you, modeling effective coping skills helps your child know what to do.

Coping strategies you can model with your child:

- Take three deep breaths.
- Remember, most things aren't perfect—and that's okay!
- Ask yourself how long you should be stuck on this feeling: a short time or a long time?
- Give yourself a few minutes—take a break.
- Get unstuck and move on (refocus on your big picture goals).
- Relax.
- Think about the big picture—is this a big deal or a little deal? How can we make it a little deal?
- Think about something good.
- Come up with a compromise.
- Remember that disappointment and frustration come and go.

Share your experiences: Share examples from your life in which you needed to let go of disappointment or frustration. Use real situations if possible, but you can also make up examples or use the following examples:

I wanted to get my favorite cereal at the store, but I couldn't find it. I'm feeling disappointed. What can I do to let go of my disappointment? Encourage your child to offer ideas for coping with disappointment—or model effective coping skills using the list above. *"Okay, I'm going to take three deep breaths and think about the big picture; I guess it isn't really a big deal. Also, I can try a Plan B this weekend—I can try another store."*

I wanted to get the grass mowed today, but I ran out of time. *"I'm disappointed, but I'm going to get unstuck and move on. It isn't a big deal—I can do it tomorrow. That is big picture thinking."*

TOPIC 1.6   Putting a Plan on Trial (Checking Your Plan Before Trying It Out)

> **BIG PICTURE SUMMARY**

In this topic, the students will plan two parties—a ridiculously bad party followed by a good Plan B party. The students put both the bad party plan and then the good party plan "on trial," thinking through the steps of each plan to evaluate them. Framing the activity as a courtroom trial will add some fun drama as the students evaluate whether a plan is well-thought-out and complete.

Students with and without executive function difficulties sometimes struggle with checking their work and find the process frustrating. By imbuing the checking process with the fun drama of a courtroom trial, this topic aims to engage students in checking their work (and plans) in a new and fresh way. The good Plan B party will then occur during the next class as a celebration of what thoughtful planning (and checking!) can accomplish.

Key Things to Do Here are the two most important things to do in today's class:

1. **Use the following Key Vocabulary often and in fun and playful ways:**
   - Executive Function Skills/Power Skills
   - Planning
   - Plan A/Plan B
   - Putting the Plan on Trial (Checking to See if It Works)
   - Power
   - Managing Frustration/Disappointment
   - Kindness to Yourself and Others
   - Flexible
   - Flexible Thinking
   - Stuck/Unstuck
   - Stuck on a Detail
   - Big Picture

2. **Find ways to spontaneously model executive function skills (flexibility and planning)** *at least once* **during class today.** Make this fun and engaging! Use flexibility and planning skills with your students to solve challenges that come up naturally or challenges that you've invented. For example, tell students, *"I am feeling **stuck** because a friend had to cancel our lunch plans today. Can you help me think of a way to deal with my disappointment and get **unstuck**?"*

 Consider what is realistic for both today's ridiculously bad party and next session's good Plan B party. Before class, prepare a list of items and activities that can work for each party, with a focus on activities and treats that will appeal to the students for the good party. It is important for them to feel that when they plan, there is a meaningful payoff.

Materials

- Unit 1 Daily Self-Awareness Rating (this worksheet can be copied for each student or found in the Student Workbook)
- PowerPoint for Topic 1.6, projected
- Power Equation Poster, posted
- Power Level card. Affix the card to the bottom of the Power Equation Poster Power Arrow.
- Ridiculously bad party materials: paper plates (with no food!), boring textbooks (make sure they are boring to everyone, even students who like to read), an uncooked raw potato, and/or other unappealing items and activities
- Optional: Courtroom props to get the students excited about putting plans on trial (e.g., a gavel, a judge's robe, images of popular courtroom TV shows)
- Optional: How to Boost Our Power Level: Reminder List (printed from Topic 1.1 or located in the front cover of the Student Workbook)

EDUCATOR PLAN

Goal: Practice planning by organizing two parties: a ridiculously bad party and then a good Plan B party. Evaluate each plan by checking each step of the plan. The good Plan B party will take place next class. Have students use power skills (Plan A/Plan B, kindness to self and others, flexibility, managing frustration/disappointment) during the discussions so feelings are not hurt and everyone feels supported.

Why: People with executive function difficulties may struggle with generating plans and checking their work. A fun visual routine can help build students' enthusiasm and skill for planning and checking work.

Plan: Do the following before class:

- Post the Power Equation Poster and place the Power Level card at the bottom part of the Power Arrow on the poster. (You'll move it up when students are flexible, are kind to themselves or others, show planning skills, or manage their frustration and disappointment.)
- Project the PowerPoint for Topic 1.6.

CLASS LESSON PLAN

Slide 1: Blank Power Plan

1. **Ask students to fill out the Unit 1 Daily Self-Awareness Rating worksheet.** Point to the blank Power Plan visual and explain to the students that it is blank today because they will be doing the planning themselves.

BLANK POWER PLAN: For topics that require the class to plan an event, the Power Plan visual is blank and will be filled in during the planning process. You may still wish to review today's schedule at the beginning of class, but explain to the students that because they are now doing the planning, they will fill in the Power Plan themselves with your support.

Slide 2: Power Equation Review

2. **Review the Power Equation.** Remind students that they are working to have more power in their lives, both for themselves and to make the world a better place.

   Here are some key discussion points for the three parts of the Power Equation:

   ★ **Part 1 of the Power Equation:** Being flexible increases our power. Briefly discuss the following skills: Plan A/Plan B, being kind to themselves and others, and getting unstuck.

    When a student offers an idea, raise the Power Level card with a praising statement, such as *"That was a good example of flexible thinking—our power is going up!"*

   ★ **Part 2 of the Power Equation:** Thinking about your big picture goal or the main idea increases your power. Ask students to discuss how noticing when they're stuck on a detail and then shifting back to the big picture helps them reach their goals.

    Continue to praise students when they contribute, raising the Power Level card and saying why you are raising the card (e.g., *"Thanks for helping us think about the big picture—the group's power is going up!"*).

   ★ **Part 3 of the Power Equation:** Setting goals and making plans to reach our goals increases our power. Review with the class how frustration and disappointment are a normal part of life when working toward goals. Discuss with students their coping strategies (from Topic 1.4) and the three flexible thinking tricks for managing frustration and disappointment (from Topic 1.5). Ask students to share coping strategies and if they remember the three flexible thinking tricks. If they don't remember, remind them:

   - **Flexible Thinking Trick 1:** When I'm frustrated or disappointed, I can ask myself, "How long should I be stuck on being frustrated or disappointed? For a short time or a longer time?" (It depends on the situation!)

- **Flexible Thinking Trick 2:** When I'm frustrated or disappointed, I can ask myself, "How can I get unstuck and refocus on my big picture goal?"
- **Flexible Thinking Trick 3:** When I'm frustrated or disappointed, I need to remember that there's always a Plan B (a way of getting unstuck).

Continue raising Power Level cards when you notice students using skills (e.g., *"Thanks for helping us understand how to manage frustration and disappointment—our power is going up!"*)

Explain to students that today they will be using all of these power skills (also known as executive function skills) to practice planning a party together.

POWER LEVEL CARDS: As in all sessions, continue moving Power Level cards up throughout the remainder of today's class. As you praise students for being flexible, planning, participating, engaging in big picture thinking, or being kind to themselves or others, raise the Power Level card part of the way up the Power Arrow. Be careful to explain why the card is going up so the group hears what they're doing well. Find a way to praise every student by the end of group.

Slide 3: Planning a Party and Putting the Plan on Trial

3. **Introduce the two parties and the idea of putting the plan on trial:** *"Today we are going to plan two parties! First, we'll plan a ridiculously bad party, and then we'll plan a good Plan B party. We are going to put both of these parties on trial—that's our fun way of figuring out if the plans work or don't work. And then next class, we're going to actually throw the good Plan B party that we plan today! Now, let's think about what makes a good plan and what makes a not-so-good plan."*

Discuss with your students the qualities of a good plan (referring to the POWERFUL PLAN column of the PowerPoint):

★ A plan is powerful if we've checked each step.

★ A plan is powerful if it's not missing any important details.

★ A plan is especially powerful if we come up with a Plan B in case the plan doesn't work exactly as we expected.

Remember to continue praising students while raising the Power Level card.

Then discuss with students the qualities of a not-so-good plan (referring to the PROBLEM PLAN column of the PowerPoint):

★ A plan may have problems if we didn't check each step.

★ A plan will not work if we missed important details.

★ A plan may have problems if we don't come up with a Plan B in case our Plan A doesn't work out.

Briefly discuss with students how putting a plan on trial (i.e., checking it step-by-step) helps us find problems in the plan and fix them. Refer to the horizontal arrow at the bottom of the PowerPoint slide, "Can I fix the PROBLEM PLAN to make it A POWERFUL PLAN?"

Finally, you may wish to discuss the following questions about the importance of checking a plan for problems:

- ★ Have you ever found an error when you were checking your answers on a test? Did checking and finding the error increase your power? How?

- ★ Can you think of an example where someone didn't check a plan carefully and it led to a bad outcome?

- ★ Do you have any strategies for checking for errors in your work?

 Praise students for examples/strategies they offer while raising the Power Level card (e.g., *"Great example of planning! Power boost."*).

Slide 4: Learning How to Plan by Planning a Ridiculously Bad Party

4a. Plan a bad party. With students' help, fill in today's blank Power Plan (students can type with educator assistance):

- ★ Fill in the goal with something like "Plan a ridiculously bad party."

- ★ Discuss with the class whether planning the bad party is a short-term goal or long-term goal (located next to the Goal section of the blank Power Plan visual). Because the goal is to plan and try out the ridiculously bad party today, this is a short-term goal.

- ★ Introduce the planning process, reminding the students to think about the who, what, where, when, and how of the party. The written steps of the plan will be mostly about the how.

- ★ Let the students know that you have a few supplies for the ridiculously bad party: paper plates (with no food!), boring textbooks, an uncooked raw potato, and/or other unappealing items and activities.

- ★ Brainstorm with the class a plan for the ridiculously bad party. Type the steps as a numbered list under Plan in the blank Power Plan visual. Encourage students to come up with as many funny ideas as possible to ensure the party is a total disaster. Here's an example of a bad party plan in case students need help generating ideas:

    1. Write a sign announcing the party with the wrong time/date.
    2. Get the supplies. (Terry will bring plates but forget to bring the food; Sam will bring two boring textbooks without thinking about what people would really want to do.)
    3. Set up the supplies.
    4. Read boring textbooks for main party activity!

 Remember to keep praising students for their planning (and flexibility) and raising the Power Level card accordingly. Remind the group why you are raising the card, and always try to link praise to the Key Vocabulary (flexible, unstuck, big picture, goal, plan, kindness to yourself and others).

Once the class has completed the bad party plan, tell them it's time to check out the plan by putting it on trial.

4b. Put the bad party plan on trial. Help students act as the judge and jury as they put the class's bad party plan on trial. Encourage students to use power skills such as flexibility, kindness to yourself and others, and managing frustration, so no feelings are hurt during this mock trial. Here are the steps to follow:

- Set up the courtroom props.
- Quickly flip back to Slide 3 (with the putting the plan on trial image) and refer to the qualities of a powerful plan and problem plan.
- Then flip back to Slide 4, the students' bad party plan. Review each step of the class's bad party plan, referring to the props (e.g., plates, potato, textbooks) whenever possible. You can appoint a student to be the judge who reads each step of the plan one by one, and the rest of the class can be the jury who votes on whether each step meets the goal or not.
- Step by step, have the class check to see if each step in the plan leads to the goal of having a ridiculously bad party. (Remind students that your goal was to throw a ridiculously bad party, so the plan is a good one if it meets that goal.)
- Put a check in the box on the Power Plan under the Check section for each part of the plan that meets the goal of planning a bad party.

 Keep praising students for their planning and big picture thinking and raise the Power Level card accordingly.

Slide 5: Learning How to Plan by Planning a Good Party (the Plan B Party)

5a. Plan a good party (the Plan B party). Explain to the students that the goal has changed, and that they will now work together to plan a fun party that will happen next class. With students' help, fill in the Power Plan with the details of the good Plan B party (students can type, or the educator can type):

- Write in a goal such as: "Plan a good party for next class." If possible, students should help with filling in the Power Plan.
- Discuss with the class whether planning a good party is a short-term goal or long-term goal (located next to Goal in the Power Plan visual). Because the goal is to plan a fun party that will happen next class, this is a short-term goal.
- Point to the Check section of the Power Plan, explaining: *"After we plan our fun Plan B party, we'll put it on trial to check to make sure it's a good plan that is likely to succeed."*
- Remind the students to think about the who, what, where, when, and how of the fun party. The written steps of the plan will be mostly about the how.
- Let the students know what supplies are available for the party they will plan. These might include a few snacks, a short video or videos, a game, music, a trip outside, etc.

- ★ Ask the class to brainstorm a step-by-step plan for the fun party. With student help, type the steps as a numbered list under Plan in the blank Power Plan visual. Remember to praise students as they plan and are flexible, and remember to raise the Power Level card, telling them why the power is going up. Here's an example of a good party plan in case students need help generating ideas:

    1. Bring plates and food.
    2. Set up the videos, games, etc.
    3. Be sure to use flexible thinking skills and kindness skills so everyone gets a chance to enjoy the party.
    4. Have fun!
    5. Clean up.

Students may suggest ideas for the party that are impossible or unrealistic. In these situations, use the flexible thinking vocabulary and ask them to come up with a Plan B. When they come up with a Plan B, raise the Power Level card and praise them for their flexible Plan B thinking.

Important Note

Remember to Use the Stuck on a Detail Routine: When students get stuck on specific off-topic details, ask: *"Do we want to get stuck on that detail or get back to the big picture?"* or *"How long should we be stuck on that interesting detail?"* See Topic 1.1 for an explanation of how to use a stopwatch to time how long they want to be stuck (30 seconds or 1 minute). Also consider using the "How long should we be frustrated/disappointed?" routine, always with empathy and patience, as described in Topic 1.5.

5b. **Put the good party plan on trial to see whether it meets the goal.** Help students act as the judge and jury as they put the class's good party plan on trial. Encourage students to use power skills such as flexibility, kindness, and managing frustration, so no feelings are hurt during this mock trial. Here are the steps to follow:

- ★ Continue the courtroom theme with appropriate props and visuals.
- ★ Quickly flip back to Slide 3 and review the putting the plan on trial routine.
- ★ Then flip back to Slide 5 (the students' good party plan). Have the students go through each step of the plan and put a check in the Check column if the step meets the goal of planning a good party or place an X next to any step that needs to be reworked. Once again, you can appoint a student to be the judge who reads each step of the plan one by one, and the rest of the class can be the jury who votes on whether each step meets the goal or not.
- ★ As the class evaluates each step of the plan, classroom volunteers can act out each step.
- ★ Encourage the students to come up with alternate ideas for steps that they feel should be improved.

 As always, praise students for their flexibility, planning, and checking and raise the Power Level card each time.

Remind the class that when we put a plan on trial, we make the plan stronger because we find any problems and fix them. Ask students to think of a way to keep track of their plan, so they don't lose or forget it (e.g., copy it down, take a picture of it, save it on the computer, write it on the board where it won't be erased). Say to the class: *"How can we keep track of our great plan so we don't lose or forget it? Next class, we'll need to have the plan ready to throw our party, so what are some ways we can keep track of the plan?"*

In addition to the method that your students come up with, make sure you privately save a copy of the plan just in case.

5c. Ask the students why we had the goal of learning how to plan and check our plan.

Point to the Why section of the Power Plan and ask students to fill in the answer or just discuss. Consider with students why putting a plan on trial (i.e., checking it step-by-step) is critical to reaching our goals—if we don't think ahead before jumping into a plan, there might be mistakes and it could even be dangerous. Also, discuss how students might use the skills they learned today (i.e., planning and checking their plans) in other classes and at home. Encourage a rich and engaged discussion.

By now, the group's Power Level card should have reached the top of the Power Arrow on the Power Equation Poster. Make sure you are praising each student. Even if a student has difficulties during a class, say things like, *"Nice job. You made it through the lesson today. It wasn't easy, but you were flexible, even when it was frustrating. You helped our group's power go up!"*

Point out to the class that because they all showed lots of power building skills today, the group's power went up. Celebrate the fact that when their power goes up, they can achieve more of what they want and need for themselves and make the world a better place. One example of this is that now that they've planned a party, they will be able to enjoy the party next class.

5d. Send Home Extension for Topic 1.6 home with students or e-mail it to parents.

5e. Look for generalization opportunities in other classes. Share copies of the blank Power Plan (located at the end of this topic) with your students' other educators. Encourage educators to use the Power Plan for class projects and activities. For example, educators may draw the Power Plan on the board to present the goal of the day's topic and the plan to reach that goal. They may also ask the class to consider why the learning goal for the day is important. The Power Plan may also be used to help students organize their individual class projects. For example:

Goal: Write a three-paragraph essay on Abraham Lincoln.

Why: I want to be a scientist when I grow up, and scientists need to be able to write.

Plan: 1. Brainstorm ideas.
2. Write an outline.
3. Write the topic sentence of each paragraph.
4. Complete each paragraph.

Check: Read and check for errors.

> **CHECK:** How are my students doing?
> Do I need to make any adjustments for the next class?

See Appendix A for a list of questions to guide your self-reflection and refer to the Troubleshooting section (Appendix B) to address common problems or any challenges that may have arisen with the curriculum.

TOPIC 1.6: Putting a Plan on Trial (Checking Your Plan Before Trying It Out)

DAILY SELF-AWARENESS RATING: UNIT 1

NAME: _____

Executive Function Skills

Flexibility + Big Picture Thinking + Goals and Planning = POWER

Mark an X on the arrow to show how you feel today:

How flexible are you today?

Stuck   Somewhat Flexible   Very Flexible

Are you stuck on details today?

Stuck on Details   Somewhat Stuck on Details   Focused on the Big Picture

Topic 1.6: Putting a Plan on Trial (Checking Your Plan Before Trying It Out)

HOME EXTENSION FOR TOPIC 1.6: PUTTING A PLAN ON TRIAL (CHECKING YOUR PLAN BEFORE TRYING IT OUT)

In order to achieve most goals, it is important to have a plan. Plans require thinking through the required steps to reach the goal. Although some students have difficulty setting goals and making plans to reach goals, these skills can be practiced. Goal setting and planning are examples of executive function skills.

In today's topic, your child's class planned a party together. The students then put the plan for the party "on trial," thinking through the steps of the plan to evaluate whether the plan was well thought out. Planning skills are critical. Below are some ideas for how to help your child become more comfortable with goal setting and planning.

Key Vocabulary/skills:

Putting the Plan on Trial (Checking to See if It Works) *Executive Function Skills/Power Skills*

Goal   *Plan(ning)*   *Plan A/Plan B*   *Managing Frustration/Disappointment*

Stuck   *Flexible*   *Stuck on a Detail*   *Big Picture*

How to use the Key Vocabulary:

1. **Use the vocabulary of setting goals and making plans in positive ways at home. For example:**

   "I'm proud of you for planning to meet up with your friend."
   "What do you want to accomplish? What is your goal?"
   "Do we need a Plan B?"
   "It doesn't look like this is working. Was there something wrong with our plan?"

2. **Share your experiences.** Are you planning anything like a visit to see a friend or a trip to the movies? Model effective planning skills by saying your plans and goals out loud and by asking your child to help you make plans and check to see if they are working. For example:

   "My goal is for us to get to _____ on time. My plan is to _____. I need your help to put the plan on trial to see if it works. Can we do that now, or would you like to have some free time first?"

   (one of your child's preferred activities or school/Scouts/practice/family member's house)

   "Well, this isn't how I planned it, but I can be flexible."
   "My goal is to make it to Back to School Night this year. I plan to leave work early."
   "My plan to go to the grocery store tonight is still possible. We have just enough time."

TOPIC 1.6: Putting a Plan on Trial (Checking Your Plan Before Trying It Out)   Blank Power Plan

POWER

CHECK:

PLAN:

Plan B?

GOAL:

WHY:

STUCK?

TOPIC 1.7   Celebration Day! The Plan B Party

> **BIG PICTURE SUMMARY**
>
> This topic focuses on celebrating the class's use of goal-setting and planning skills. It's also a celebration of many other power/executive function skills, including flexible thinking, Plan A/Plan B, and managing frustration and disappointment. The goal for today is for all students to leave the class knowing their new planning and flexibility skills have given them the power to succeed in planning and experiencing today's fun party.

Key Things to Do Here are the two most important things to do in today's class:

1. **Use this Key Vocabulary often and in fun and playful ways:**
   - ★ Executive Function Skills
   - ★ Goal
   - ★ Plan
   - ★ Putting the Plan on Trial (Checking to See if It Works)
   - ★ Power
   - ★ Plan A/Plan B
   - ★ Flexibility
   - ★ Flexible Thinking
   - ★ Managing Frustration/Disappointment
   - ★ How Long Should I Be Disappointed?
   - ★ Stuck/Unstuck
   - ★ Stuck on a Detail
   - ★ Big Picture

2. **Find ways to spontaneously model executive function skills (flexibility and planning) *at least once* during class today.** Make this fun and engaging! Use flexibility and planning skills with your students to solve challenges that come up naturally or challenges that you've invented. For example, talk with your students about how being flexible can feel challenging, even when it's just the "small stuff." Describe how the small stuff can feel like a really big deal sometimes. You could say something like:

   "I have a favorite coffee that I drink every morning. Today, I went to make my first cup, and I was all out of coffee. I had to use my backup coffee—it's older, and I don't like the flavor as much. It was really disappointing, but I used flexible thinking. I told myself: 'I can have my favorite coffee next time, but right now, I don't want to get stuck and be late to work.' I took some deep breaths to get unstuck and got on with my day."

Materials

- Unit 1 Daily Self-Awareness Rating (this worksheet can be copied for each student or found in the Student Workbook)

- PowerPoint for Topic 1.7, projected
- Power Equation Poster, posted
- Power Level card. Affix the card to the bottom of the Power Equation Poster Power Arrow.
- The good/fun party (Plan B party) materials (as planned last class)
- Optional: Courtroom props to get the students excited about putting plans on trial (e.g., a gavel, a judge's robe, images of popular courtroom TV shows)

- Optional: How to Boost Our Power Level: Reminder List (printed from Topic 1.1 or located in the front cover of the Student Workbook)

EDUCATOR PLAN

Goal: Celebrate the Plan B party to help students feel good about their goal-setting and planning skills. Use other power skills, including putting the plan on trial, flexibility, Plan A/Plan B, and managing frustration and disappointment, as any challenges arise during the party.

Why: It's important for the students to experience goal setting and planning as attainable, successful, and relatively easy. Future topics will involve greater planning challenges, but this topic focuses on showing students that when they use goal-setting and planning skills, it pays off.

Plan: Use the standard classroom setup as described in the previous topic.

POWER LEVEL CARD: As in all sessions, continue moving the Power Level card up throughout the remainder of today's class. As you praise students for being flexible, planning, participating, engaging in big picture thinking, or being kind during class, raise the Power Level card part of the way up the Power Arrow. Be careful to explain why the card is going up, so they know what the group is doing well. Find a way to praise every student by the end of class. You may opt to give your students a reward at the end of the group (e.g., free time, time on computer) for reaching the Power Zone (the top of the Power Arrow). For now, continue to only move the Power Level card up the Power Arrow and avoid moving it down.

CLASS LESSON PLAN

Slide 1: Blank Power Plan

1a. Ask students to fill out the Unit 1 Daily Self-Awareness Rating worksheet. Point to the blank Power Plan visual and explain that it's blank because the class made their own plan for today's party.

"Last class you planned a ridiculously bad party to practice your planning skills. And then after that, you planned a fun party. We are going to celebrate the fun party that you planned today. That's what today is all about—celebrating your goal setting and planning! Let's start out by remembering our goal and plan. You had a strategy for remembering the plan for the party. What was it?"

Praise the class for the strategies they used for remembering their plan for the party from last class (writing it down, taking a picture, etc.). If necessary, help them remember and clarify any points of confusion about the plan. Have the students enter the goal and plan into the blank Power Plan. Have them review the plan for the party.

 As always throughout the curriculum, when a student offers an idea, raise the Power Level card with a praising statement, such as *"Great job remembering an important part of our plan—our power is going up!"*

1b. Remind the class that planning is powerful and fun, but that part of planning is dealing with the unexpected: *"We may need a Plan B if things don't go as expected. Are you ready to come up with Plan Bs if things don't go as expected?"* Students may wish to come up with some Plan Bs for things that might go wrong.

Consider building one or two unexpected surprises into today's class (without preparing your students in advance). For example, you could forget to bring plates, so the class will have to use flexible thinking for how to serve the food (e.g., paper towels, napkins). Later, you could surprise the class with a special visit from another educator or the principal. Ask them to come up with a Plan B for how to include the visitor in the party activities.

1c. Have the class set up the party, following the steps on the Power Plan visual. Work to make the party a success for all students. If students get stuck, encourage them to use skills like flexibility, Plan A/Plan B, and managing frustration and disappointment. When they use these skills (even if prompted to do so), remember to praise them and raise the Power Level card. Use the stuck on a detail routine if the class gets stuck.

1d. At the end of the class, put the plan on trial. (Optional: Set up the courtroom props.)

Briefly review the idea of putting a plan on trial (using Slide 2 to review). Then switch back to Slide 1 and tell the students: *"Let's put our plan on trial. Let's check it. Did we meet our goal of having a fun party?"* Invite the students to go step-by-step through their plan, checking off each step that was successful. Discuss how the class can put the plan on trial before *and* after they carry it out. Ask students why it is powerful to do both. Explain to the class that checking your plan before allows you to avoid problems and checking it after allows you to learn from your mistakes and see what to do differently next time.

1e. Praise the students for their wonderful use of planning and flexibility skills. Let them know that today's party is just the beginning; next class, you are going to learn the skills to plan an even bigger party or event.

1f. Ask students why they had a goal to plan a party. Point to the Why section of the Power Plan and ask students to fill in the answer or just discuss. Gently lead discussion to focus on topics related to practicing planning skills and flexibility. Encourage students to discuss how they are using (or could use) the goal-setting and planning skills at home, in other classes, and to get more choice and power in their lives. Discuss with the class how goal setting, planning, and flexibility are all known as executive function skills. Be sure to affirm the variety of thoughts and opinions the students give, so all of the students feel heard and celebrated. Remember that the Power Level card should make it to the top of the Power Arrow on the Power Equation Poster by the end of class.

1g. Send Home Extension for Topic 1.7 home with students or e-mail to parents.

1h. Look for generalization opportunities in other classes. Check with other educators to see if they've been able to make use of the blank Power Plan in class (located at the end of Topic 1.6). Provide educators with additional copies, and brainstorm further ways that the visual can be integrated into class and assignments. Do the students have a longer-term project that needs to be broken down into steps? Can the Power Plan visual be integrated into the educator's lesson? Here's an example for a science lesson:

Goal: Learn about the scientific method.

Why: The scientific method is a powerful way to study and learn things. The scientific method has made it possible for people to learn a lot about how things in the world work.

Plan A:

1. Learn key words and vocabulary.
2. Learn the steps of the scientific method.
3. Use the scientific method to test a hypothesis.
4. Write up the results.

Plan B: If we run out of time, we will finish this next class.

Check: Did we reach our goal? What did we learn about the scientific method?

> **CHECK:** How are my students doing?
> Do I need to make any adjustments for next class?

See Appendix A for a list of questions to guide your self-reflection and refer to the Troubleshooting section (Appendix B) to address common problems or any challenges that may have arisen with the curriculum.

TOPIC 1.7: Celebration Day! The Plan B Party

DAILY SELF-AWARENESS RATING: UNIT 1

NAME: _____

Executive Function Skills

Flexibility + Big Picture Thinking + Goals and Planning = POWER

Mark an X on the arrow to show how you feel today:

How flexible are you today?

Stuck   Somewhat Flexible   Very Flexible

Are you stuck on details today?

Stuck on Details   Somewhat Stuck on Details   Focused on the Big Picture

TOPIC 1.7: Celebration Day! The Plan B Party

HOME EXTENSION FOR TOPIC 1.7: CELEBRATION DAY! THE PLAN B PARTY

Today's topic focused on celebrating the students' use of goal setting, planning, and flexible thinking skills. We threw a fun and successful Plan B party together. The goal was for your child to leave the class knowing their new skills have given them the power to succeed in planning.

Key Vocabulary/skills:

Goal   *Plan*   *Setting a Goal and Making a Plan to Reach the Goal*

How to use the Key Vocabulary:

1. **Whenever possible, start a discussion with your child about planning events.** You could talk about events in the news or on TV, cultural or sports events, or a family event or activity. For example:

   "What was their goal?"
   "How many people had to work together to plan this?"
   "What would have happened if every person had a different plan for the event?"
   "Do you think any of the people planning this event had to ask for help?"

2. **Include your child in the planning of an upcoming event.** The more practice your child gets with planning, the better they'll get over time. If you take over planning and scheduling everything for your child (and you wouldn't be alone if you have), they won't get to practice. But without some help with planning, they may struggle and get frustrated. Try to get a just-right balance of support and practice with this idea:

   - Set up a social event with your child, like meeting a friend in the park or having cousins over to play. Before the event, ask your child to help you plan activities for the get-together, and be sure to come up with Plan Bs in case it rains, or if their friend doesn't want to do what your child wants to do.

   - Here is a sample plan you can use:

     Goal: To have fun with my friend.
     Why: So my friend will want to hang out again. I like to be a good friend!
     Plan:

     1. Invite my friend to meet up.
     2. Ask my friend what they want to do and do that first because they are the guest.
     3. Suggest we play on the computer.
     4. Compromise if we need to.
     5. Have a snack.

     Do: Follow the plan. (Let's have fun!)
     Check: How did it go? Did we need to make a Plan B?

UNIT 2

Compromise

TOPIC 2.1 Compromising Is a Win-Win

BIG PICTURE SUMMARY

This topic teaches why compromising is useful and outlines four different strategies people can use to compromise. It ends with a game to practice the compromise strategies.

Key Things To Do Here are the two most important things to do in today's class:

1. **Use this Key Vocabulary often and in fun and playful ways:**

    ★ Executive Function Skills

    ★ Flexible

    ★ Plan A/Plan B

    ★ Goal, Why, Plan, Check

    ★ Use Coping Strategies and Flexible Thinking When Needed

    ★ Big Picture

    ★ Stuck on a Detail

    ★ How to Compromise:

      • Each Gets Part.

      • Combine Ideas.

      • Take Turns.

      • Do Something Different You Both Like.

Key Vocabulary

The Key Vocabulary is a critical part of the curriculum; it is more important than the actual activities in each topic! The Key Vocabulary should be spoken as often as possible and presented in fun and enjoyable ways. Avoid punitive uses of the Key Vocabulary because that can interfere with student buy-in and use of the words and skills. The goal is to get your students to want to use the Key Vocabulary in their everyday lives.

Important Note: New Key Vocabulary is introduced throughout the curriculum. Although a specific list of Key Vocabulary is provided for each topic, continue to use and reinforce all the Key Vocabulary from the curriculum in your interactions with the students. Be sure to make explicit connections that their use of Executive Function Skills gets them more power so they can get what they want. For example, you could say, *"I noticed you used a coping strategy so that you could refocus on your **big picture goal** to finish your homework during school. Great work boosting your power!"*)

2. **Find ways to spontaneously model executive function skills (compromise, flexibility, and planning)** *at least once* **during class today.** Make this fun and engaging! Use

compromise, flexibility, and planning skills with your students to solve challenges that come up naturally or challenges that you've invented. For example: *"It looks like we are missing a few people today from group, but I don't want to get stuck on feeling disappointed. My **Big Picture Goal** is to learn about **Compromising** today, so let's get started."*

Materials

 ★ Unit 2 Daily Self-Awareness Rating (worksheet copied for each student or found in the Student Workbook)

 ★ PowerPoint for Topic 2.1, projected

★ Power Equation Poster, posted

★ Power Level card. Affix the card to the bottom of the Power Arrow.

★ Failure to Compromise video ("Dr. Seuss' The Zax"): https://www.youtube.com/watch?v=dZmZzGxGpSs

EDUCATOR PLAN

Goal: Students will learn what a compromise is, why it is useful to compromise, and how to compromise.

Why: Many students with executive function challenges don't know how to compromise, nor do they understand that compromising is a tool for getting what is most important to them while giving up less important details. This topic incorporates both direct instruction and practice to build on students' areas of strength and show them that compromise allows for win-win solutions.

Plan: Do the following before class:

★ Post the Power Equation Poster and place the Power Level card at the bottom of the Power Arrow on the poster.

★ Pull up the link for the Dr. Seuss' The Zax video so it's ready to view.

★ Project the PowerPoint for Topic 2.1.

CONTINUE USING THE POWER LEVEL CARD AND SPECIFIC PRAISE:
Remember to continue using the Power Level card. Focus on celebrating or noticing when the students are doing well. However, when you need to provide corrective feedback, it's essential—and scientifically supported—to provide praise four times for every one instance of corrective feedback. Do NOT lower the Power Level card. Rather, help students notice that they are stuck and refer them back to the key executive function skills they have learned and the Power Equation. You might say, *"Our Power Level is **stuck**—let's look at the Power Equation to see what we can do to get **unstuck**. I wonder if a **compromise** would help here."*

CLASS LESSON PLAN

Slide 1: Power Plan

1a. Ask students to fill out the Unit 2 Daily Self-Awareness Rating worksheet and review the Power Plan for Topic 2.1.

1b. **Tell students that they will be planning a bigger and better event and then discuss what the event could be.** Offer several options that are practical for the class, such as another party, a meeting with the vice principal to tell them what is easy or hard about school, a public service event, or a field trip. Briefly discuss some ideas for the event, so the students get excited about it. Students will have more time to select and plan the event in future topics.

Slide 2: The Power Equation: The Compromise Skill

2. **Explain to the class that in order to plan your new event, you will need to practice some new executive function skills.** Tell the students that the important new skill they will practice today is the skill of compromise. Point to compromise in the Power Equation (located under the Be Flexible heading). Note that compromise is a new tool for getting more power and more of what you want and need.

Slide 3: The Compromise Skill

3. **Start a discussion to introduce the concept of Compromise.** Ask students why they think compromise is useful. Will everyone want exactly the same things in the new event that we plan? Here are some key points to cover with the class:

   ★ Compromise allows the group to communicate and come up with a plan that everyone likes.

   ★ Compromise is different than giving in. With compromise, everyone gets some of what they want. We call that a win-win.

   ★ Compromising helps when you have to make a decision with another person.

   ★ When people don't compromise, no one gets anything (a lose-lose), or someone gets what they want, while other people get much less or none of what they want and then feel bad.

   ★ Ask the class to tell you what compromise means to them, and then have the students identify several ways they can compromise (or if they have ever had to compromise).

 Remember to always praise students when you notice them using skills like flexible thinking, big picture thinking, kindness, and compromise. Tell students what they've done well while raising the Power Level card on the Power Arrow of the Power Equation Poster. Continue this routine throughout all classes.

Topic 2.1: Compromising Is a Win-Win   87

Slide 4: Compromise Video

4a. **Show a video about a failure to Compromise, such as "Dr. Suess' The Zax."** Synopsis: The north-going Zax and the south-going Zax meet at the midpoint. Neither Zax is willing to walk around the other Zax, so they stand there for years, unwilling to compromise. As a result, the rest of the world moves on without them. Years later, they're still left stuck and frustrated in the middle of the highway.

4b. **Discuss the video with the students and pose questions like these:**

- ★ Has a situation similar to this one ever happened to you?
- ★ Did the north-going Zax get what he wanted? What about the south-going Zax?
- ★ Was either Zax flexible in their ideas?
- ★ Did either Zax communicate what they wanted? Was it effective?
- ★ Did each Zax want something that conflicted with what the other Zax wanted? Could both Zaxes get exactly what they want at the same time? If two people want things that conflict, does it help to say, "I never budge?"
- ★ Did either Zax gain any power in the story?
- ★ What did the Zaxes lose by not compromising?
- ★ Is there a way they could have compromised and each gotten what they wanted? What if one Zax took one step to the side?
- ★ Can you think of other times when people refuse to budge, and it doesn't work? (For example, sports lockouts, traffic gridlock, filibusters in Congress.) **Note:** Be prepared for students to complain about their parents in response to this question. You can respond by moving the group forward: *"Okay, we all struggle with compromising, but the payoff is big when you get a win-win—when both people get some of what they want."* Alternatively, you can talk through options for discussing true compromise with parents—for example, students can teach their parents about compromise using the Home Extension for this topic.
- ★ Does compromising mean you should never stick to your idea, and you should always go with what the other person wants? (The answer is no.)

Compromise is when we keep our eye on the big picture, stay flexible, and communicate to come up with a win-win compromise that works for everyone. It is one of the most powerful of the skills we will learn and practice.

 Remember to continue praising students and the group while raising the Power Level card. Be sure to explain why you're increasing the Power Level.

Slide 5: How to Compromise

5. **Discuss different ways to Compromise.** Reference the 4 Ways to Compromise visual in the PowerPoint and discuss the example with the class. You can also use an example of compromise from your own life—sharing personal examples can increase student buy-in.

Explain to the students that a win-win compromise is when everybody is flexible and communicates with kindness to get some of they want, either now or later.

For example: Two brothers are at the grocery store with their mom, who says, "The two of you can pick out dessert for after dinner tonight." One brother wants chocolate cupcakes, but the other brother wants vanilla ice cream. These are a few examples of win-win **Compromises** they could come up with:

* **Each Gets Part:** Have a small chocolate cupcake and a little vanilla ice cream.
* **Combine Ideas:** Get vanilla cupcakes.
* **Take Turns:** Respectfully convince mom to let them pick two desserts: chocolate cupcakes for tonight and vanilla ice cream for tomorrow night.
* **Do Something Different You Both Like:** Get chocolate chip cookies instead!

 Reminder: Keep using the Power Level card to praise students.

Slide 6: A Graphic of the Four Ways to Compromise

6. **Discuss the Compromise graphic.** Ask the class to consider how each of the four pictures on the **Compromise** graphic remind us of the related skills. For example, the green circle reminds us of **Combining Ideas** because it combines the yellow and blue colors. The red square reminds us of **Doing Something Different** because it is different than the yellow and blue circles.

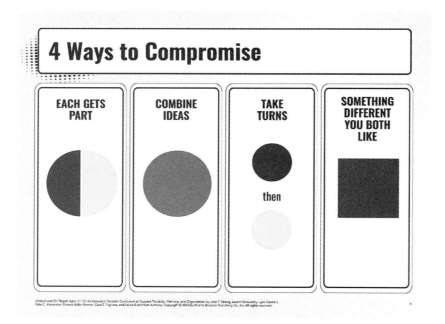

Slide 7: Compromise Competition and Scenario 1

7. **Compromise Competition Activity**
   * There are eight compromise challenges presented on the following eight PowerPoint slides. The scenarios have been designed for the class to practice coming up with win-win compromises as a group. Encourage students to use other power

skills like being kind and flexible (e.g., taking turns and listening) when practicing compromise strategies.

- ★ Discuss several examples from the scenarios as a group without being timed. For each of the eight scenarios, we've provided examples of each type of compromise (i.e., each gets part, combine ideas, take turns, something different you both like). Only share the answers with the students if they are stuck or if they need examples of how to play the game. Sometimes the compromise is silly, so feel free to laugh with the students.

- ★ Once students understand the game, race the clock to see how many compromises they can come up with for the remaining scenarios in 5 minutes.

- ★ If no answers are provided by the students, then read out the answers below.

Important Note

Stuck on a Detail Routine: As described in Topic 1.1, use the **Stuck on a Detail** routine whenever a student (or instructor!) gets stuck on a detail, like a specific off-topic idea (e.g., a video game, a special interest). Ask one of the following questions: *"How long do we want to be stuck on that interesting detail?"* or *"Do we want to get stuck on that detail or get back to the big picture?"* If the class wants to get stuck on the detail, you can say, *"Great! Do we want to be stuck on it for 30 seconds or 1 minute?"* Then use a timer to count 30 seconds or 1 minute. When time's up you can say, *"Great! We were stuck on the detail for 1 minute, and now we can get back to the big picture."* This gentle approach to getting back on task can help improve the self-regulation skills of students who struggle with maintaining the big picture topic and being flexible to improve their self-regulation skills.

Scenario 1: I want to play a video game, but my friend wants to go outside.

- ★ **Each Gets Part:** Play video games for 30 minutes and then go outside for 30 minutes.

- ★ **Combine Ideas:** Go to an arcade and play video games.

- ★ **Take Turns:** If the weather is bad, play video games and then go outside tomorrow. If weather is good, go outside and then play video games tomorrow.

- ★ **Do Something Different You Both Like:** Watch a movie.

Slide 8: Scenario 2

Scenario 2: I want to go outside, but my dad wants me to do my homework.

- ★ **Each Gets Part:** Go outside for 10 minutes for every 30 minutes of doing homework.

- ★ **Combine Ideas:** Lie on the grass outside to do homework.

- ★ **Take Turns:** Today, finish homework first and then go outside. Tomorrow, go outside first and then do homework.

- ★ **Do Something Different You Both Like:** Walk the dog.

Slide 9: Scenario 3

Scenario 3: I want to read comics, but my friend wants to play soccer.

- ★ **Each Gets Part:** Play soccer for 30 minutes and then read comics for 30 minutes.
- ★ **Combine Ideas:** Go to the soccer field and read comics on the bench while waiting for my friend to finish playing soccer.
- ★ **Take Turns:** Read comics today and play soccer tomorrow.
- ★ **Do Something Different You Both Like:** Watch a video tutorial and learn how to build an awesome new paper airplane.

Slide 10: Scenario 4

Scenario 4: I want to watch my favorite show, but my friend wants to watch his favorite show.

- ★ **Each Gets Part:** Watch 20 minutes of my favorite show and then 20 minutes of my friend's favorite show.
- ★ **Combine Ideas:** Watch a show that is similar to both of our favorite shows.
- ★ **Take Turns:** Watch the friend's favorite show this week and then watch my favorite show next week.
- ★ **Do Something Different You Both Like:** Watch a completely different show.

Slide 11: Scenario 5

Scenario 5: I want to get pizza at a restaurant for dinner, but Mom wants to eat dinner at home.

- ★ **Each Gets Part:** Get mozzarella sticks from the pizza restaurant and have a later dinner at home with Mom.
- ★ **Combine Ideas:** Make pizza at home.
- ★ **Take Turns:** Eat at home tonight and go out for pizza later in the week.
- ★ **Do Something Different You Both Like:** Order Chinese food.

Slide 12: Scenario 6

Scenario 6: My little brother and I want to play the piano at the same time.

- ★ **Each Gets Part:** I teach my little brother a piece that he doesn't know how to play and let him practice afterward.
- ★ **Combine Ideas:** Play a piece that two people can play together, like Chopsticks.
- ★ **Take Turns:** My little brother plays for 20 minutes, and then I play for 20 minutes.
- ★ **Do Something Different You Both Like:** Play a two-player video game.

Slide 13: Scenario 7

Scenario 7: I want to wear sweatpants, but Mom wants me to wear khakis.

- ★ **Each Gets Part:** Wear sweatpants at home and wear khakis to go outside.
- ★ **Combine Ideas:** Wear khaki-colored sweatpants.
- ★ **Take Turns:** Wear khakis today and wear sweatpants some other time.
- ★ **Do Something Different You Both Like:** Wear jeans.

Slide 14: Scenario 8

Scenario 8: I want to skip breakfast, but Dad wants me to eat pancakes, bacon, and strawberries.

- ★ **Each Gets Part:** I eat a pancake but no bacon or strawberries.
- ★ **Combine Ideas:** I skip breakfast at home but take it with me to eat later when I'm hungry.
- ★ **Take Turns:** I eat Dad's breakfast today, but tomorrow I just have juice.
- ★ **Do Something Different You Both Like:** Make a big midmorning snack.

Slide 15: Topic 2.1 Wrap-Up: Why Is Compromise Powerful?

15a. **Ask students to consider how and why Compromising will build power in their lives at school, at home, and in the future (e.g., getting a job).** Point to the Why section of the Power Plan and ask students to fill in the answer or just discuss. Knowing how to compromise gives you power because it helps you make decisions that work for everyone without giving in or getting stuck in lose-lose conflicts. Knowing how to compromise gives you power because it helps you be kind to yourself and others and get some of what you want even when you disagree with someone.

15b. **Send Home Extension for Topic 2.1 home with students or e-mail it to parents.**

15c. **Look for generalization opportunities in other classes.** Ask your students' other instructors to use the blank Power Plan (introduced at the end of Topic 1.6) with students for their individual work (e.g., making a plan for how a student will complete a project or assignment). Ask the instructors to help the students fill out the Power Plan (printed or on a computer). Emphasize the importance of using at least four positive statements for every correction or command when using the Power Plan so students will come to enjoy using it. Here's an example for a science project:

Goal: Complete your science project.

Why: Science is interesting and fun. Doing a science project helps you learn how to complete larger, longer-term projects.

Plan A:

1. Come up with a practical idea for your project.
2. Talk to your teacher about your idea.

3. Plan out the different parts of the project.
4. Split up the parts so you complete one part each day.

Plan B: If you get stuck, talk to your teacher about plans for how to get the project done.

Check: Did you reach your goal? Did you work on and complete your science project?

CHECK: How are my students doing?
Do I need to make any adjustments for the next class?

See Appendix A for a list of questions to guide your self-reflection and refer to the Troubleshooting section (Appendix B) to address common problems or any challenges that may have arisen with the curriculum.

TOPIC 2.1: Compromising Is a Win-Win

DAILY SELF-AWARENESS RATING: UNIT 2

NAME: _____

Executive Function Skills

Flexibility + Big Picture Thinking + Goals and Planning = POWER

1. How much do you think you can compromise today?

Mark an X on the arrow to show how you feel today:

⟵———○———————————○———————————○———⟶

Can't Compromise   Can Compromise Some   Can Compromise
(I'm Feeling Too Stuck)

2. Which executive function skills do you plan to use today? (Check all that apply.)

Making Plan Bs when Plan As don't work ☐

Focusing on the big picture (instead of being stuck on details) ☐

Being flexible ☐

Using coping strategies and flexible thinking if needed ☐

Compromising ☐

TOPIC 2.1: Compromising Is a Win-Win

HOME EXTENSION FOR TOPIC 2.1: COMPROMISING IS A WIN-WIN

In this topic, students learned why compromising is useful and were taught four ways that people can compromise so that everyone gets some of what they want.

Key Vocabulary/skills:

Compromise or *Win-Win Compromise*

How to Compromise (Four Ways):

1. *Each Gets Part*
2. *Combine Ideas*
3. *Take Turns*
4. *Do Something Different You Both Like*

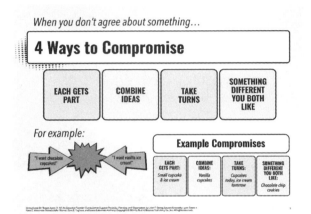 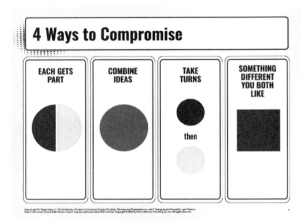

How to use the Key Vocabulary:

Compromise is an easy word to use on a daily basis and is probably already common in your vocabulary. Remember that compromise is a way for both people to get part of what they want. One example discussed in the class was the following:

Two brothers are at the grocery store with their mom, who says, "The two of you can pick out dessert for after dinner tonight." One brother wants chocolate cupcakes, but the other brother wants vanilla ice cream. Here are a few examples of win-win compromises they could come up with:

- **Each Gets Part:** Have a small chocolate cupcake and a little vanilla ice cream.
- **Combine Ideas:** Get vanilla cupcakes.
- **Take Turns:** Respectfully convince mom to let them pick two desserts: chocolate cupcakes for tonight, and vanilla ice cream for tomorrow night.
- **Do Something Different You Both Like:** Get chocolate chip cookies instead!

TOPIC 2.1: Compromising Is a Win-Win (continued)

HOME EXTENSION FOR TOPIC 2.1: COMPROMISING IS A WIN-WIN

1. Apply these compromise options to situations that come up in your everyday life and discuss them with your child. For example, if you and a family member want to watch different things on TV, you can discuss how compromise is a way for everyone to get a little of what they want and take turns or watch a third option instead. Mention that compromise is a powerful flexibility skill.

2. Ask your child to help you come up with Compromise options when you want something different from someone else. For example, suppose you want Indian food and your friend/partner/spouse wants Italian food. Can your child come up with some possible compromises for the two of you? Make sure to provide praise for any attempts or ideas they offer.

TOPIC 2.2   Should I Compromise?

BIG PICTURE SUMMARY

In the previous topic, students learned how to **compromise** and what positive outcomes can result from successful compromise. Some students don't compromise enough (they are overly inflexible), and some students compromise too much (they are too accommodating). In this topic, students will use the **"Should I compromise?"** formula to decide when and when not to compromise. Students will practice gathering information about a situation and the other person's perspectives, and they'll use this information to weigh their options and make a decision about a compromise.

Key Things to Do Here are the two most important things to do in today's class:

1. **Use this Key Vocabulary often and in fun and playful ways:**
   - Executive Function Skills
   - Flexible
   - Plan A/Plan B
   - Be Kind to Yourself and Others
   - Should I Compromise?
   - Is it a Big Deal or a Little Deal (or a Medium Deal)?
   - Let it Go
   - Stick to Your Idea

2. **Find ways to spontaneously model executive function skills (compromise, flexibility, and planning)** *at least once* **during class today.** Make this fun and engaging! Use compromise, flexibility, and planning skills with your students to solve challenges that come up naturally or challenges that you've invented. For example: *"Oh no! A fire drill. This is definitely not a compromise situation. Let's go!"*

Remember, new Key Vocabulary is introduced throughout the curriculum. Although a specific list of Key Vocabulary is provided for each topic, continue to use and reinforce all the Key Vocabulary from the curriculum in your interactions with the students (in group/class, other classes, etc.).

Materials

 ★ Unit 2 Daily Self-Awareness Rating (worksheet copied for each student or found in the Student Workbook)

Topic 2.2: Should I Compromise?

- PowerPoint for Topic 2.2, projected
- Power Equation Poster, posted
- Index cards (or half-sheets of paper): three for each student, for the "Should they compromise?" lightning round
- Power Level card, affixed to the bottom of the Power Arrow on the Power Equation Poster

EDUCATOR PLAN

Goal: Students learn to use the "Should I compromise?" formula to help them decide whether it's best to compromise or not.

Why: Students with executive function challenges may struggle with knowing when to compromise. When students have this difficulty, they may be overly passive or too rigid, which can interfere with their ability to build relationships and may reduce their success in and satisfaction with social situations.

Plan: Do the following before class:

- Post the Power Equation Poster and place the Power Level card at the bottom of the Power Arrow on the poster. Raise the Power Level card when students use executive function skills (i.e., compromise, flexibility, kindness, planning, or use coping strategies and flexible thinking if needed).
- Project the PowerPoint for Topic 2.2.

POWER LEVEL: Remember to continue using the Power Level card. Focus on celebrating or noticing when the students are doing well. However, when you need to provide corrective feedback, it's essential—and scientifically supported—to provide praise four times for every one instance of corrective feedback. Do NOT lower the Power Level card. Rather, help students notice that they are stuck and refer them back to the key executive function skills they have learned and the Power Equation. You might say, *"Our Power Level is **stuck**—let's look at the Power Equation to see what we can do to get **unstuck**. I wonder if a **compromise** would help here."*

CLASS LESSON PLAN

Slide 1: Power Plan

1. Ask students to fill out the Unit 2 Daily Self-Awareness Rating worksheet and review the Power Plan for Topic 2.2.

Slide 2: "Should I Compromise?" Formula

2a. **Introduce the idea to the class that sometimes it is helpful to compromise, and other times it is helpful to stick to your idea or to let it go:**

"Last time we learned how to compromise. Compromising with another person can be very powerful, but it isn't always best to compromise. Sometimes it's best to stick to your first idea and not compromise with someone. And sometimes it's best to let your idea go and not work out a compromise. You may need to talk it through to figure out if it's better to compromise or not."

2b. **Explain that kindness, listening, and including others to talk it through can be helpful when people disagree.** Ask students to identify what skills might be helpful when two people do not agree. Explore what happens when people disagree about something and things get heated or intense—for example, people can get into arguments, hurt each other's feelings, or fail to work out a solution, which means at least one person may not get anything they want instead of everyone getting some of what they want. It can also get in the way of gaining power and building relationships. Listening and being kind and respectful doesn't mean giving in. In fact, being kind and listening usually helps others listen to *our* ideas better.

2c. **Explain the "Should I compromise?" formula (referring to the PowerPoint).** Use the examples below or create your own examples to illustrate the steps of deciding whether or not to compromise (as indicated in the "Should I compromise?" formula).

- ★ **Don't compromise; just let it go:** My friend wanted to see one movie, but I wanted to see a different movie. My friend had been waiting to see his movie for months, and I only sort of wanted to see my movie. It was a big deal to her; she said it was a 2 (in the "Should I compromise?" formula). It was only a 1 for me, so I let my idea go and we watched her movie. Because I let go of my idea, we didn't need to come up with a Compromise.

- ★ **Don't compromise, but instead stick to your idea:** A friend suggested that we go out for dinner, but I had to grade tests and didn't have time to go out. It was a big deal for me. It was definitely a 2 (in the "Should I compromise?" formula). My friend wanted to go out to dinner, but he said we could go a different night. He said it was only a 1 for him, so I stuck with my idea of staying in and grading. I didn't compromise because it mattered a lot more to me than to my friend.

- ★ **Examples of Compromise:** When we disagree and both care the same amount about our choices, then it can be helpful to compromise. If I care somewhat about my choice and you care somewhat about your choice, that means we are both 1s in the "Should I compromise?" formula and should try to compromise. If we both care a lot about our choices, that means we are both 2s in the "Should I compromise?" formula and should try to compromise.

Ask the class to come up with an example of a situation in which two people disagree but should compromise because they care the same amount about their choices (e.g., you and your friend wanted to see a different movie; you and your friend wanted something different for dinner).

Slide 3: Compromise Detective—Figuring Out When to Compromise

3. **Discuss how to figure out how much a person cares about something (i.e., whether they are a 0, 1, or 2 in the "Should I compromise?" formula).** How do you decide when to compromise? Review the following steps with the class, pointing to each step on the PowerPoint slide:

    ★ The first step is to get information about the situation (the first three boxes on the PowerPoint slide). Discuss the following steps with the class:

    - What is your original idea or preference? (What is your Plan A?)
    - How important is it to you to stick to your idea, or how much do you care about your Plan A? (Are you a 0, 1, or 2?)
    - **Listen:** What is the other person saying about their preference?
    - **Think:** What do you know about the other person's feelings and preference? Does the other person understand your feelings and preference?
    - **Talk It Through:** Are there questions you can ask to help you understand what the other person wants or how much they care? Is there anything else you can tell the other person so that they understand what you want and how much you care?
    - Overall, using the listen, think, and talk it through steps, do you feel the other person is a 0, 1, or 2 about this (how strong is their preference for it)?

    ★ The final step is to figure out whether you should compromise. Use the "Should I compromise?" formula to figure out who cares more (the fourth box on the PowerPoint slide). Discuss the following steps with the class:

    - **Compromise:** If you both feel roughly the same about the idea, a compromise is a good way to go.
    - **Let it go:** If the other person cares more than you do about the idea, you might want to let it go.
    - **Stick to your idea:** If you feel more strongly than the other person about the idea, it might make sense to stick to your idea.

Slide 4: Compromise Detective—Use the Listen, Think, and Talk It Through Steps to Figure Out How Much the Other Person Cares

4. **Do a role-play based on the following scenario, acting out the role of Ethan.** You'll act it out twice, but how much Ethan cares is different each time.

    ★ The first time, act as though Ethan doesn't really care so much about his preference (he's a 0). Encourage students to be detectives and pay attention to what Ethan says to figure out how much Ethan cares. Ask a student to act out the part of the person who wants to play the video game, pretending to care somewhat (a 1). After you act out the scenario with the student, ask the class if they need more information and what questions they might ask. Once they have no other questions, ask how much Ethan cared about playing chess: a 0, 1, or 2? Ask students what helped them decide how much Ethan cared. Then tell them that you were trying to act out a 0. Ask the class to consider what should happen when Ethan is a 0 and the other person is a 1 (Ethan lets his choice go, and the other person sticks with their idea).

- ★ Repeat the same scenario acting out Ethan's role as a 2 (cares a lot). Ask a student to act out the other person's role as a 1 (cares somewhat) and repeat as above.

Slide 5: Important Times Not to Compromise

5. **Explain to the class that there may be situations in which there is no safe compromise, and they should stick to their idea.** For example:

   - ★ You never have to compromise about being touched. If someone wants to touch you and you don't want them to, do not compromise and do not allow it.

   - ★ Others never have to compromise about being touched. If they don't want to be touched, don't push them to compromise and don't touch them.

   - ★ You should do what law enforcement officers or police tell you to do because it can be very dangerous if you don't.

   - ★ You should not share your personal information with strangers on the Internet. Be kind to yourself and protect your information even when they pressure you to compromise.

Important Note: Consider any policies your school has regarding personal safety and health education as well as the needs of your group members. Depending on these factors, you can adjust the above items as needed to best fit your group. You could also collaborate with your school's personal safety and health instructor to see how the concept of "times not to compromise" connects with their content.

Slides 6–9: "Should They Compromise?" Lightning Round Scenarios

6. **Play a "Should they compromise?" lightning round.** Hand out three index cards to each student and ask them to write a 0 on one, a 1 on another, and a 2 on the final card. Refer to the "Should I compromise?" formula (Slide 2), reminding students that 0 means "don't really care, no strong preference," 1 means "care somewhat," and 2 means "care a lot, strong preference." Tell students they will have 5 minutes to solve as many compromise situations as they can.

   Start by reading the two-person scenario to the class. Then the students will vote by holding up the index card they feel best represents how much each person in the scenario cares (0, 1, or 2). Have them vote separately for each person in the scenario. You or a student should record the vote totals for each person in the scenario on the board. Write <, =, or > between the numbers to show which person in the scenario cares more (e.g., 0 < 2). You or the student writing on the board will break any ties. Once the equation is on the board, students discuss whether it's a compromise situation or if either of the people should be flexible and give up their idea.

Here are a few lightning round scenarios:

- **(Slide 6):** The teacher brings in donuts for the class because they have done a good job being flexible. Half the donuts are glazed, and the other half are jelly-filled. Just as David is reaching for the last jelly-filled donut, Maria says that she wants it. David stares at her with a serious look and says, "Sorry, I hate glazed donuts, but I love jelly-filled donuts. Could I have it?" Maria smiles and says she actually likes both.

- **(Slide 7):** Ben tells his twin brother Tyrone that it is Tyrone's turn to walk the dog. Tyrone says he has a big test tomorrow and really needs time to study for it. Ben isn't that busy.

- **(Slide 8):** The teacher tells her students that each of them has to pick an animal to write a report on, and Jamie calls out, "I want to write on sharks!" Greg's favorite thing in the whole world is sharks. He talks about them all the time and knows more about them than anyone. Greg says, "No! I really, really want to write about sharks."

- **(Slide 9):** Sue and Arianna meet at lunch. Sue says, "Let's go to my house after school. I really want to show you my new model spaceship I got for my collection." Arianna says, "No, let's go to the park and play soccer. We need to get ready for the school tryouts." Sue leans in toward her friend and says, "We can do that tomorrow, come see my model spaceship today." Arianna wrinkles her forehead and says, "No, I have to babysit tomorrow."

Slide 10: Topic 2.2 Wrap-Up: Why Is It Important to Know When to Compromise?

10a. **Ask students why it's important to know when to compromise. How can students use this skill to build power in their lives at school, at home, and in the future?** Point to the Why section of the Power Plan and ask students to fill in the answer or just discuss. Prompt students to consider what happens if someone always gives in and lets go of their choice (they aren't being kind to themselves and risk getting mistreated by others, who may take advantage of them—i.e., get treated like a pushover or a doormat). What if someone never lets go of their idea (they aren't being kind to others and risk damaging their relationships and losing power)? What if someone doesn't know when to compromise?

10b. **Send Home Extension for Topic 2.2 home with students or e-mail it to parents.**

10c. **Look for curriculum generalization opportunities in other classes.** Ask your students' other instructors about whether they've had a chance to use the blank Power Plan with students for their individual work (e.g., making a plan for how a student will complete a project or assignment). Provide any necessary coaching to help instructors use the Power Plan with the students for planning out assignments or projects. Emphasize the importance of using at least four positive statements for every correction or command when using the Power Plan so students will come to enjoy using it. Here's an example for a book report:

Goal: Write your book report.

Why: It's a part of your grade for the class. Practicing your reading and writing are powerful ways to have more success in the future.

Plan A:

1. Choose the book that you're going to read. Ask your teacher if you need help deciding which book you'll read.//
2. Read a chapter a day.
3. After you read each chapter, write three sentences about what happened in the chapter. Keep those notes in a notebook or in the same folder on your computer.
4. Once you're done with the book, use your notes from each chapter to help you write your book report.
5. Meet with your teacher before the book report is due to work on organizing and editing your writing.

Plan B: If you get stuck, talk to your teacher about how to get your book report done.

Check: Did you reach your goal? Did you work on and complete your book report?

> **CHECK:** How are my students doing?
> Do I need to make any adjustments for the next class?

See Appendix A for a list of questions to guide your self-reflection and refer to the Troubleshooting section (Appendix B) to address common problems or any challenges that may have arisen with the curriculum.

TOPIC 2.2: Should I Compromise?

DAILY SELF-AWARENESS RATING: UNIT 2

NAME: _____

Executive Function Skills

Flexibility + Big Picture Thinking + Goals and Planning = POWER

1. How much do you think you can compromise today?

Mark an X on the arrow to show how you feel today:

Can't Compromise   Can Compromise Some   Can Compromise
(I'm Feeling Too Stuck)

2. Which executive function skills do you plan to use today? (Check all that apply.)

Making Plan Bs when Plan As don't work ☐

Focusing on the big picture (instead of being stuck on details) ☐

Being flexible ☐

Using coping strategies and flexible thinking if needed ☐

Compromising ☐

TOPIC 2.2: Should I Compromise?

HOME EXTENSION FOR TOPIC 2.2: SHOULD I COMPROMISE?

In this topic, students used a simple method to decide when to compromise and when not to compromise.

Key Vocabulary/skills:

Plan A/Plan B *When to Compromise* *Who Cares More?*

Compromise (Plan B) *Let It Go* *Stick to Your Idea*

How to use the Key Vocabulary:

When talking about compromising, it can be helpful to attach numbers to how much people care about the particular situation. Follow these steps to help your child decide, "Should I compromise?":

Step 1: How big of a deal is this? How strong is your preference (0, 1, or 2)?

   0 = Little deal, no strong preference

   1 = Care a bit, some preference

   2 = Big deal, strong preference

Step 2: What should we do? Should we compromise?

   Person A cares more (Person A's preference number is higher) = Person A sticks with their idea. Person B lets go of their idea.

   Person A and Person B care the same (preference numbers are the same) = **Compromise.**

   Person B cares more (Person B's preference number is higher) = Person B sticks with their idea. Person A lets go of their idea.

Apply these steps to situations that come up in your everyday life and discuss them with your child. Use the numbers (0, 1, 2) to make your examples concrete for your child. Start by choosing a situation where you don't care too much, so you can let it go and your child can practice their compromising skills on something easy. Here's an example in which you and your child want different things for dinner:

Tell your child that you're thinking of making chicken for dinner and ask them what they feel like having. If they suggest pasta, you could ask, *"How important is this to you: 0, 1, or 2?"* Once your child answers, say that it matters less to you (*"It's a little deal to me—that means 0"*), so you're going to let go of the idea of making chicken for dinner and make pasta instead.

TOPIC 2.3 Try Out Your Compromise Skills

> **BIG PICTURE SUMMARY**

In the previous two topics, students learned how and when to **Compromise**. To determine whether they should **Compromise** in a certain situation, they practiced gathering information to learn how strongly the other person feels about their choice or preferences. In today's topic, students will practice these skills using the compromise guide and work through compromise opportunities by playing a game called "The Compromiser."

Key Things to Do Here are the two most important things to do in today's class:

1. **Use this Key Vocabulary often and in fun and playful ways:**

   ★ Executive Function Skills

   ★ Flexible

   ★ Plan A/Plan B

   ★ Be Kind to Yourself and Others

   ★ Should I Compromise?

   ★ Is It A Big Deal or a Little Deal (or a Medium Deal)?

   ★ Let It Go

   ★ Stick to Your Idea

   ★ How to Compromise:
   - Each Gets Part.
   - Combine Ideas.
   - Take Turns.
   - Do Something Different You Both Like.

Educator Note

Remember, new Key Vocabulary is introduced throughout the curriculum. Although a specific list of Key Vocabulary is provided for each topic, continue to use and reinforce all the Key Vocabulary from the curriculum in your interactions with the students (in group, class, other classes, etc.).

2. **Find ways to spontaneously model Executive Function Skills (Compromise, Flexibility, and Planning)** *at least once* **during class today.** Make this fun and engaging! Use Compromise, Flexibility, and Planning skills with your students to solve challenges that come up naturally or challenges that you've invented. For example, *"This morning, my*

*friend wanted to stop and get donuts on the way to work, but I wanted to get to work early to get ready for the day. We had to figure out, '**Should We Compromise**?' They cared a bit, but it was a **Big Deal** to me, and I cared a lot, so we **Stuck with My Idea**, and my friend **Let It Go**."*

Materials

- Unit 2 Daily Self-Awareness Rating (worksheets copied for each student or found in the Student Workbook)

- PowerPoint for Topic 2.3, projected
- Power Equation Poster, posted
- Power Level card. Affix the card to the bottom of the Power Arrow on the Power Equation Poster.
- The Compromiser Scenario cards (found at the end of this topic), printed and cut out
- Sticky notes or small pieces of paper

EDUCATOR PLAN

Goal: Using the "Should I compromise?" formula, students will apply their compromising skills in a role-playing game.

Why: Compromising may be difficult for people with executive function challenges because it requires understanding that giving in is not the same thing as being flexible so that you can achieve your goals and work with others. We are teaching it here as a systematic process that students can use. Learning to compromise will initially require practice during relaxed, low-pressure situations, until students develop their skills enough to use them in more challenging real-world scenarios.

Plan: Do the following before class:

- Post the Power Equation Poster and place the Power Level card at the bottom of the Power Arrow on the poster. Raise the Power Level card when students use Power Skills, or **Executive Function Skills**, like when they **Compromise**, are **Flexible** or kind, show **Planning** skills, or manage their frustration and disappointment.

- Project the PowerPoint for Topic 2.3.

- Read through "The Compromiser" game instructions and consider the following:

  • "The Compromiser" game awards students group points for correct answers. Determine if this system will work for your group and think about how you would like the students to be able to redeem the points. For example, will students earn a minute of free time at the end of class for each point? Consider what your group finds especially important and motivating.

  • If your students have difficulty with role-playing or don't want to act for the game, you can be the actor. Alternatively, you can record the interactions ahead of time.

 **POWER LEVEL:** Remember to continue using the Power Level. Focus on celebrating or noticing when the students are doing well, and when you need to provide corrective feedback, it's essential and scientifically supported to provide praise four times for every one instance of corrective feedback. The Power Level system helps you catch students doing well, particularly when they use the skills and Key Vocabulary taught in the curriculum. If students are struggling to use **Executive Function Skills**, you could state, *"Our Power Level is Stuck—let's look at the Power Equation to see what we can do to get Unstuck."*

CLASS LESSON PLAN

Slide 1: Power Plan

1. Ask students to fill out the Unit 2 Daily Self-Awareness Rating worksheet and review the Power Plan for Topic 2.3.

Slide 2: Review the "Should I Compromise?" Formula

2. Review the steps of deciding whether to Compromise. (Reference the "Should I compromise?" formula.)

   ★ You can make this a game by asking students to review the formula for 2 minutes and then covering up the slide (or switching to another slide) and asking them questions about the contents.

   ★ Review how to use kindness, listening, and including others to talk it through when **Compromising** to increase the likelihood of others listening to your message.

Slide 3: Review the How to Compromise Visual

3. Review the four ways to Compromise. (Reference the How to Compromise visual.) You can make this a game by asking students to review the visual for 2 minutes and then covering up the slide and asking them questions about the contents.

Slide 4: Review the Graphic of the Four Ways to Compromise

4. Ask the class to consider how each of the four pictures on the Compromise graphic—that is, remind us of the related skills. For example, the green circle reminds us of **Combining Ideas** because it combines the yellow and blue colors. The red square reminds us of **Doing Something Different** because it is different than the yellow and blue circles.

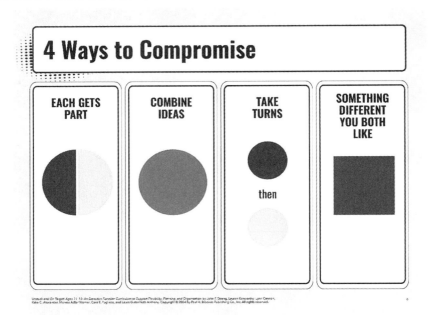

Slide 5: "The Compromiser" Game Rules

5a. Introduce the rules to the game:

1. Select two students (or one educator and one student). Each of the players receives an actor's card (i.e., Round 1, Actor A and Round 1, Actor B).

2. Players read their card, using the information on their card to help them determine how they are going to act out their scene (how strongly they feel about a situation).

3. Hand out sticky notes or small pieces of paper to the "audience" members.

4. The two actors take turns acting out the information on their card.

5. Thinking about how strongly each actor feels about their situation, audience members vote by writing down a number for each actor (0, 1, or 2) on their sticky note or paper.

    Example:

Actor A	Actor B
0	2

6. Audience members reveal their votes.

7. Record their answers on the board. If the majority of students select the correct answers for Actors A and B, the class earns a point for each of them. A maximum of 2 points can be earned per round.

8. Based on the correct answer (e.g., Actor A = 0; Actor B = 2), students determine if Actor A should **Let It Go, Stick to Their Idea,** or **Compromise.**

9. If the majority of students select the correct outcome, the class earns a point.

10. If the numbers are equal, a **Compromise** is necessary. Each student (actors included) should think of a **Compromise** solution and share it with the class.

Topic 2.3: Try Out Your Compromise Skills   109

Each new idea for a **Compromise** earns the class an extra point, with the possibility of many points being earned if each student comes up with a different plausible **Compromise**.

5b. **Ask follow-up bonus questions from the list below. Students can earn more extra points for the class by offering thoughtful answers.**

- ★ What happens if your friend feels very strongly about every situation? Will you want to continue to hang out with that friend?
- ★ What happens if both people refuse to **Compromise** and insist on **Sticking to Their Ideas?**
- ★ What happens if you have a really good compromise strategy in a conflict situation, but you don't use **Executive Function Skills** (or Power Skills) to boost the Power Level?
- ★ What would happen to your ability to build relationships and increase your Power Level if you always **Stuck to Your Ideas?**
- ★ Are you more likely to want to hang out with someone who can be kind to themselves and others to **Compromise,** or someone who always insists on **Sticking to Their Idea?**

Slide 6: The Compromiser Game

6. Lead the students through three rounds of the game (as described above).

Slide 7: Topic 2.3 Wrap-Up: Why Are We Practicing Compromise?

7a. **Ask students why we are practicing compromise.** Point to the Why section of the Power Plan and ask students to fill in the answer or just discuss. Ask students to talk about which areas of their lives they can enhance with compromise skills and what kinds of power they can build by knowing when and how to compromise. Ask students what happens if someone is always a 2 about everything, meaning everything is a big deal to them. Explain how always being a 2 would make a person lose power and seem selfish.

7b. Send Home Extension for Topic 2.3 home with students or e-mail it to parents.

7c. **Look for curriculum generalization opportunities in other classes.** Check in with other educators to learn how they are using the Power Plan visual with students for group and individual work (e.g., making a plan for how to get a project or assignment done).

> **CHECK:** How are my students doing?
> Do I need to make any adjustments for the next class?

See Appendix A for a list of questions to guide your self-reflection and refer to the Troubleshooting section (Appendix B) to address common problems or any challenges that may have arisen with the curriculum.

TOPIC 2.3: Try Out Your Compromise Skills

DAILY SELF-AWARENESS RATING: UNIT 2

NAME: _____

Executive Function Skills

Flexibility + Big Picture Thinking + Goals and Planning = POWER

1. How much do you think you can compromise today?

Mark an X on the arrow to show how you feel today:

Can't Compromise (I'm Feeling Too Stuck)   Can Compromise Some   Can Compromise

2. Which executive function skills do you plan to use today? (Check all that apply.)

- ☐ Making Plan Bs when Plan As don't work
- ☐ Focusing on the big picture (instead of being stuck on details)
- ☐ Being flexible
- ☐ Using coping strategies and flexible thinking if needed
- ☐ Compromising

TOPIC 2.3: Try Out Your Compromise Skills

HOME EXTENSION FOR TOPIC 2.3: TRY OUT YOUR COMPROMISE SKILLS

In this topic, students continued to practice the skills of deciding when to compromise and how to compromise.

Key Vocabulary/skills:

How Important Is This to You?

When to Compromise?

How to Compromise?

How to use the Key Vocabulary:

If you see something on TV or hear something on the news, or your child is talking about something that is going on at school, use one of the following discussion questions to start a conversation with your child about the importance of compromise:

What happens if both people refuse to compromise and insist on sticking to their ideas? Think about sports stars' contracts, world leaders, local politicians, or your co-workers.

Are you more likely to want to hang out with someone who can flexibly make compromises or someone who always insists on sticking to their idea? Use examples from your family or your child's social group. Think about people who are easy or difficult to get along with (friends, neighbors, family, teachers). Be careful not to let the conversation get too negative.

TOPIC 2.3: Try Out Your Compromise Skills   The Compromiser Scenario Cards

---

Round 1, Actor A

I love soccer. In fact, if I could do one thing all day, every day, I would play soccer. All of my friends know I love soccer because I talk about it all of the time. My friend who will be going outside with me today also likes soccer. He mentioned that he learned to play basketball over the weekend. I can't wait to play soccer after school today.

My Plan A: to play soccer

I feel like a: 2

Round 1, Actor B

I just learned how to play basketball. I wanted to learn after I went to a game with my dad. I think it might be fun to play after school today. I love all sports, though, so I would be cool with playing anything. I'll be going outside today with my friend who loves soccer. He talks about it all of the time and plays it almost every day.

My Plan A: to play basketball

I feel like a: 1

Round 2, Actor A

I am starving! I can't wait to have a snack after school. Maybe my mom will stop at a restaurant with us. A milkshake and fries sounds really good right now. The more I think about it, the hungrier I get!

My Plan A: to go to a restaurant

I feel like a: 1

Round 2, Actor B

I am going home with my good friend today. I am pretty hungry but I don't really want to go to a restaurant. I think I'd rather get something to eat at home.

My Plan A: eat at home

I feel like a: 1

Round 3, Actor A

I love to play video games when I get home. I am working really hard to beat my last level, and I really want to play before I start my homework. It is really important to me to have some time playing the game.

My Plan A: to play video games after school.

I feel like a: 2

Round 3, Actor B

My cousin just lent me the movie I have been wanting to see more than anything. I am going home with my friend after school and can't wait to watch the movie with him. It's going to be so great, and I don't think I can wait any longer.

My Plan A: to watch my new movie

I feel like a: 2

TOPIC 2.4 Plan Another Special Event Together Using Compromise Skills (Two Sessions)

BIG PICTURE SUMMARY

In Topic 2.4, students will have an opportunity to practice using their compromise skills as they plan a second event (the first event was the Unit 1 party). The Unit 2 event should be something more meaningful than the party; it will help students tap into their desire to have the power to make the world, their school, or their lives a little better.

Key Things to Do (This topic will likely take two class periods)

Here are the two most important things to do in today's class:

1. **Use this Key Vocabulary often and in fun and playful ways:**
   - ★ Executive Function Skills
   - ★ Plan A/Plan B
   - ★ Be Kind to Yourself and Others
   - ★ How Long Should I Be Disappointed?
   - ★ Should I Compromise?
   - ★ Is It a Big Deal or a Little Deal (or a Medium Deal)?
   - ★ How Important Is This to You?
   - ★ Let It Go
   - ★ Stick to Your Idea
   - ★ How to Compromise:
     - Each Gets Part.
     - Combine Ideas.
     - Take Turns.
     - Do Something Different You Both Like.
   - ★ Stuck on a Detail

Remember, new Key Vocabulary is introduced throughout the curriculum. Although a specific list of Key Vocabulary is provided for each topic, continue to use and reinforce all of the Key Vocabulary in the curriculum in each topic and all interactions with the students (in group, class, other classes, etc.).

2. **Find ways to spontaneously model executive function skills (compromise, flexibility, and planning) *at least once* during class today.** Make this fun and engaging! Use

compromise, flexibility, and planning skills with your students to solve challenges that come up naturally or challenges that you've invented.

Special instructions for today's class:

★ Decide on the framework for the Unit 2 event. How much money, if any, is available to spend on the event? Do you want to provide students with a few ideas for the type of event it could be (e.g., party, cooking, craft, public service activity, game day)?

★ If you think your students might have difficulty letting go of an idea they come up with for the event, have a positive reinforcement system set up for those students who can let go of an idea (e.g., a ticket for a turn in a prize bag or a minute of free time).

Materials

★ Unit 2 Daily Self-Awareness Rating (worksheets copied for each student or found in the Student Workbook)

★ Whiteboard, chart paper, or projected board to write down student ideas for possible activities

★ PowerPoint for Topic 2.4, projected

★ Power Equation Poster, posted

★ Power Level card. Affix to the bottom of the Power Arrow on the Power Equation Poster.

★ Optional: Courtroom imagery to get the students excited about putting plans on trial (a gavel, a judge's robe, images of popular courtroom TV shows)

EDUCATOR PLAN

Goal: Use the how to compromise visual and "Should I compromise?" formula to plan a special class event.

Why: Practicing compromising and planning together helps students integrate their social and executive function skills.

Plan: Do the following before class:

★ Post the Power Equation Poster and place the Power Level card at the bottom of the Power Arrow on the poster. Raise the Power Level card when students compromise, are flexible or kind to themselves or others, show planning skills, or use coping strategies and flexible thinking if needed.

★ Project the PowerPoint for Topic 2.4.

Blank Power Plan: For topics that require the class to plan an event, the Power Plan visual is blank and will be filled in during the planning process. Explain to the students that because they are now doing the planning, they will fill in the Power Plan themselves (or with your support). You may still wish to review today's schedule/plan at the beginning of class.

Topic 2.4: Plan Another Special Event Together Using Compromise Skills (Two Sessions)   115

Important Note

Remember to Use the Stuck on a Detail Routine: When discussions get stuck on specific off-topic details, ask: *"Do we want to get stuck on that detail or get back to the big picture?"* or *"How long should we be stuck on that interesting detail?"* See Topic 1.1 for an explanation of how to use a stopwatch to time how long the class wants to be stuck (30 seconds or 1 minute). Also consider using the how long should we be frustrated/disappointed routine, always with empathy and patience, as described in Topic 1.5.

Power Level: Remember to continue using the Power Level card. Focus on celebrating or noticing when the students are doing well. However, when you need to provide corrective feedback, it's essential—and scientifically supported—to provide praise four times for every one instance of corrective feedback. Do NOT lower the Power Level card. Rather, help students notice that they are stuck and refer them back to the key executive function skills they have learned and the Power Equation. You might say, *"Our Power Level is **stuck**—let's look at the Power Equation to see what we can do to get **unstuck**. I wonder if a **compromise** would help here."*

CLASS LESSON PLAN

Slide 1: Blank Power Plan

1a. **Ask students to fill out the Unit 2 Daily Self-Awareness Rating worksheet.** Point to the Power Plan and explain that it is blank today because the class will be doing the planning themselves:

   "Today is the day we will set our goal for a special event. We will use our compromise skills so we can pick a goal for the event together. Your job today is to figure out the Goal, the Why, and the Plan for our special event. Then we'll have the event on another class day."

1b. **Review the steps of deciding whether to compromise (reference the how to compromise and the "Should I compromise?" formula/visual [Slide 2]).** Make this a game to encourage participation. For example, for each question the group answers, they earn 25 cents toward the party/event expenses. Review the following questions and discussion starters with the class:

   ★ Name all of the compromise strategies.

   ★ Tell us about a situation in which you had to think about compromising.

   ★ What happens if everyone feels like a 2?

- ★ What happens if everyone feels strongly about every choice?
- ★ If I feel strongly and you feel strongly, we need to come up with a ____?
- ★ If I feel strongly and you feel strongly and we don't come up with a compromise, what will happen?
- ★ If I don't care and you care a lot, what should I do?

1c. Tell students they will be using their compromise skills to plan a big picture goal for the special event.

- ★ **Have the class brainstorm different possible events and record the ideas on the board.** Provide structure by suggesting ideas for the event, like a public service project, a field trip, or a larger party for a special teacher. Let students know if there is a budget and remind them to only make suggestions that cost little to no money (i.e., make your own decorations, free entertainment like a video or board game). Tell students they are going to have the opportunity to share how strongly they feel about a particular idea for the event and why, using the 0, 1, 2 scale.

- ★ **Because an abundance of 2s can lead to challenges, encourage the class to aim for 0s and 1s when possible.** Remind students that if they don't feel too strongly about an idea or if everyone agrees on an item, it allows us to move along more quickly and have more fun. Remind students that more extreme feelings are okay from time to time, but if you are always a 2, it could get in the way of boosting power and building relationships. Reward students for expressing moderate interests (0s or 1s) and for making flexible statements (e.g., *"I want to do X, but I'm open to other ideas"*) by raising the Power Level card and offering praise. Consider using flexibility prompts such as *"I know you feel really strongly. What would help you feel a little less strongly about this?"*

- ★ **One veto per student is allowed.** Some students may have incredibly strong feelings about certain suggestions (e.g., playing laser tag might be overwhelming for a student with sensory processing issues). Honor these strong feelings by giving each student one veto that allows them to remove an idea from the board, either because they feel strongly about not wanting to do it or because they simply cannot do it. Explain to the students that it's okay to have strong feelings occasionally and that your friends will be flexible about this as long as you don't always insist on your own preferences.

Here are a few educator prompts to support your students' planning. Be careful not to direct these prompts toward a specific student or in a blaming way:

- ★ *"What happens to your power if you insist on your own way for every item?"*
- ★ *"Is this an event for just you, or is this an event for the whole group?"*
- ★ *"Do you have to give a suggestion for every category?"*
- ★ *"What happens if we get stuck on every item and we run out of time to plan for the event?"*
- ★ *"Are you more likely to want to hang out with someone who includes others and can make compromises or someone who continuously insists on sticking to their idea without including others' ideas or preferences?"*
- ★ *"What can you do to help move this process along?"*

Present all of the group's ideas, asking the students to use the 0, 1, 2 scale to identify how strongly they support each idea and why. This will allow students to practice listening to and understanding each other's preferences. Write down key information on the blackboard or whiteboard, as shown in this example:

Event Activity	Asaad	Kim	Olivia	Total
Throw a party for a special teacher	2	0	2	
Clean up a playground	0	2	1	
Watch a movie about the Earth	0	1	0	

Remind students that if the class cares the same amount (has matching scores) for two or more ideas, they can decide to compromise so each gets part of what they want. Students can use compromise options from the How to Compromise visual.

After students rate how strongly they feel about each option (using the 0, 1, 2 scale), add the numbers and see which options have the highest scores. Then ask the class to use the compromise strategies (each gets part, combine ideas, take turns, or do something different you both like) to develop a final goal for the event.

Example:

Event Activity	Asaad	Kim	Olivia	Total
Throw a party for a special teacher	2	0	2	4
Clean up a playground	0	2	1	3
Watch a movie about the Earth	0	1	0	1

You can say something like: *"Our top choices are throwing a party and cleaning up the playground. It looks like there is a little more interest in the party. Should we go with the party, or should we compromise?"* If the class decides to compromise, have them use the How to Compromise visual (from Topic 2.1 or 2.3) to select the winning event. Type (or have students type) the finalized event goal into the blank Power Plan. Be sure to praise the students for using compromise skills to decide on the goal, raising the Power Level card when possible.

1d. **Next, the class should decide on the steps of the plan to achieve their goal.** The plan will consist of the various steps necessary for the event to happen and be successful. You might want to come up with categories before you start the brainstorm to help focus the students. For example, if they choose to throw a party, then help the class brainstorm the necessary parts of a party: decorations, food, entertainment, etc. Follow a similar procedure as above with each category, starting with brainstorming, any vetoes, rating (0, 1, 2) how strongly they like each choice, deciding based on the sum of the ratings, and compromising if two choices are close. Remind the students that strong feelings about every choice (ratings of 2) can get in the way of boosting our Power Level and sometimes our ability to build relationships.

1e. **Put the plan for the special event on trial (see Slide 3; same procedures as in Topic 1.5).** Here's a sample script you can use:

"Let's check our plan by putting it on trial. Will we reach our goal? Did we come up with a good plan for reaching our goal? While we're checking our plan, let's make sure

to use flexibility skills and be kind to ourselves and others, so everyone is included. Let's see if the plan works, or if there are any problems we need to fix."

Create a courtroom feel with courtroom visuals and, if the class wants to, a judge and jury. Have the students go through each step of the plan and put a check in the Check column if the step is good or place an X next to any step that needs to be reworked. As the class evaluates each step of the plan, you can ask for classroom volunteers to act out each step. Encourage the students to come up with another idea for steps they feel should be improved.

Praise the students for their flexibility, planning, and checking, raising the Power Level card each time. Explain to the class:

"When we put a plan on trial, we make our plan better because we find all of the problems and fix them. Next class, we get to celebrate with the wonderful event you planned."

1f. **Ask students to think of a way to keep track of the plan for the special event, so they don't lose or forget it (e.g., copy it down, take a picture of it, save it on the computer, write it on the board where it won't be erased).** Say to the class:

"How can we keep track of our great plan so we don't lose or forget it? Next class we'll need to have the plan ready so we can do our special event. So what are some ways we can keep track of our plan?"

1g. **Ask students why we planned an event using compromise and put that plan on trial.** Point to the Why section of the Power Plan and ask students to fill in the answer or just discuss. Gently lead the discussion to focus on how planning and checking our plan help us gain more power. Make sure to affirm the variety of thoughts and opinions the students give so all of your students hear their successes and areas of strength reflected back to them. Praise and reinforce their persistence and problem solving.

1h. **Send Home Extension for Topic 2.4 home with students or e-mail it to parents.**

1i. **Look for generalization opportunities in other classes.** Discuss with other educators how hard it can be for students to check their work. Describe how the students in your group have been practicing the skill of checking by putting their plan on trial. Explain that the trial imagery makes checking more playful and enjoyable. Ask educators to consider using the plan on trial Key Vocabulary to reinforce the students as they check their work. For example, if a student has written a paragraph, they can check it or put it on trial to look for errors.

> **CHECK:** How are my students doing?
> Do I need to make any adjustments for the next class?

See Appendix A for a list of questions to guide your self-reflection and refer to the Troubleshooting section (Appendix B) to address common problems or any challenges that may have arisen with the curriculum.

TOPIC 2.4: Plan Another Special Event Together Using Compromise Skills

DAILY SELF-AWARENESS RATING: UNIT 2

NAME: _____

Executive Function Skills

Flexibility + Big Picture Thinking + Goals and Planning = POWER

1. How much do you think you can compromise today?

Mark an X on the arrow to show how you feel today:

Can't Compromise   Can Compromise Some   Can Compromise
(I'm Feeling Too Stuck)

2. Which executive function skills do you plan to use today? (Check all that apply.)

Making Plan Bs when Plan As don't work ☐

Focusing on the big picture (instead of being stuck on details) ☐

Being flexible ☐

Using coping strategies and flexible thinking if needed ☐

Compromising ☐

TOPIC 2.4: Plan Another Special Event Together Using Compromise Skills

HOME EXTENSION FOR TOPIC 2.4: PLAN ANOTHER SPECIAL EVENT TOGETHER USING COMPROMISE SKILLS

In today's topic, students continued to practice their compromise skills by planning a special event together.

Key Vocabulary/skills:

Plan A/Plan B   *Flexible Thinking*   *Compromise*

Stuck on a Detail   *Big Picture*   *Checking the Plan*

How to use the Key Vocabulary/skills:

1. Ask your child to tell you what they've learned in group about the power of compromising. Ask about the event the class planned. Is your child excited about getting to plan a group event?

2. Have you, as an adult, ever had to make compromises when planning an event? Think of events like birthday parties, family holiday gatherings, and weddings.

   - Tell your child about why it was important to compromise and how things worked out for the better because you did.
   - You can also talk about a time when you didn't compromise and regretted it.
   - Try to avoid talking about a time when you compromised but it didn't work. Save that conversation for another time.

TOPIC 2.5 The Special Event

BIG PICTURE SUMMARY

In Topics 2.1–2.4, students learned how and when to compromise. They had opportunities to practice their compromise skills using kindness and flexible thinking. Students also practiced the planning and big picture skills first taught in Unit 1 (the stuck on a detail routine, using coping strategies and flexible thinking when needed, Goal-Why-Plan-Check, putting your plan on trial). Now, in Topic 2.5, students will enjoy the special event they planned. There may be a need for some flexibility—and opportunities for Plan Bs—during today's event.

Key Things to Do Here are the two most important things to do in today's class:

1. **Use this Key Vocabulary often and in fun and playful ways:**
   - ★ Executive Function Skills
   - ★ Plan A/Plan B
   - ★ Be Kind with Yourself and Others
   - ★ Use Coping Strategies and Flexible Thinking if Needed
   - ★ Should I Compromise?
   - ★ Is It a Big Deal or a Little Deal (or a Medium Deal)?
   - ★ How Important Is This to You?
   - ★ Let It Go
   - ★ Stick to Your Idea
   - ★ How to Compromise:
     - Each Gets Part.
     - Combine Ideas.
     - Take Turns.
     - Do Something Different You Both Like.
   - ★ Stuck on a Detail?

2. **Find ways to spontaneously model executive function skills (compromise, flexibility, and planning)** *at least once* **during class today.** Make this fun and engaging! Use compromise, flexibility, and planning skills with your students to solve challenges that come up naturally or challenges that you've invented. For example:

   "Last night my partner and I couldn't agree on what ice cream to get at the store. I wanted chocolate, and they wanted mint chocolate chip. I asked them whether they were a 0, 1, or 2. They don't like chocolate at all, so they chose 2. I like both, so I chose 1 and decided to let it go. We got mint chocolate chip, watched a movie, and had a good time together."

Special instructions for today's class:

1. Decide if students will do any of the preparations for the event (such as deciding when the event will be held and what materials you'll need).

2. Some students may have certain expectations for what a special event will be like. To help manage expectations for students, provide them with a framework for this event (this will vary based on the type of event you are having). Think about what might pose a problem and help them manage their expectations and understand that they can still have a good time by using flexible thinking and compromise. Here are some examples of what you might say to the class:

   - *"Are you up for a flexibility challenge today?"*
   - *"All parties are different, and there's a chance we won't be able to finish the video during our event."*
   - *"If the decorations don't look exactly like you envisioned them, can we still have fun?"*
   - *"Disappointment is an important feeling. How long should we be stuck on it? How should we let go of disappointment and move on?"*

Materials

- Unit 2 Daily Self-Awareness Rating (worksheets copied for each student or found in the Student Workbook)

- PowerPoint for Topic 2.5, projected
- Power Equation Poster, posted
- Power Level card, affixed to the bottom of the Power Arrow on the Power Equation Poster
- Optional: Camera or video-recording device

EDUCATOR PLAN

Goal: Have a successful second event.

Why: These events are important for the students to feel connected and practice the skills in ways that allow them to generalize their new skills outside the classroom.

Plan: Do the following before class:

- Post the Power Equation Poster and place the Power Level card at the bottom of the Power Arrow on the poster. Raise the Power Level when they compromise, are flexible or kind, show planning skills, or use coping strategies or flexible thinking if needed.
- Project the PowerPoint for Topic 2.5.
- If appropriate, you may want to record or take pictures of today's event so during the next class you can review with students all of the skills they used and challenges they faced during the event.

Topic 2.5: The Special Event

> **CLASS LESSON PLAN**

Slide 1: The Power Equation

1a. Ask students to fill out the Unit 2 Daily Self-Awareness Rating worksheet.

1b. **Remind students that today is the special event they planned.** Refer to the Power Equation and brainstorm with the students what they need to do to make this a successful event.

Slide 2: Blank Power Plan

2a. **Have the class help you recreate the plan for today's event on the blank Power Plan.**

"We are about to have our special event! That's what today is all about—celebrating your goal setting and planning for the special event! Let's start out by remembering our goal and plan. You had a strategy for remembering the plan for our special event. What was it?"

Praise the class for any strategies they used for remembering their plan for the special event from last class (e.g., writing it down, taking a picture). If necessary, help them remember and clarify any confusion about the plan. Have the students enter the goal and plan in the blank Power Plan. Review the plan for the special event with the class.

During the event, remember to praise individual students for all of the power and executive function skills they use, raising the Power Level up a bit. For example, if a student is flexible and lets go of their idea because others have another plan they feel strongly about (a level 2), praise the student for their flexibility and raise the Power Level card. Also, there may be opportunities during today's event for students to compromise using one of the four compromise strategies (each gets part, combine ideas, take turns, do something different you both like).

2b. Discuss why the class learned about compromise as a way to plan an event.

2c. Send Home Extension for Topic 2.5 home with students or e-mail it to parents.

2d. **Look for generalization opportunities in other classes.** Continue the discussion with educators about students checking their plans and work or putting them on trial. Encourage educators to use these terms. Remind educators that the Power Plan has a Check column (a visual support/reminder for checking) and remind them to use the Power Plan visual (Goal-Why-Plan-Check) with the students to help complete and check their projects and assignments.

> **CHECK:** How are my students doing?
> Do I need to make any adjustments for the next class?

See Appendix A for a list of questions to guide your self-reflection and refer to the Troubleshooting section (Appendix B) to address common problems or any challenges that may have arisen with the curriculum.

TOPIC 2.5: The Special Event

DAILY SELF-AWARENESS RATING: UNIT 2

NAME: _____

Executive Function Skills

Flexibility + Big Picture Thinking + Goals and Planning = POWER

1. How much do you think you can compromise today?

Mark an X on the arrow to show how you feel today:

Can't Compromise (I'm Feeling Too Stuck) — Can Compromise Some — Can Compromise

2. Which executive function skills do you plan to use today? (Check all that apply.)

- Making Plan Bs when Plan As don't work ☐
- Focusing on the big picture (instead of being stuck on details) ☐
- Being flexible ☐
- Using coping strategies and flexible thinking if needed ☐
- Compromising ☐

TOPIC 2.5: The Special Event

HOME EXTENSION FOR TOPIC 2.5: THE SPECIAL EVENT

In today's topic, students enjoyed a special event that they planned during the last class. This project gave them an opportunity to celebrate the power of using their goal setting, planning, flexibility, big picture thinking, and compromise skills.

Key Vocabulary/skills:

    Goal   *Plan*   *Plan A/Plan B*

    Compromise (When We Disagree, Figuring Out How We Can Both Get Some of What We Want)

How to use the Key Vocabulary/skills:

1. Ask your child to explain to you how the event in today's group session went. Did everything go as your child expected? Were people flexible?

2. Pick a time this week when you are planning to do something with your child (going somewhere special, making dinner, etc.). Help them make predictions about what could go wrong and how to handle challenges using flexibility and planning. Here are a few examples of what you might say to your child:

"Is there a chance that I might burn dinner? What will we eat if I do?" (Be flexible; try a Plan B; let go of being disappointed.)

"Is there a chance that you won't get to school on time today? What will we do if you are late?" (Be flexible and try a Plan B—write a note; let go of being upset.)

"Is there a chance that the store will be out of _____? What should be our Plan B?"

TOPIC 2.6 Reviewing the Special Event

BIG PICTURE SUMMARY

In Topic 2.5, students celebrated their special event—a sign of their success with setting a goal, compromising, and planning. In this topic, the class will review the event from last session, identifying all of the skills they used during the event.

Key Things to Do Here is the most important thing to do in today's class:

Use this Key Vocabulary often and in fun and playful ways:

- ★ Executive Function Skills
- ★ Flexible
- ★ Unstuck
- ★ Plan A/Plan B
- ★ Be Kind to Yourself and Others
- ★ Goal
- ★ Plan
- ★ Putting Your Plan on Trial (Checking Your Plan)
- ★ Use Coping Strategies and Flexible Thinking if Needed
- ★ Should I Compromise?
- ★ Is It a Big Deal or a Little Deal (or a Medium Deal)?
- ★ Let It Go
- ★ Stick to Your Idea
- ★ How to Compromise:
  - Each Gets Part.
  - Combine Ideas.
  - Take Turns.
  - Do Something Different You Both Like.
- ★ Stuck on a Detail?
- ★ Big Picture

Materials

 ★ Unit 2 Daily Self-Awareness Rating (worksheets copied for each student or found in the Student Workbook)

- PowerPoint for Topic 2.6, projected
- Power Equation Poster, posted
- Power Level card, affixed to the bottom of the Power Arrow on the Power Equation Poster
- Video or pictures from the special event (if recorded during last class)

EDUCATOR PLAN

Goal: Students will reflect on the special event from last class, considering what executive function and power skills they used during the event and areas to improve on in the future.

Why: Self-reflection is an important skill for growth. Today's reflection on the last group's event provides the students an opportunity to remember what skills they used and to consider what skills they might continue to practice moving forward.

Plan: Do the following before class:

- Post the Power Equation Poster and place the Power Level card at the bottom of the Power Arrow on the poster.
- Project the PowerPoint for Topic 2.6.
- For today's class, consider writing all of the Key Vocabulary and phrases from the list above on the board. Or you can use the list on the second PowerPoint slide if you are not using the screen to show video or pictures from the special event.
- If pictures or videos were taken during the special event, you can review them before class to highlight certain photos or clips that show students using executive function and power skills. Try including a few examples of challenges that came up during the special event so the students can think through what they might do differently next time.
- If no pictures or videos were taken of the special event, consider writing on the board an outline of key moments from the event that highlight various skills the students used and challenges they faced. This outline can help prompt the students to remember the event with greater clarity and meaning.

CLASS LESSON PLAN

Slide 1: Power Plan

1. **Ask students to fill out the Unit 2 Daily Self-Awareness Rating worksheet.** Review the Power Plan for Topic 2.6.

Slide 2: Review the Special Event

2. **Review the special event from last class, having the class circle (or highlight) each of the skills they used from the Key Vocabulary list.** If video or pictures were taken of the special event, review them one at a time with the class—or, using the outline on the board, have the class recall key moments from the event from memory. For each photo, ask the students to consider which skills and Key Vocabulary they used (or could have used). For example, while watching the video, freeze-frame to make comments and ask questions:

   "What skill is Jack using here? That's right—he showed flexibility by coming up with a Plan B when the music wouldn't play."

   "Dashawn, you did a nice job managing disappointment there. I could tell that was disappointing, but you stayed calm. Can anyone identify which power skills Dashawn was using?"

   Encourage students to lead the discussion and see how many of the skills they can identify. Make sure to focus on the students' successes and the challenges that they successfully faced. Ask them to consider which Key Vocabulary and skills they could do a better job with next time.

Slide 3: Preparing for Unit 3: Beginning to Think About a Longer-Term Group Goal

3. **Tell the class they will have the chance to plan for a longer-term goal.** The students can begin to brainstorm possible goals at the end of today's class. The Unit 3 goal should be larger in scope and more meaningful than the special event they celebrated last class. Many classes decide to focus on a goal that aims to make the world a better place. Altruistic goals may be highly motivating for students and engage them at a deeper level than a simple party. For example, some groups have planned a public service project or a field trip, planted a school garden, made care packages for overseas active-duty military, and created presentations about how to support the environment. Explain to the students:

   "Next class we will be thinking about a longer-term project goal. We will have more time to plan this project. This could be something that makes a difference in the world. For example, [give examples of possible types of projects]. Do you want to brainstorm a few ideas for possible projects and then we can think more about them next class?"

   Keep a copy of any ideas they come up with for use in the next class.

Slide 4: Topic 2.6 Wrap-Up: Why Are We Practicing Goal Setting and Planning?

4a. **Ask students why planning events together is good practice for the future.** Point to the Why section of the Power Plan and ask students to fill in the answer or just discuss. Ask students to think about what they are learning from planning events together. Discuss what kinds of power they can gain by setting a goal and making plans to reach the goal.

4b. Look for generalization opportunities in other classes. Continue to encourage your students' other educators to use Key Vocabulary from the Executive Function Skills List (found at the end of Topic 1.1). If educators have misplaced the skills list, provide them with a new copy. Here are some critical questions to ask other educators:

- ★ Have they been able to post the Executive Function Skills List in their classrooms?
- ★ Have they come up with creative ways of reinforcing the Key Vocabulary and skills?
- ★ Do they find the Key Vocabulary and skills useful in their own lives (this can be a great motivator for using them more naturally with students)?

> **CHECK:** How are my students doing?
> Do I need to make any adjustments for the next class?

See Appendix A for a list of questions to guide your self-reflection and refer to the Troubleshooting section (Appendix B) to address common problems or any challenges that may have arisen with the curriculum.

TOPIC 2.6: Reviewing the Special Event

DAILY SELF-AWARENESS RATING: UNIT 2

NAME: _____

Executive Function Skills

Flexibility + Big Picture Thinking + Goals and Planning = POWER

1. How much do you think you can compromise today?

Mark an X on the arrow to show how you feel today:

Can't Compromise　　　　　Can Compromise Some　　　　　Can Compromise
(I'm Feeling Too Stuck)

2. Which executive function skills do you plan to use today? (Check all that apply.)

Making Plan Bs when Plan As don't work　☐

Focusing on the big picture (instead of being stuck on details)　☐

Being flexible　☐

Using coping strategies and flexible thinking if needed　☐

Compromising　☐

UNIT 3

Efficient Planning

TOPIC 3.1   Getting (and Staying) Excited About a Future Goal

BIG PICTURE SUMMARY

In Topic 3.1, students will start thinking about the challenges of maintaining focus on and sustaining enthusiasm for a longer-term goal, even when the current situation is distracting. Their goal will be planning a group project or event on a larger scale than the event they planned in Unit 2. Today's topic brings together many skills taught in this program: setting a goal, compromising, and staying excited about a long-term goal. Students will need to use kindness and flexible thinking skills during the goal-setting and compromise process.

Key Things to Do Here are the two most important things to do in today's class:

1. **Use this Key Vocabulary often and in fun and playful ways:**

    ★ Executive Function Skills

    ★ Long-Term Goal

    ★ Quick Reward OR Long-Term Payoff

    ★ Eyes on the Prize

    ★ Goal

    ★ Plan

    ★ Big Picture

    ★ Should I Compromise?

    ★ How to Compromise:
      - Each Gets Part.
      - Combine Ideas.
      - Take Turns.
      - Do Something Different You Both Like.

    ★ How Long Should I Be Stuck on This Feeling?

2. **Find ways to spontaneously model executive function skills (compromise, flexibility, and planning)** *at least once* **during class today.** Make this fun and engaging! Use compromise, flexibility, and planning skills with your students to solve challenges that come

Key Vocabulary

The Key Vocabulary is a critical part of the curriculum; it is more important than the actual activities in each topic! The Key Vocabulary should be spoken as often as possible and presented in fun and enjoyable ways. Avoid punitive uses of the Key Vocabulary because that can interfere with student buy-in and use of the words and skills. The goal is to get your students to want to use the Key Vocabulary in their everyday lives.

up naturally or challenges that you've invented. For example: At the end of this lesson, when identifying ways to stay focused and excited about the group goal (see Slide 11), you could say to the class: *"I want to make a poster celebrating our cool goal, but I'm open to compromising. Do you have other ideas?"*

Special Instructions for Today: Have a range of ideas for possible group projects or events in mind (e.g., a special lunch, a volunteer activity). Encourage the group to be creative within the boundaries of what is realistic for your setting. Consider highly motivating events that will tap into the class's desire to make their community or world a better place. Goals that previous groups have chosen include making care packages for overseas active-duty military, planting a school garden, helping raise collections for a community food emergency program, and developing a plan to reduce carbon emissions at their school.

Important Note: The group's Unit 3 event should require the students to engage in a greater level of planning, independence, and consideration of important details than their Unit 1 and 2 events. For example, if the group plans a lunch for their teachers, then their planning should include coming up with a budget, coordinating a date that works for everyone, deciding who will bring what, developing reminders for bringing things on the day of the event, assigning cleanup duties, and so forth. The group should be responsible not only for deciding what they want to do, but also for how they will do it. Although the students will put the plan for their project or event on trial in Topic 3.4, encourage the class to spontaneously put parts of their plan on trial each week, thinking through and checking to see if they are missing any important parts of the plan. The Unit 3 event should be generally successful, but also allow the students a greater degree of independence to learn from their mistakes.

Materials

- Unit 3 Daily Self-Awareness Rating (worksheets copied for each student or found in the Student Workbook)

- PowerPoint for Topic 3.1, projected
- Power Equation Poster, posted
- Power Level card: Affix the card to the bottom of the Power Arrow on the Power Equation Poster.
- Optional: Materials (e.g., posterboard, magazines) for students to make a visual aid that encourages them to keep their eyes on the prize (see Slide 11).

EDUCATOR PLAN

Goal: Students will learn how longer-term planning builds power in their lives. Using the compromise skills they learned in Unit 2, the class will decide together on a longer-term goal. Students will also design a visual to help keep them excited and keep their eyes on the prize over the next few sessions as they plan their longer-term event.

Why: Many students with executive function challenges struggle with delaying gratification and staying focused on longer-term goals. Focusing on longer-term goals may mean passing up quick rewards in order to plan for a long-term payoff. This topic helps students develop thinking strategies to maintain their excitement about a more distant goal, even as immediate temptations distract from that goal.

Plan: Do the following before class:

- ★ Post the Power Equation Poster and put the Power Level card at the bottom of the Power Arrow on the poster. Raise the Power Level card when students compromise, are flexible or kind, show planning skills, or successfully manage their frustration and disappointment.
- ★ Project the PowerPoint for Topic 3.1.

CLASS LESSON PLAN

Slide 1: Power Plan

1a. Ask students to fill out the Unit 3 Daily Self-Awareness Rating worksheet.

1b. **Briefly review the Power Plan for Topic 3.1.** Remind the class that they'll be using their planning and flexibility skills to plan a longer-term project or event. Remind them that the longer-term goal will be bigger and more exciting than the previous events the class planned. Explain that because this is a bigger goal, it will take a little longer to plan.

1c. **If helpful, model excitement for the class by discussing one or two long-term goals that you have planned in the past.** For example, describe a vacation that took several weeks to plan. You can share an exciting visual like a picture of a beach that helped you stay excited about the vacation you were planning. Link this excitement to the class's opportunity to plan a meaningful event or project over the next few classes.

Slide 2: Comparing Short-Term and Longer-Term Goals

2. **Have the class fill in the two columns marked short-term goals and longer-term goals.** Brainstorm short-term and longer-term goals with your students, including recreational, school, and life goals (e.g., finishing a homework assignment, saving up to buy a game, graduating from college, getting a job as a computer programmer).

Slide 3: Keeping Your Eyes on the Prize: A Phrase to Stay Focused on Our Goal

3. **Introduce the powerful executive function skill of keeping your eyes on the prize (i.e., staying focused on an important goal).** Describe the saying "keep your eyes on the prize" and its importance for the U.S. civil rights movement:

   ★ The rights of Black people in the United States were unfairly limited in the past.

   ★ Although some things may be getting better over time—because of the work of great heroes like Dr. Martin Luther King Jr. and many others—there is still a lot of injustice and racism.

   ★ The civil rights movement, with leaders like Dr. Martin Luther King Jr. and many others, is a powerful movement in the United States—and it continues today. It started out to help Black people to be treated more fairly, and it expanded to work for the rights of many different people, including people with disabilities, autistic people, and many others.

   ★ It was not easy to plan the steps to get basic civil rights for Black people. It took a great deal of planning, and it took time. And all of the people involved in the civil rights movement had to keep their eyes on the prize.

   ★ The saying "eyes on the prize" was very popular during the 1950s and 1960s (it was the title of a popular song) as a way for the civil rights movement to stay focused on the goal of more freedom.

   ★ Let's look at this simple time line of a few years of the civil rights movement:

     - 1955: Rosa Parks, a Black woman, refused to give up her bus seat to a white man. This led to the Montgomery bus boycott, during which Black people refused to use the unfair, racially segregated bus system in Montgomery, Alabama. Rosa Parks and her allies in the boycott were keeping their eyes on the prize of ending racism and discrimination. Racism and discrimination wouldn't just end in one day, but she was working toward that long-term goal step by step through the boycott.

     - 1963: Dr. Martin Luther King Jr. delivered his "I Have a Dream" speech during the March on Washington for Jobs and Freedom. His speech emphasized the importance of ending racism and discrimination, and it inspired many people to work for justice. He was keeping his eyes on the prize of ending racism and discrimination, working toward that long-term important goal.

     - 1964: The Civil Rights Act was passed to outlaw discrimination based on race, color, religion, sex, or national origin. Many people had kept their eyes on the prize for years, planning and working to make this happen.

     - 1965: The Voting Rights Act was passed to outlaw racial discrimination in voting. Again, many people had kept their eyes on the prize of achieving this goal.

   ★ What do you think eyes on the prize means?

   ★ In the civil rights movement, what prize (or prizes) do you think they were working toward?

   ★ We can use the image of keeping your eyes on the prize to help us stay focused on important and powerful goals. This saying can help remind us of our important goals so that we don't forget to work toward them, even when it is hard.

Slides 4–8: Quick Rewards Versus Long-Term Payoff

4. **Discuss how quick rewards are fine, but longer-term planning can give you much more power and lead to more rewards.** Review with the class the following real-world examples of the benefits of longer-term planning:

    ★ (Slide 4): Rush through a test, so I can read my book (quick reward) or take my time and go over my answers before turning it in and get a better grade (long-term planning = bigger reward).

    ★ (Slide 5): Spend money on candy each day (quick reward) or save up money for a special game (long-term planning = long-term payoff).

    ★ (Slide 6): Play games all the time (quick reward) or finish my schoolwork before playing games and get better grades (long-term planning = long-term payoff).

    ★ (Slide 7): Get stuck talking about my interests every day (quick reward) or listen to other people's interests too and improve my friendships (long-term planning = long-term payoff).

    ★ (Slide 8): Throw recycling in the trash because it's easier (quick reward) or sort your recycling each day and put it in the recycling bin (long-term planning = long-term payoff = knowing that you are doing better for the Earth).

Slide 9: Deciding on an Important Longer-Term Goal Using Compromise Skills

9a. **Help the class get excited about planning for a larger and more meaningful event over the next few classes.** Discuss with students how they will need to keep their eyes on the prize during the planning process so they don't lose sight of accomplishing their important longer-term goal.

9b. **Have the class brainstorm different possible events (refer to the list the class started in Topic 2.6).** Provide some structure for the brainstorming session by suggesting possible events (e.g., a public service project, a field trip, planting a school garden, creating a care package for overseas military personnel). Record students' ideas on the board and tell them they are going to have the opportunity to share how strongly they feel about a particular idea and why, using the 0, 1, 2 scale (from the "Should I compromise?" formula). Go over these pointers with the students:

    ★ Aim for 0s and 1s (because if most people are a 2, it can lead to challenges). Remind students that if they don't feel too strongly about an idea (or if everyone agrees on an item), it allows us to move along more quickly and have more fun. Remind students that more extreme feelings are okay from time to time, but if you are always a 2, then you will lose power and potentially hurt relationships. Reward students for expressing moderate interests (0s or 1s) and for making flexible statements (e.g., "I want to do X, but I'm open to other ideas") by raising the Power Level card and offering praise. Consider using flexibility prompts such as, *"I know you feel really strongly. What would help you feel a little less strongly about this?"*

    ★ One veto allowed per student. Some students may have incredibly strong feelings about certain suggestions (e.g., playing laser tag might be overwhelming for a student with sensory processing challenges). Honor these strong feelings by giving each student one veto that allows them to remove an idea from the board, either because they feel strongly about not wanting to do it, or because they simply cannot do it. Explain to the students that it's okay to have strong feelings occasionally and that your friends will be flexible about this if you don't always insist on your own preferences.

★ Here are a few prompts to support the students' planning. Be careful not to direct these prompts toward a specific student or in a blaming way:

1. *"What happens to the group's power if people insist on their own way for every item?"*
2. *"Is this an event for just one person, or is this an event for the whole group?"*
3. *"Does everyone have to give a suggestion for every category?"*
4. *"What happens if we get stuck on every item and we run out of time to plan for the event?"*

9c. Present all of the group's ideas, asking the students to use the 0, 1, 2 scale to identify how strongly they feel about each idea and why. This will allow students to practice listening to and understanding each other's preferences. Write down key information on the blackboard/whiteboard.

Remind students that if the class cares the same amount (has matching scores) for two or more ideas, they can decide to compromise so each person gets part of what they want. Students can use compromise options from the how to compromise visual.

After students use the 0, 1, 2 scale to rate how strongly they feel about each option, add the numbers to determine which options have the highest scores**.** Then ask the class to use the compromise strategies (each gets part, combine ideas, take turns, or do something different you both like) to develop a final goal for the event.

You can say something like: *"Our top choices are raising money for an animal shelter and having a special lunch for educators. How can we compromise? We could combine ideas by making a special lunch for educators and donating the money we make to an animal shelter."*

Slide 10: Finalizing the Goal for the Longer-Term Event/Project

10. When the final goal is decided, enter it in the blank Power Plan visual. Provide lots of praise for the students' use of compromise, kindness, and flexible thinking skills to decide on their shared goal (raising the Power Level card as appropriate).

Ask students to think of a way to keep track of the goal for the longer-term event/project, so they don't lose or forget it (e.g., copy it down, take a picture of it, save it on the computer, write it on the board where it won't be erased). Say to the class: *"How can we keep track of our great plan so we don't lose or forget it? Next class we'll need to have the plan ready so we can do our special event. So what are some ways we keep track of our plan?"*

Slide 11: Remember, and Stay Excited About, the Goal (a Strategy to Keep Our Eyes on the Prize)

11. **The class should now discuss strategies to stay excited about and focused on their goal for the longer-term event or project.** This could be a visual reminder to keep them enthusiastic about their longer-term goal over the next few sessions. The visual could be a small poster with cutouts from magazines, a PowerPoint, or another idea the class comes up with. The class may also choose to select a phrase that will serve as their "cheer" when they need more motivation during the planning process (e.g., "keeping our eyes on the prize of planting our school's new garden.") Help the students keep these strategies in mind throughout the upcoming planning sessions (Topics 3.2–3.4).

Slide 12: Topic 3.1 Wrap-Up: Why Learn to Keep Our Eyes on the Prize for Longer-Term Goals?

12a. **Ask students to consider why keeping their eyes on the prize is important for different kinds of goals in their lives.** Encourage students to think about times in their own lives when they kept their eyes on the prize and followed through with projects. Where have they already used longer-term planning successfully in their personal lives? How does keeping your eyes on the prize increase your power? Point to the Why section of the Power Plan and have the students fill in the answer, or just discuss it.

12b. **Send Home Extension for Topic 3.1 home with students or e-mail it to parents.**

12c. **Look for generalization opportunities in other classes.** Explain to the students' other educators that over the next few weeks, they'll be learning the skills necessary to stay focused on a longer-term goal. Ask if they'll be assigning any upcoming projects that are longer-term (such as a larger project, science experiment, or research paper). If the answer is yes, suggest using the Power Plan to make a plan and the eyes on the prize motivational phrase to help students stay focused on the plan over time. Provide educators with more blank copies of the Power Plan visual found at the end of this lesson.

> **CHECK:** How are my students doing?
> Do I need to make any adjustments for the next class?

See Appendix A for a list of questions to guide your self-reflection and refer to the Troubleshooting section (Appendix B) to address common problems or any challenges that may have arisen with the curriculum.

TOPIC 3.1: Getting (and Staying) Excited About a Future Goal

DAILY SELF-AWARENESS RATING: UNIT 3

NAME: _____

Executive Function Skills

Flexibility + Big Picture Thinking + Goals and Planning = POWER

Mark an X on the arrow to show how you feel today:

Are you focused on the group's goal today?

Stuck on Details   Stuck on Some Details   Eyes on the Prize

Will you plan today?

Rush in With No Plan   Plan Some   Plan and Check to Make Sure the Plan Will Work

TOPIC 3.1: Getting (and Staying) Excited About a Future Goal

HOME EXTENSION FOR TOPIC 3.1: GETTING (AND STAYING) EXCITED ABOUT A FUTURE GOAL

In this topic, the students considered how long-term goals can be very powerful, but reaching them sometimes requires more patience and time to plan. The students were introduced to the idea of "keeping their eyes on the prize"—that is, staying focused and excited about a long-term goal. Today, the class decided on a long-term goal to plan for as a group. They shared their ideas and preferences and then used compromise skills to decide on a final goal.

Key Vocabulary/skills:

Long-Term Goal   *Eyes on the Prize*

Big Picture   *Power Plan* (i.e., the next page of this Home Extension handout)

How to use the Key Vocabulary/skills at home:

- Talk with your child about a long-term goal that you are currently working toward or have previously accomplished (especially one that they would be interested in). Talk about how you have to stay excited and keep working toward your goal (i.e., keep your eyes on the prize) to accomplish it. Consider writing out the goal and plan on a piece of paper.

- Use the Power Plan chart (i.e., the next page of this Home Extension handout) to develop a long-term goal and plan with your family. Perhaps you're saving money for a new TV or computer, or planning for a trip to visit Grandma. Have your child help you fill out the Power Plan chart, including writing in the goal (for example, plan a trip to Grandma's house) and brainstorming ideas for your Plan A. Also make sure to include a Plan B (for example, if it snows and we can't make the trip, our Plan B will be to visit Grandma in the spring). Consider using this Power Plan chart (which will be the next page of the Home Extension handout for the next several classes) to plan for different goals for your entire family (for example, a weekend trip, a homework schedule, a research project, a meeting with your boss).

TOPIC 3.1: Getting (and Staying) Excited About a Future Goal (continued)

POWER

CHECK:

PLAN:

Plan B?

GOAL:

WHY:

STUCK?

TOPIC 3.2   Efficient Planning—Staying Focused on the Big Picture Goal

BIG PICTURE SUMMARY

Related to the skill of keeping your eyes on the prize (practiced in Topic 3.1) is the ability to avoid getting stuck on unimportant details. Students will learn how to evaluate whether they are focused on their big picture goal and making progress toward their longer-term project or are stuck on off-topic details.

Key Things to Do Here are the two most important things to do in today's class:

1. **Use this Key Vocabulary often and in fun and playful ways:**
    * Executive Function Skills
    * Plan
    * Eyes on the Prize
    * Focused on the Big Picture Goal Versus Stuck on an Off-Topic Detail
    * Is This an Important Detail?
    * Efficiency = Doing a Task Well and Fairly Quickly

2. **Find ways to spontaneously model executive function skills (efficiency, compromise, flexibility, and planning)** *at least once* **during class today.** Make this fun and engaging! Use efficiency, compromise, flexibility, and planning skills with your students to solve challenges that come up naturally or challenges that you've invented.

Important Note

The purpose of Unit 3 is to teach students more independent planning skills. Support your students as they work out each step of the plan, like strategies for remembering to bring key supplies (e.g., phone calendar reminders, reminder buddies). They also need to learn to anticipate problems with their plan. Encourage the class to spontaneously put parts of their plan on trial each week, thinking through and checking to see if they are missing any important steps. The Unit 3 project or event should be generally successful, but should also allow your students a greater degree of independence to learn from their mistakes.

Materials

* Unit 3 Daily Self-Awareness Rating (worksheets copied for each student or found in the Student Workbook)
* **PPT** PowerPoint for Topic 3.2, projected
* Power Equation Poster, posted

Topic 3.2: Efficient Planning—Staying Focused on the Big Picture Goal   143

- ★ Power Level card: Affix the card to the bottom of the Power Arrow on the Power Equation Poster.
- ★ Eyes on the prize motivational memory aid from the last topic (Topic 3.1, Slide 11)
- ★ Optional: Materials for making two signs to hold up during class: a "focused on the big picture goal" sign and a "stuck on off-topic details" sign)

EDUCATOR PLAN

Goal: Students will begin to plan the steps for their longer-term project. They will keep their eyes on the prize (big picture goal) to encourage efficient planning.

Why: Students with executive function challenges may have difficulty staying focused on their big picture goal. Providing a framework for evaluating whether they are focused on their goal or stuck on an off-topic detail teaches students self-monitoring skills.

POWER LEVEL CARD: Remember, the Power Level card only moves up, and it should be moved up frequently. Focus on celebrating or noticing when the students are doing well, instead of focusing on problematic behaviors (i.e., Power Losses). The system should be used primarily for highlighting flexibility and problem solving, particularly when they use the skills and Key Vocabulary taught in the curriculum.

Plan: Do the following before class:

- ★ Post the Power Equation Poster and place the Power Level card at the bottom of the Power Arrow on the poster. Raise the Power Level card when students compromise, are flexible or kind, show planning skills, or manage their frustration and disappointment.
- ★ Project the PowerPoint for Topic 3.2.

CLASS LESSON PLAN

Slide 1: Blank Power Plan

1a. **Ask students to fill out the Unit 3 Daily Self-Awareness Rating worksheet.** Prompt the students to remember the group project or event they chose last class and fill in the Goal section of the blank Power Plan. If needed, remind students of the memory aid they came up with last class for remembering the goal. Also remind students that this is a longer-term goal that will take more time to plan, which is why they made their eyes on the prize visual aid last class—to stay excited about and focused on this longer-term goal. Have the students post their eyes on the prize poster from last class in a visible location (or do their cheer) to stay excited about the long-term goal.

1b. **Discuss the importance of efficiency.** Here are some key points to cover for the class discussion:

- What does efficient mean?
- Efficiency = doing a task well and fairly quickly
- Over the next few classes, the students will have to be efficient in their planning, or they might not finish the plan for their longer-term goal.
- If we aren't efficient, we won't get things done.
- Being efficient requires that we stay focused on the big picture, and not get stuck on details—even if interesting—for too long.

1c. **Have the class decide on visual cues to show when they are focused on the big picture goal versus when they are stuck on off-topic details.** Give the students several options for showing whether they are focused on the big picture goal (i.e., planning their upcoming event or project) or stuck on off-topic details. For example, the class could make paper signs for when they are focusing on the big picture (successfully planning) versus when they are getting stuck on off-topic details (such as a video game discussion that isn't relevant to the plan). Or the students might come up with simple hand signals, like a thumbs up or thumbs down for when they are focused on their big picture goal or when they are getting stuck on off-topic details, respectively.

During class, you (and eventually your students) can evaluate whether the class is focused on the goal of planning or stuck on off-topic details by showing the corresponding sign or hand signal.

Slide 2: Practice the Self-Monitoring System (Example 1)

2. **Practice the new self-monitoring system using the following examples.** (Note: If the students grasp the concept, they can improvise their own story about getting stuck on details.) The first example should be read by a student, while you show the appropriate big picture or stuck on off-topic details visual cues (see above). You should read the second example, with a student or students showing the appropriate visual cues (e.g., raising the stuck on off-topic details sign versus the focused on big picture goal sign at different points in the example):

- **Example 1:** *"Our goal is to make a pizza. So we first have to go to the store to get the ingredients and then come back and make the pizza. Speaking of stores, I went to the video game store the other day and they have an awesome new game called Mystic Flies where you have to gather these gold stones out of bird nests. It is so cool! But oh yeah, we were talking about pizza. So we need to go to the store and get cheese and tomato sauce and crust. I love pizza! The last time I had pizza was last Thursday. It was a large and I shared it with my dad. Wow, it was so good, we ate all of it that night. So getting back to the goal for today, once we get the ingredients, we'll come back and make the pizza."*

Slide 3: Practice the Self-Monitoring System (Example 2)

★ **Example 2:** Have a student in the group ask, "How did you plan your vacation?" Answer the question using the following script, making sure to say each sentence slowly enough so the students can give the cue indicating whether the statement is currently focused on the big picture or stuck on an off-topic detail:

"I planned my vacation by first thinking about my goal—I wanted to do something I've never done before. Then I made a list of some of the things I've never done before. Oh, by the way, I had pizza last night—it was so yummy! Oh, sorry, I was talking about my plans for vacation—so I made the list and then I picked my top three choices—going to the mountains, going sailing, or going to see a volcano in Hawaii. Then I focused on the one that I liked the most—Hawaii. Oh, actually, last summer I went to Canada—that was fun. I could tell you a story about Canada, but I should get back to the big picture. So I started to plan my trip to Hawaii and I first figured out when I could go. Then I scheduled my flight and my hotel room."

Back to Slide 1

4a. **Encourage the class to begin planning their long-term goal by entering the details of the plan in the blank Power Plan.** Encourage the students to think about the who, what, where, when, and how of the project or event. Remind the class that this is a long-term goal that may take several classes to plan.

4b. **Use the visual cues during the class's planning.** Remind the students that in order to plan efficiently, you will use visual cues (signs or hand signals) to help the class notice when they are focused on the big picture goal or stuck on an off-topic detail. Add verbal reminders if helpful. For example:

   ★ *"I'm holding up the focused on the big picture goal sign because you are focused on the big picture—nice work!"*

   ★ *"I held up the stuck on an off-topic detail sign because we are stuck on a detail—is it an important detail? Or is it off-topic?"*

   ★ *"This seems like an off-topic detail; that's why I'm holding up this sign. How long should we be stuck on it?"*

4c. **Allow the students to self-monitor using the big picture goal versus stuck on an off-topic detail cues.** This may work best with one student controlling the cues, but some classes may be able to do this as a group. It may be useful to validate that sometimes the off-topic details are interesting, but it is still important to notice if they are helping you reach the big picture goal. Provide support as necessary.

4d. **Encourage and support the planning process as necessary.** Allow the students to make decisions and use planning and compromise skills. Provide structure and reminders as necessary, and fade support whenever possible. Remember, the students' plan may be intricate and involve multiple steps given the larger scope of this project. You may need to transfer the written plan to the board to allow for more room to write out the steps of the plan.

4e. Near the end of class, ask the students how they will remember planning they've done today. Help the class develop a strategy for remembering, like taking a picture of the Power Plan visual or writing it down. If helpful, briefly discuss how the students remember other important details from their day like homework or projects.

4f. Ask students why efficiency is important for planning different goals in their lives. Have students think about situations where they got stuck on details and it derailed their plan. Why is efficiency so important at school, for homework, and in other areas of their lives? Ask them to consider how getting stuck on off-topic details might get in the way of them accomplishing their goals. Consider how getting stuck on off-topic details can make us all stuck and lead to failing to accomplish our goals.

4g. Send Home Extension for Topic 3.2 home with students or e-mail it to parents.

4h. Look for generalization opportunities in other classes. Discuss the focused on the big picture goal versus stuck on an off-topic detail routine with other classroom educators. Encourage them to use this Key Vocabulary with their class to help the students focus on the main idea and most important information during a lesson. For examples, an educator could say, "Great job focusing on the big picture goal!" or "It seems we're stuck on off-topic details. Can we get back to the big picture?"

> **CHECK:** How are my students doing?
> Do I need to make any adjustments for the next class?

See Appendix A for a list of questions to guide your self-reflection and refer to the Troubleshooting section (Appendix B) to address common problems or any challenges that may have arisen with the curriculum.

TOPIC 3.2: Efficient Planning—Staying Focused on the Big Picture Goal

DAILY SELF-AWARENESS RATING: UNIT 3

NAME: _____

Executive Function Skills

Flexibility + Big Picture Thinking + Goals and Planning = POWER

Mark an X on the arrow to show how you feel today:

Are you focused on the group's goal today?

Stuck on Details | Stuck on Some Details | Eyes on the Prize

Will you plan today?

Rush in With No Plan | Plan Some | Plan and Check to MakeSure the Plan Will Work

TOPIC 3.2: Efficient Planning—Staying Focused on the Big Picture Goal

HOME EXTENSION FOR TOPIC 3.2: EFFICIENT PLANNING— STAYING FOCUSED ON THE BIG PICTURE GOAL

The class is now planning for their long-term group goal. Today's topic focused on efficiency—the importance of staying focused on the big picture and not getting stuck on details.

Key Vocabulary/skills:

Efficiency   *Big Picture*   *Stuck on Off-Topic Details*

How Long Should I Be Stuck on This Detail?

How to use the Key Vocabulary/skills:

- Ask your child to teach you about the difference between focusing on the big picture goal and being stuck on off-topic details. Ask them to tell you about efficiency and how getting stuck on details can slow you down.

- Use the "stuck on off-topic details" Key Vocabulary at home in fun ways. When you notice someone (including yourself!) getting stuck on a detail, say in a positive voice, *"That's an interesting detail! How long should we be stuck on it? One minute or 2 minutes?"* Show genuine interest in the detail until 1 or 2 minutes are up (time it on your phone), and then ask, *"Should we get back to the big picture?"* One of the best ways to use this technique is to practice it in front of your child with your spouse, partner, or other family members. For example, a family member could intentionally get stuck on a detail (such as talking too much about football stats), and you could respond by saying, *"Fascinating detail! How long should we be stuck on it?"*

- Use the Power Plan chart (i.e., the next page of this Home Extension handout) to develop a plan or model making a plan. For example, you might plan your Saturday errands and post it on the refrigerator. Or you might make a plan to go on an outing with the family. Don't forget to make a Plan B!

TOPIC 3.2: Efficient Planning—Staying Focused on the Big Picture Goal (continued)

POWER

CHECK:

PLAN:

Plan B?

GOAL:

WHY:

STUCK?

TOPIC 3.3   Efficient Planning—Watching the Clock

> **BIG PICTURE SUMMARY**
>
> In the previous Unit 3 topics, the students learned about and practiced keeping their eyes on the prize (staying excited about a goal) and staying focused on the big picture goal versus getting stuck on off-topic details. In this topic, students will learn the value of efficiency and watching the clock—keeping track of how much time it's taking to plan in order to do the task well and fairly quickly.

Key Things to Do   Here are the two most important things to do in today's class:

1. **Use this Key Vocabulary often and in fun and playful ways:**
   - Executive Function Skills
   - Watching the Clock
   - Efficiency
   - Efficient Planning
   - Focused on the Big Picture Goal Versus Stuck on Off-Topic Details
   - Is This an Important Detail?
   - Stuck on an Off-Topic Detail
   - Eyes on the Prize
   - Should We Compromise?
   - How to Compromise:
     - Each Gets Part.
     - Combine Ideas.
     - Take Turns.
     - Do Something Different You Both Like.

2. **Find ways to spontaneously model executive function skills (compromise, flexibility, and planning) *at least once* during class today.** Make this fun and engaging! Use compromise, flexibility, and planning skills with your students to solve challenges that come up naturally or challenges that you've invented. For example:
   - *"I'm keeping my eyes on the prize and made a schedule to make sure we get through all of our lessons, so we have time for an end-of-year celebration."*
   - *"I know we all want to get to the game at the end of class today. Let's watch the clock, stay focused on the lesson's big picture goal, and try not to get stuck on off-topic details."*
   - *"I love the way you stayed focused on the big picture goal and tabled that detail for another time."*

Topic 3.3: Efficient Planning—Watching the Clock

Special Instructions for Today: Continue the visual system that the students developed last class to show whether they're focused on the big picture goal or stuck on off-topic details. Practice the timing reminders (see Slide 3) before class.

Important Note

The group's Unit 3 plan should require the students to engage in a greater level of planning, independence, and consideration of important details than the Unit 1 and 2 events. For example, if the group plans a lunch for their teachers, then their planning should include coming up with a budget, coordinating a date that works for everyone, deciding who will bring what, developing reminders for bringing things on the day of the event, and assigning cleanup duties. The group should be responsible not only for deciding what they want to do, but also for how they will do it. Although the students will put the plan for their project or event on trial in Topic 3.4, encourage the class to spontaneously put parts of their plan on trial each week, thinking through and checking to see if they are missing any important parts of the plan. The Unit 3 event should be generally successful, but also allow the students a greater degree of independence to learn from their mistakes.

Materials

- Unit 3 Daily Self-Awareness Rating (worksheets copied for each student or found in the Student Workbook)

- PowerPoint for Topic 3.3, projected
- Power Equation Poster, posted
- Power Level card: Affix the card to the bottom of the Power Arrow on the Power Equation Poster.
- Kitchen timer, stopwatch, or other timer
- Eyes on the prize motivational aid from Topic 3.1, Slide 11
- Focused on the big picture goal versus stuck on off-topic details signs or signals from Topic 3.2, Slide 1

EDUCATOR PLAN

Goal: Students will continue to plan for their longer-term project or event. They will focus on their big picture goal and watch the clock to achieve efficient planning.

Why: Because young people with executive function challenges tend to struggle with efficient planning, self-reminders to focus on moving the process along (watching the clock) can help them plan more quickly and become less frustrated by the planning process.

 **POWER LEVEL CARDS:** Remember, the Power Level card only moves up, and it should move up frequently. Focus on celebrating or noticing when the students are doing well, and ignore problematic behaviors whenever possible. The system should be used primarily for being flexible, particularly when they use the skills and Key Vocabulary taught in the curriculum.

Plan: Do the following before class:

- ★ Post the Power Equation Poster and place the Power Level card at the bottom of the Power Arrow on the poster. Raise the Power Level card when students compromise, are flexible or kind, show planning skills, or manage their frustration and disappointment.
- ★ Project the PowerPoint for Topic 3.3.

CLASS LESSON PLAN

Slide 1: Power Plan

1a. Ask students to fill out the Unit 3 Daily Self-Awareness Rating worksheet.

1b. **Today's Power Plan is completely blank.** Students should fill in the missing words (Goal, Why, Plan, Plan B, Check, Stuck, Power) from memory. Give them hints if necessary.

1c. Explain to the students: *"Today we are going to continue planning for our longer-term goal. We want to get most of our planning for the project done today, so we're going to learn how to watch the clock so that we don't run out of time."*

Slide 2: Efficiency and Watching the Clock

2. **Explain that the class will have to be efficient in planning for their goal, or they might not finish the plan in time to do the event or project.** Review the meaning of the word efficient (doing a task well and fairly quickly) and write the definition on the board. Engage the students in discussion about the three concepts below:

- ★ Eyes on the prize. Briefly review that keeping your eyes on the prize means staying excited about a longer-term goal. Refer to the class's eyes on the prize visual aid or cheer that they came up with for the longer-term event.
- ★ Focused on the big picture goal versus stuck on an off-topic detail. Ask the class to describe the two visual cues they developed last class for indicating whether they're focused on the big picture goal or getting stuck on an off-topic detail.
- ★ Efficiency: watch the clock. Discuss why watching the clock is important. Ask the class if they've ever had to plan something quickly and to consider what happens if we lose track of the time while we're planning.

Slide 3: Continue Planning for the Big Event/Project

3a. **Explain that you will be watching the clock to help the class plan efficiently.** Tell the students that a timer will go off every 5 minutes to remind everyone to stay focused on finishing the planning.

3b. **Have the class use their memory strategy from last class to pull up the parts of the plan that are already complete.** They can type the Goal, Why, and Plan into the PowerPoint slide or pull up a saved file from last class.

3c. **Students should continue planning their long-term goal, entering the different steps in the Power Plan as efficiently as possible.** If needed, prompt the students to use the "Should we compromise?" formula and how to compromise skills. Remind the class that there will be a few timing reminders while they're planning. At the end of each 5-minute period, show students the stopwatch or timer and remind them of the importance of watching the clock:

  ★ After the first 5-minute planning period, praise the class by saying, *"Good job watching the clock! We want to make sure we are efficient and don't get stuck."* Through a show of hands, ask the class to self-assess whether they have been focused on the big picture goal of planning for the event or stuck on off-topic details.

  ★ After the second 5-minute period, praise students again for watching the clock. Repeat the routine from above, asking them to vote on whether they were focused on the goal or stuck on off-topic details.

  ★ After the third 5-minute period, tell the class that they've been planning for 15 minutes, and time is getting close to running out. Remind them that it is powerful to plan efficiently.

  ★ After the final 5-minute period, praise the students for excellent planning and watching the clock. Repeat the voting process from above.

Important Note: If useful during the planning process, employ the signs or hand signals the class developed in Topic 3.2 to show when they are focused on the big picture goal versus when they are stuck on off-topic details.

3d. **Ask students to think of a way (or use a method from a previous session if it worked well) to keep track of the planning they've done, so they don't lose or forget it.** For example, have them copy it down, take a picture of it, save it on the computer, or write it on the board where it won't be erased. Discuss how having a strategy for remembering important information builds power and ask students about strategies they already use for remembering homework and other important details.

3e. **Ask students why watching the clock is important for planning different goals in their lives.** Why is watching the clock important for getting things done? How about keeping your eyes on the calendar? How can these skills help with finishing school projects? Could they improve your grades? Could they increase your power to help make the world a better place?

3f. **Send Home Extension for Topic 3.3 home with students or e-mail it to parents.**

3g. **Look for generalization opportunities in other classes.** Discuss the watch the clock Key Vocabulary with your students' other classroom educators, emphasizing that focusing on the clock should be presented in a positive and supportive manner with students. Encourage educators to use the Key Vocabulary with their class to support the students' focus on efficiency, praising them with statements like, *"Nice job watching the clock and getting the work done!"*

> **CHECK:** How are my students doing?
> Do I need to make any adjustments for the next class?

See Appendix A for a list of questions to guide your self-reflection and refer to the Troubleshooting section (Appendix B) to address common problems or any challenges that may have arisen with the curriculum.

TOPIC 3.3: Efficient Planning—Watching the Clock

DAILY SELF-AWARENESS RATING: UNIT 3

NAME: _____

Executive Function Skills

Flexibility + Big Picture Thinking + Goals and Planning = POWER

Mark an X on the arrow to show how you feel today:

Are you focused on the group's goal today?

Stuck on Details   Stuck on Some Details   Eyes on the Prize

Will you plan today?

Rush in With No Plan   Plan Some   Plan and Check to Make Sure the Plan Will Work

TOPIC 3.3: Efficient Planning—Watching the Clock

HOME EXTENSION FOR TOPIC 3.3: EFFICIENT PLANNING—WATCHING THE CLOCK

The class continued to work on their plan for achieving a long-term group goal. Planning a fun and meaningful event together teaches them how to plan for long-term projects at school and in life. This topic continued the focus on efficiency—this time encouraging the students to complete their plan on time by "watching the clock" and not getting stuck on off-topic details.

Key Vocabulary/skills:

Efficiency

Watching the Clock

Stuck on an Off-Topic Detail

Should We Get Back to the Big Picture Goal?

How to use the Key Vocabulary/skills:

For some students, homework is especially challenging because they get stuck on details. Students may struggle with developing a plan for how to complete their homework efficiently. Consider supporting your child's homework efforts with pre-planning and reminders about being efficient. Use the Power Plan chart (i.e., the next page of this Home Extension handout) to write out the goal of getting homework done fairly quickly and well, and then develop a plan with your child to help them complete it as efficiently as possible.

You might consider adding time limits for each part of the homework (for example, 15 minutes of math followed by a 5-minute break). Help your child time the segments. Encourage your child to consider when they are getting stuck on details, such as a video game, Internet searching, or less important parts of the assignment. It can be helpful to identify a time in the near future when they can go back to their personal interests (for example, *"Once you are finished with the assignment, you can play your video game"*).

TOPIC 3.3: Efficient Planning—Watching the Clock (continued)

POWER

CHECK:

PLAN:

Plan B?

GOAL:

WHY:

STUCK?

TOPIC 3.4 Pulling It All Together—Using All the Key Vocabulary/Skills to Finalize the Plan

BIG PICTURE SUMMARY

In this topic, students finalize the plan for their longer-term goal using all of the skills taught in the curriculum: efficiency skills (keeping your eyes on the prize, staying focused on the big picture goal, and watching the clock), compromise skills, and the skill of checking to see if a plan will work (putting the plan on trial).

Key Things to Do (This topic will take more than one class period to complete)

Here are the two most important things to do in today's class:

1. **Use this Key Vocabulary often and in fun and playful ways:**
   - ★ Executive Function Skills
   - ★ Eyes on the Prize
   - ★ Focused on the Big Picture Goal Versus Stuck on Off-Topic Details
   - ★ Stuck on a Detail
   - ★ Watch the Clock
   - ★ Efficiency
   - ★ Efficient Planning
   - ★ Should We Compromise?
   - ★ How to Compromise:
     - Each Gets Part.
     - Combine Ideas.
     - Take Turns.
     - Do Something Different You Both Like.
   - ★ Putting the Plan on Trial (Check Your Plan to See if It Will Work)

2. **Find ways to spontaneously model executive function skills (compromise, flexibility, and planning)** *at least once* **during class today.** Make this fun and engaging! Use compromise, flexibility, and planning skills with your students to solve challenges that come up naturally or challenges that you've invented. Here are a few examples:
   - ★ *"I'm worried I am not going to be able to get through today's lesson, so I am going to be very efficient. I've also put a time goal next to each part of the plan so I can watch the clock and make sure we finish."*
   - ★ *"I love the way you used your plan to stay focused on your big picture goal."*
   - ★ *"That was an interesting off-topic detail. You did a great job ending that conversation so you could focus on your big picture goal."*

Topic 3.4: Pulling It All Together—Using All the Key Vocabulary/Skills to Finalize the Plan 159

Special instructions for today: Continue the visual system that the students developed in a previous class to indicate whether they're focused on the big picture goal or stuck on off-topic details. Continue the timing reminder system from last class.

Important Note

The group's plan for their longer-term event is completed in today's lesson. There may be some additional legwork that students will need to do (and you may need to help with) in preparation for the big event next class. In some cases, the big event day is not so much an event, but the finalization of the project (e.g., packing up and sending the care packages to overseas active-duty military, planting the school garden). Some projects like the school garden may take more than one class to complete and could potentially be scheduled on a weekend.

Materials

- Unit 3 Daily Self-Awareness Rating (worksheets copied for each student or found in the Student Workbook)

- PowerPoint for Topic 3.4, projected
- Power Equation Poster, posted
- Power Level card: Affix the card to the bottom of the Power Arrow on the Power Equation Poster.
- Kitchen timer, stopwatch, or other timer
- Eyes on the prize motivational aid from Topic 3.1, Slide 11 (e.g., poster to stay motivated about the longer-term goal the students picked)
- Focused on the big picture goal versus stuck on off-topic details signs or signals from Topic 3.2, Slide 1

EDUCATOR PLAN

Goal: Students will finalize their plan for their longer-term goal. They will keep their eyes on the prize to stay focused on their big picture goal and watch the clock to be efficient. They will also put their plan on trial to make sure it will work and there are no missing steps.

Why: To promote the use of executive function skills in different settings, it is essential to practice the integration of skills and their self-directed application.

Plan: Do the following before class:
- Post the Power Equation Poster and place the Power Level card at the bottom of the Power Arrow on the poster. Raise the Power Level card when students compromise, are flexible or kind to themselves or others, show planning skills, or manage their frustration and disappointment.
- Project the PowerPoint for Topic 3.4.

CLASS LESSON PLAN

Slide 1: Eyes on the Prize, Big Picture Thinking, and Efficiency

1a. Ask students to fill out the Unit 3 Daily Self-Awareness Rating worksheet.

1b. **Remind students about the importance of efficiency so they can finalize their plan for the longer-term event today.** Review the three concepts below, allowing the class to describe them:

- **Eyes on the Prize:** Staying excited about our longer-term goal

- **Focused on the big picture goal versus stuck on an off-topic detail:** Noticing whether we are focused on the big picture goal or stuck on an off-topic detail

- **Efficiency: Watch the Clock**: Planning quickly and carefully

Slide 2: Blank Power Plan

2a. **Encourage the students to remember their goal and the planning they've done for their upcoming group event or project.** Use the same memory strategy from the end of the previous class (e.g., taking a picture, writing it down). Praise the class for any strategies they used for remembering their plan for the special event from last class. If necessary, help them remember and clarify any confusions about the plan. Have the students enter the goal and steps of the plan in the blank Power Plan. Review the plan for the special event with the class.

Use the same self-monitoring system the class developed in Topic 3.2 (e.g., signs or hand signals) to show when they're focused on the big picture goal versus when they are stuck on off-topic details.

2b. **Encourage the students to finish planning for the longer-term goal, with a focus on efficiency.** As in Topic 3.3, tell the students the planning session will be divided into three 5-minute time periods. Before each period, show the stopwatch and remind the class of the importance of watching the clock:

- After the first 5-minute planning period, praise the class by saying: *"Good job watching the clock! We want to make sure we are efficient and don't get stuck."* Through a show of hands, ask the class to self-assess whether they have been focused on the big picture goal of planning for the event or stuck on off-topic details.

- After the second 5-minute period, praise students again for watching the clock. Repeat the routine from above, asking them to vote on whether they were focused on the goal or stuck on off-topic details.

- After the final 5-minute period, praise the students for excellent planning, watching the clock, and finishing their plan.

Topic 3.4: Pulling It All Together—Using All the Key Vocabulary/Skills to Finalize the Plan

2c. **After the plan has been finalized, tell students they are going to put the plan on trial.**

   ★ *"Let's check our plan by putting it on trial. Will we reach our goal? Did we come up with a good plan for reaching our goal? While we're checking our plan, let's make sure to use flexibility and kindness, so everyone feels respected. Let's see if the plan works, or if there are any problems we need to fix."*

2d. **Putting the plan on trial:** If students are eager, consider again creating a fun courtroom feel with courtroom visuals and a judge and jury. Have the students go through each step of the plan and put a check in the Check column if the step is good or place an X next to any step that needs to be reworked. As the class evaluates each step of the plan, classroom volunteers can act out each step. Encourage the students to come up with other ideas for steps that they feel should be improved. Allow the class to do as much of the checking process as they can on their own, adding support when necessary.

2e. **Praise the students for their thinking into the future and their use of executive function skills:**

   "When we put a plan on trial, we can make our plan better because we find all of the problems and fix them. Next class, we get to celebrate with the wonderful event/project you planned."

2f. **Ask students to keep track of the planning they've done, so they don't lose or forget it (e.g., copy it down, take a picture of it, save it on the computer, write it on the board where it won't be erased).** Discuss how having a strategy for remembering important information builds power and ask students about strategies they already use for remembering homework and other important details.

2g. **Ask students why we've learned how to plan efficiently.** Why is it important to be efficient in planning different goals in their lives? Why is it important to put plans on trial before doing them?

2h. **Send Home Extension for Topic 3.4 home with students or e-mail it to parents.**

2i. **Look for generalization opportunities in other classes.** Review the three efficiency skills with educators, asking them to emphasize all three in their classes: eyes on the prize, focused on the big picture goal versus stuck on off-topic details, and watching the clock. Remind educators to use this vocabulary and the Power Plan visual to support class planning and projects.

> **CHECK:** How are my students doing?
> Do I need to make any adjustments for the next class?

See Appendix A for a list of questions to guide your self-reflection and refer to the Troubleshooting section (Appendix B) to address common problems or any challenges that may have arisen with the curriculum.

TOPIC 3.4: Pulling It All Together—Using All the Key Vocabulary/Skills to Finalize the Plan

DAILY SELF-AWARENESS RATING: UNIT 3

NAME: _____

Executive Function Skills

Flexibility + Big Picture Thinking + Goals and Planning = POWER

Mark an X on the arrow to show how you feel today:

Are you focused on the group's goal today?

Stuck on Details ←——————— Stuck on Some Details ———————→ Eyes on the Prize

Will you plan today?

Rush in With No Plan ←——————— Plan Some ———————→ Plan and Check to Make Sure the Plan Will Work

TOPIC 3.4: Pulling It All Together—Using All the Key Vocabulary/Skills to Finalize the Plan

HOME EXTENSION FOR TOPIC 3.4: PULLING IT ALL TOGETHER— USING ALL THE KEY VOCABULARY/SKILLS TO FINALIZE THE PLAN

Today the class finalized their plan for their long-term group event. They also carefully checked their plan for errors by putting it on trial like in a courtroom. Over the last few sessions, they have kept their eyes on the prize, working hard and staying excited about the long-term group event.

Key Vocabulary/skills:

Goal

Putting the Plan on Trial (Checking the Plan)

Plan

Eyes on the Prize

How to use the Key Vocabulary/skills:

- Ask your child to tell you about the group plan for their event. How has the planning been going? Did they check their plan? How did they stay excited and keep their eyes on the prize? Did they have to compromise? Provide significant praise for your child's planning in the group, including their ability to plan for a long-term goal.

- Your child and teacher will be deciding soon on a personal goal to work toward using the techniques that have been practiced in this program. You may wish to consult with your child and their teacher to discuss ideas for the personal goal (this can be a goal at school or home, or one that is helpful for both). It is important that your child's personal goal be:
    - Achievable in a few days/weeks
    - Reasonably simple, but also meaningful to your child
    - Highly motivating for your child (something that they want to do)

- Use the Power Plan (i.e., the next page of this Home Extension handout) to make a plan or model making a plan. It can be silly, like a plan to brush your teeth (and a Plan B for running out of toothpaste), or more substantive, like a plan for going to visit a sick relative or friend.

TOPIC 3.4: Pulling It All Together—Using All the Key Vocabulary/Skills to Finalize the Plan (continued)

POWER

CHECK:

PLAN:

Plan B?

GOAL:

WHY:

STUCK?

TOPIC 3.5   The Longer-Term Event/Project—Efficient Planning = Power!

BIG PICTURE SUMMARY

In Topics 3.1–3.4, students learned how to maintain their excitement for a longer-term goal and efficiently complete their plan. They also practiced putting their plan on trial to look for missed details and made appropriate changes to their plan. They have used compromise skills and flexible thinking throughout the process, and they managed frustration and disappointment when things didn't go as expected. Today, the group celebrates their successes with the event or project they have planned.

Key Things to Do Here are the two most important things in today's class:

1. **Use this Key Vocabulary often and in fun and playful ways:**
   - ★ Executive Function Skills
   - ★ Eyes on the Prize
   - ★ Flexible Thinking
   - ★ Be Kind
   - ★ Plan A/Plan B
   - ★ Managing Frustration and Disappointment
   - ★ Should We Compromise?
   - ★ How to Compromise:
     - Each Gets Part.
     - Combine Ideas.
     - Take Turns.
     - Do Something Different You Both Like.

2. **Find ways to spontaneously model executive function skills (compromise, flexibility, and planning)** *at least once* **during class today.** Make this fun and engaging! Use compromise, flexibility, and planning skills with your students to solve challenges that come up naturally or challenges that you've invented.

Special instructions for today: Some students may have certain expectations for what this project or event will be like. To help manage student expectations and minimize disappointment, you can provide them with a framework for this event (this will vary based on the type of event you are having). Think about what might pose a problem and help students manage their expectations and understand that they can still use flexible thinking and compromise to have a good time.

Materials

 ★ Unit 3 Daily Self-Awareness Rating (worksheets copied for each student or found in the Student Workbook)

- PowerPoint for Topic 3.5, projected
- Power Equation Poster, posted
- Power Level card: Affix the card to the bottom of the Power Arrow on the Power Equation Poster.
- Optional: Camera or video-recording device

EDUCATOR PLAN

Goal: Have a successful longer-term event or project.

Why: It is important for students to be able to enjoy the event or project they have spent time planning, so they can associate positive feelings with the longer-term planning process.

Plan: Do the following before class:

- Post the Power Equation Poster and place the Power Level card at the bottom of the Power Arrow on the poster. Raise the Power Level card when students compromise, are flexible or kind, show planning skills, or manage their frustration and disappointment.
- Project the PowerPoint for Topic 3.5.

CLASS LESSON PLAN

Slide 1: The Longer-Term Event/Project Is Celebrated Today

1a. **Ask students to fill out the Unit 3 Daily Self-Awareness Rating worksheet.** Praise the class for their efficient planning and explain to them that because they were efficient, they had the power to complete their plan. Review the following points with students:

- They kept their eyes on the prize and planned a larger event.
- They stayed focused on the big picture instead of getting stuck on off-topic details.
- They watched the clock and planned quickly, while also doing a good job.
- They put the plan on trial, which helped them think through any problems with the plan.

1b. **Ask the students to fill in the blank Power Plan with their plan for today's event or project.** Encourage students to use their strategy from last topic for remembering the details of their plan and praise them for any strategies they used (e.g., writing it down, taking a picture). If necessary, help them remember and clarify any confusion about the plan.

1c. Remind the students of flexible thinking skills (e.g., using a Plan B if Plan A doesn't work) and managing frustration and disappointment. Discuss how this will help them if things do not go as expected with today's event or project.

1d. Enjoy the event or project. You (or a student volunteer) can document the event with pictures or video to be used in the next class to reflect on what parts of the plan worked and what steps could have been done differently.

1e. Ask students why we have learned how to plan efficiently. Point to the Why section of the Power Plan and fill in if desired.

1f. Send Home Extension for Topic 3.5 home with students or e-mail it to parents.

1g. Look for generalization opportunities in other classes. Encourage educators to ask students about the longer-term goal they planned in class. Educators can praise the students for using flexibility, compromise, planning, and efficiency skills to plan a successful event or project.

> **CHECK:** How are my students doing?
> Do I need to make any adjustments for the next class?

See Appendix A for a list of questions to guide your self-reflection and refer to the Troubleshooting section (Appendix B) to address common problems or any challenges that may have arisen with the curriculum.

TOPIC 3.5: The Longer-Term Event/Project—Efficient Planning = Power!

DAILY SELF-AWARENESS RATING: UNIT 3

NAME: _____

Executive Function Skills

Flexibility + Big Picture Thinking + Goals and Planning = POWER

Mark an X on the arrow to show how you feel today:

Are you focused on the group's goal today?

Stuck on Details — Stuck on Some Details — Eyes on the Prize

Will you plan today?

Rush in With No plan — Plan Some — Plan and Check to Make Sure the Plan Will Work

TOPIC 3.5: The Longer-Term Event/Project—Efficient Planning = Power!

HOME EXTENSION FOR TOPIC 3.5: THE LONG-TERM EVENT/PROJECT—EFFICIENT PLANNING = POWER!

Today the class completed their long-term project. The goal of this project was to make planning exciting and manageable for the students so they can feel more confident and comfortable when planning for projects and other long-term events.

Key Vocabulary/skills:

Goal *Plan*

Flexibility *Compromise*

Plan A/Plan B

How to use the Key Vocabulary/skills:

- Ask your child to tell you about the group's long-term project. Tell your child how proud you are of their flexibility and planning with the group. Ask if there were some unexpected challenges, and if the class used flexibility skills (Plan A/Plan B, compromise) to deal with them.

- Next week, your child and teacher will be deciding on a personal goal to work toward using the techniques that have been practiced in this program. You may wish to consult with your child and their teacher to discuss ideas for the personal goal (it can be a goal at school or home, or one that is helpful for both). It is important that your child's personal goal be:
    - Achievable in a few days/weeks
    - Reasonably simple, but also meaningful to your child
    - Highly motivating for your child (something that they want to do)

- Use the Power Plan on the next page of this Home Extension handout to keep practicing and modeling making plans, and Plan Bs, at home. This week it may be a plan to make cookies or clean up a messy room. Don't forget a Plan B.

TOPIC 3.5: The Longer-Term Event/Project—Efficient Planning = Power! (continued)

POWER

CHECK:

PLAN:

Plan B?

GOAL:

WHY:

STUCK?

TOPIC 3.6   Reviewing the Longer-Term Event/Project: Learning from Our Successes and Challenges

BIG PICTURE SUMMARY

In Topic 3.5, students celebrated their longer-term event or project—a sign of their success in setting a goal, compromising, planning, staying focused on the big picture goal, keeping their eyes on the prize, and watching the clock. In today's topic, the class reviews the event or project from last class, identifying all of the skills they successfully used from the curriculum. Each student also considers a possible personal goal to work toward for Unit 4.

Key Things to Do Here is the most important thing to do in today's class:

Use this Key Vocabulary often and in fun and playful ways:

- ★ Executive Function Skills
- ★ Flexible Thinking
- ★ Getting Unstuck
- ★ Plan A/Plan B
- ★ Goal-Why-Plan-Check
- ★ Putting Your Plan on Trial (Checking Your Plan)
- ★ Managing Frustration and Disappointment
- ★ Should I Compromise?
- ★ How to Compromise:
    - Each Gets Part.
    - Combine Ideas.
    - Take Turns.
    - Do Something Different You Both Like.
- ★ Eyes on the Prize—Staying Excited About a Longer-Term Goal
- ★ Focusing on the Big Picture Goal
- ★ Efficiency = Doing a Task Well and Fairly Quickly
- ★ Watch the Clock—Planning Quickly and Carefully

Materials

- ★ Unit 3 Daily Self-Awareness Rating (worksheets copied for each student or found in the Student Workbook)

- ★ PowerPoint for Topic 3.6, projected

- ★ Power Equation Poster, posted
- ★ Power Level card, affixed to the bottom of the Power Arrow on the Power Equation Poster
- ★ Videos and/or pictures from the special event

EDUCATOR PLAN

Goal: Students will reflect on the longer-term event or project, considering which executive function skills they used successfully during the last class and which skills to continue to work on in the future. Each student will also begin to brainstorm ideas for a personal goal they'll work toward in Unit 4.

Why: Reviewing their goal setting and planning from Unit 3 allows students time for self-reflection and self-evaluation, which are important skills for growth.

Plan: Do the following before class:

- ★ Post the Power Equation Poster and place the Power Level card at the bottom of the Power Arrow on the poster. Raise the Power Level card when students compromise, are flexible or kind to themselves or others, show planning skills, or manage their frustration and disappointment.
- ★ Project the PowerPoint for Topic 3.6.
- ★ For today's class, consider writing all of the Key Vocabulary and phrases (from the list above) on the board.
- ★ If pictures or videos were taken during the special event or project, you may want to review them before class to highlight certain photos or clips that show students using executive function skills. Also include a few examples of challenges that came up, so the students can think about what they might do differently next time.
- ★ If no pictures or videos were taken last class, consider creating an outline of key moments from the event or project that highlight various skills the students used and challenges they faced. This outline can help prompt the students to remember the event or project with greater clarity and meaningfulness.

CLASS LESSON PLAN

Slide 1: Power Plan

1. **Ask students to fill out the Unit 3 Daily Self-Awareness Rating worksheet.** Review the Power Plan for Topic 3.6.

Topic 3.6: Reviewing the Longer-Term Event/Project: Learning from Our Successes and Challenges

Slide 2: Review the Special Event/Project

2. **Review the special event or project from last class, having the class circle (or highlight) each of the executive function skills they used.** If video or pictures were taken last class period, go through them one at a time with the class. Or, with the help of an outline written on the board and prompts from you, have the students discuss key moments from the event or project from memory. For each photo or moment, ask the students to consider what skills and Key Vocabulary they used (or could have used).

   For example, while watching the video, freeze-frame and ask, *"What skill is Jack using here? That's right: He was so flexible when the music wouldn't play. So he came up with a Plan B."* Or: *"Dashawn, you did a nice job managing disappointment there. I could tell that was disappointing, but you stayed calm. Can anyone identify which powerful skills Dashawn was using?"* Encourage students to lead the discussion. See how many of the skills they can identify and circle (ideally, most of them on the board or PowerPoint). Make sure to focus on the students' successes and the challenges that they successfully faced. Ask them to consider which Key Vocabulary or skills they could do a better job with next time.

Slide 3: Preparing for Unit 4: Beginning to Think About Your Personal Goal in This Class

3a. **Let students know that everyone will be working on a goal over the next few classes.** Here is a sample script you can use: *"We've learned a lot about how to get more power in our lives by setting and reaching goals together. We just reached an important goal in our last class! For our next class, I want you to start to think about a personal goal that you'll work on. We've always done our goals together as a group, but this time, we're going to do something especially powerful and work on our own personal goal. And I'm going to set a personal goal for myself, too!"*

3b. **Help students begin to brainstorm realistic goals for themselves.** Explain to the students: *"We want to make sure your goal is something that excites you, will add power to your life, and is something that you can realistically achieve."*

   You may want to share with students some possible ideas for goals, such as:

   ★ Inviting a friend to hang out
   ★ Completing an English assignment without leaving it to the last moment
   ★ Doing a chore or small job to make some money
   ★ Getting a good grade on a quiz or a test
   ★ Doing a good deed
   ★ Learning a skill
   ★ Ordering a pizza
   ★ Compromising with a friend in an online game

   Consider writing down the ideas that the students come up with so that you can show them next class as they continue to think about their personal goals. Let the students know that next class, we'll try to finalize each person's personal goal.

Slide 4: Topic 3.6 Wrap-Up: Why Review the Special Event or Project?

4a. **Ask students why planning is good practice for the future.** Point to the Why section of the Power Plan and have students fill in the answer or just discuss. Ask students what they are learning from setting and reaching goals. Discuss what kinds of power they can gain by knowing how to set a personal goal and making plans to reach that goal.

4b. Send Home Extension for Topic 3.6 home with students or e-mail it to parents.

4c. **Consider checking in with each student's parents, caregivers, and educators to let them know that the students will be choosing a personal goal to work toward.** Let families and educators know that it is important for the student to pick a goal that is realistic and motivating to them. Parents and other educators may have some ideas about a possible personal goal for the student, which they can discuss with them prior to the next class.

> **CHECK:** How are my students doing?
> Do I need to make any adjustments for the next class?

See Appendix A for a list of questions to guide your self-reflection and refer to the Troubleshooting section (Appendix B) to address common problems or any challenges that may have arisen with the curriculum.

TOPIC 3.6: Reviewing the Longer-Term Event/Project: Learning from Our Successes and Challenges

DAILY SELF-AWARENESS RATING: UNIT 3

NAME: _____

Executive Function Skills

Flexibility + Big Picture Thinking + Goals and Planning = POWER

Mark an X on the arrow to show how you feel today:

Are you focused on the group's goal today?

Stuck on Details ⟵——————○——————○——————○——————⟶ Eyes on the Prize

Stuck on Some Details (middle)

Will you plan today?

Rush in With No Plan ⟵——————○——————○——————○——————⟶ Plan and Check to Make Sure the Plan Will Work

Plan Some (middle)

TOPIC 3.6: Reviewing the Longer-Term Event/Project: Learning from Our Successes and Challenges

HOME EXTENSION FOR TOPIC 3.6: REVIEWING THE LONG-TERM EVENT/PROJECT: LEARNING FROM OUR SUCCESSES AND CHALLENGES

In today's topic, students reviewed the special project they planned for last class, identifying the planning, flexibility, and compromise skills they used to plan and work together. They also began to brainstorm a possible personal goal to work toward over the next several classes.

Key Vocabulary/skills:

Flexible   *Plan A/Plan B*   *Managing Frustration/Disappointment*

Compromise   *Setting a Goal*   *Making a Plan*   *Checking Your Plan*

How to use the Key Vocabulary/skills:

- Your child will be selecting a personal goal to work toward over the next several classes. This goal should be motivating to them—something they are excited about. This goal should also be realistic—something they can accomplish fairly easily over several days, not something that would take months. In this activity, we are trying to get students excited about setting personal goals and learning that with just a little bit of skill, they can get more of what they want and need in their lives.

- Ask your child to explain several of the powerful words (also known as executive function skills) they have been learning in class. Have them teach you about being flexible, setting goals, planning, and compromising. Try out the skills after your child teaches them to you.

- If your family attends a special event together (a meal, a birthday, a trip), take photos and/or videos. Afterward, look at the pictures or videos together and ask your child to identify what flexibility, compromise, and planning skills they see the family using (or not using). For example, you might review pictures from a family meal where everyone compromised on what kind of restaurant to go to. You may also use the Power Plan to write down the plan that worked, or the Plan B that was used when Plan A didn't work.

UNIT 4

Making Executive Function Skills Work in Your Life

TOPIC 4.1 Developing a Personal Goal: Using Executive Function Skills in Our Real Lives

BIG PICTURE SUMMARY

This topic launches the final part of the curriculum: the opportunity for each student to practice using executive function skills to improve and enrich their own life. Students will select a personal goal to work toward in order to practice goal setting and planning as life skills. The structure of the classes in this unit will be a bit different: The students will do some planning activities as a group (e.g., reviewing one another's personal goals and plans), but will also work independently toward their goals while you float between students to offer more individualized supports.

Key Things to Do Here are the two most important things to do in today's class:

1. **Use this Key Vocabulary often and in fun and playful ways:**

   ★ Executive Function Skills

   ★ Using Executive Function Skills in Day-to-Day Life, Making the Skills Work in My Life (or the version of this phrase the students decide on during the class)

   ★ Flexible Thinking

   ★ Getting Unstuck

   ★ Plan A/Plan B

   ★ Goal-Why-Plan-Check

   ★ Putting Your Plan on Trial (Checking Your Plan)

   ★ Managing Frustration and Disappointment

   ★ Should I Compromise?

   ★ How To Compromise:
      - Each Gets Part.
      - Combine Ideas.
      - Take Turns.
      - Do Something Different You Both Like.

Key Vocabulary

The Key Vocabulary is a critical part of the curriculum; it is more important than the actual activities in each topic! The Key Vocabulary should be spoken as often as possible and presented in fun and enjoyable ways. Avoid punitive uses of the Key Vocabulary because that can interfere with student buy-in and use of the words and skills. The goal is to get your students to want to use the Key Vocabulary in their everyday lives.

- ★ Eyes on the Prize = Staying Excited About a Longer-Term Goal
- ★ Keeping Focused on the Big Picture Goal (Instead of Getting Stuck on Off-Topic Details)
- ★ Efficiency = Doing a Task Well and Fairly Quickly
- ★ Watch the Clock = Planning Quickly and Carefully

2. **Find ways to spontaneously model executive function skills (compromise, flexibility, and planning)** *at least once* **during class today.** Make this fun and engaging! Use compromise, flexibility, and planning skills with the students to solve challenges that come up naturally or challenges that you've invented.

Special instructions for today: Using the brainstormed list from Topic 3.6 and input from other educators or parents and caregivers, consider possible personal goals for each student prior to class. Each student's goal should be realistic, motivating, and able to be accomplished in about three classes. Decide on a personal goal for yourself that you'll work toward over the next few classes. Working toward your own goal will serve as a positive model for your students as they work on their own personal goal planning. Your goal should be visible to the students, appropriate to discuss with the class, and achievable in a few sessions. Here are a few examples of possible educator goals and how to explain them to the class:

- ★ *"I will use at least two executive function skills each day and report back to the class about how it's going."*
- ★ *"I will use executive function skills to plan a graduation party for the end of our program, which is coming up soon."*
- ★ *"I'm going to use executive function skills to plan an upcoming summer vacation."*
- ★ *"I'm going to use my executive function skills to make delicious cookies for the group."*
- ★ *"I'm going to use my executive function skills to clean my bedroom—and then go get a milkshake."*

 The personal Power Plan and graduation slides for Topic 4 are intended to be used by each student for their final presentation in Topic 4.5. If the students don't have individual computers in class, they can use the personal Power Plan and graduation worksheets (located in the Student Workbook and at the end of this topic).

Materials

- ★ Unit 4 Daily Self-Awareness Rating (worksheets copied for each student or found in the Student Workbook)

- ★ PowerPoint for Topic 4.1, projected
- ★ Power Equation Poster, posted

- ★ Power Level card: Affix the card to the bottom of the Power Arrow on the Power Equation Poster.

- ★ Personal Power Plan and graduation PowerPoints or worksheets for each student—available as a PowerPoint template (if each student has their own computer during class) or as a set of worksheets in the Student Workbook and at the end of this topic.
- ★ The students' brainstormed list of possible personal goals from the end of Topic 3.6

EDUCATOR PLAN

Goal: Students will develop a personal goal and a plan to accomplish it.

Why: Practicing executive function skills as a way to get more of what they want and need can help build students' confidence in using these skills in their day-to-day lives.

Plan: Do the following before class:

- ★ Post the Power Equation Poster and place the Power Level card at the bottom of the Power Arrow on the poster. Raise the Power Level card when students compromise, are flexible or kind, show planning skills, or successfully manage their frustration and disappointment.
- ★ Project PowerPoint for Topic 4.1.
- ★ Present the personal Power Plan and graduation documents to the class in one of three ways: as a PowerPoint if each student has their own computer for class, within the Student Workbook, or handed out as a packet of worksheets.

CLASS LESSON PLAN

Slide 1: Power Plan

1. Ask students to fill out the Unit 4 Daily Self-Awareness Rating worksheet and review the Power Plan for Topic 4.1.

Slide 2: Using the Executive Function Skills in Our Day-to-Day Lives

2a. Praise students for the planning they've done over the last few weeks. Here are a few discussion points to cover with the class:

- ★ We've learned and practiced flexibility, compromise, and planning so you can have more power in your lives.
- ★ How are these executive function skills powerful?
- ★ What kinds of power do these executive function skills help us get? How can these executive function skills help you now? How can these executive function skills help you in the future?

Topic 4.1: Developing a Personal Goal: Using Executive Function Skills in Our Real Lives

2b. **Introduce the idea of students using executive function skills in their day-to-day lives. Use the following points to lead a discussion with the students:**

   ★ We've learned how to get more power in our lives by using our flexibility and planning skills.

   ★ These executive function skills will not increase our power if we only use them in this class, so we have to use them in other areas of our lives.

   ★ That's why we are learning and practicing this final skill of using executive function skills in day-to-day life.

   ★ Why is this important?

   ★ What do you want to call the idea of using executive function skills in day-to-day life so you remember to use them in your lives at school and at home? Here are a few suggestions you can make if the students need help:

   - Make the skills work in your life
   - Making it real
   - Real world
   - Other ideas?

   ★ This is the most important part of our whole class—skills are only useful and powerful if we use them in every part of our lives.

Write the new Key Vocabulary or phrase that the students come up with on the board. This should be the students' motto for the rest of the curriculum, so write it in a prominent location and make sure it is seen and discussed each class!

Slide 3: Educator's Personal Goal

3. **Get the class excited about working on individual personal goals and tell them that you will also be working on your goal.** Present your own personal goal to the students. Choose a personal goal that you will be working to plan and achieve over the next few classes as a model for your students, who will also be working on their own personal goals. Your goal should be visible to the students, appropriate to discuss with your students, and achievable. While working toward your goal, model persistence and flexibility by sharing your Power Plan visual with the class and talking about your progress and any challenges you face. For a list of possible educator goals, see "special instructions for today" above.

Slide 4: Setting Students' Personal Goals

4. **Each student chooses a personal goal and develops a personal Power Plan for achieving their goal. Explain to the class:**

   "We've learned a lot about how to get more power in our lives using flexibility and planning skills. Now each of us is going to choose our personal goal to work on over the next few classes."

 Have the students pull up the personal Power Plan and graduation PowerPoint documents on their computers (or have them turn to the beginning of Unit 4 in the Student

Workbook or distribute copies of the worksheets). Encourage students to select a very simple goal to start—something they can easily achieve. Display the list of goals the students brainstormed from last class and offer additional ideas if needed (e.g., inviting a friend to hang out, completing an English assignment without leaving it to the last moment, doing a chore or job to make some money, getting a good grade on a quiz or a test, doing a good deed, learning a skill, ordering a pizza, compromising with a friend in an online game).

Ask each student to share their idea for a personal goal with the class. In an affirming, positive, and supportive way, encourage discussion of each student's goal using the following questions from the PowerPoint:

- ★ Is this a goal you can complete in the next few weeks?
- ★ Is it likely to be successful?
- ★ Is it worth your time?
- ★ Will it increase power in your life, or not so much? Why? How?

If necessary, encourage students to adjust their goals so they are short-term, likely to be successful, worthwhile, and powerful. Most importantly, make sure the goal is motivating to the student!

Ask students to fill in their goal on the personal Power Plan (page 2 of the personal Power Plan/graduation document). Then have the class discuss why they are selecting their goals. They can write the "Why" in the Why section of the personal Power Plan.

Slide 5: Building a Powerful Plan

5a. **Once students have selected their goals, tell the class they have a few minutes to think about their plan for achieving their goal.** Use the four questions on the PowerPoint to help them think about necessary steps in their plan.

- ★ Who will you work with to reach your goal (parent, teacher, friend)?
- ★ What are the materials you need to reach your goal?
- ★ Where will your goal happen?
- ★ When will your goal happen?

5b. **Allow students time to work through the steps of their plans, offering individual support as needed.** Have students enter the steps directly into the Plan section of the personal Power Plan in their personal Power Plan/graduation packet.

5c. **Make a copy of each student's completed personal Power Plan so that you can have a copy and the student can continue planning outside of class.**

Note: If the students are unable to complete all of the steps of their plan during class today, there will be time next class to do so.

Slide 6: Topic 4.1 Wrap-Up: Why Work Toward Personal Goals?

6a. **Ask the class, *"Why did we begin to plan for our personal goals?"*** What is powerful about setting and accomplishing personal goals? Will there be any challenges with accomplishing our personal goals? What skills might we use if challenges come up?

6b. **Send Home Extension for Topic 4.1 home with students or e-mail it to parents.**

6c. **Look for generalization opportunities in other classes.** Coordinate with educators or other school personnel to help support the students' personal goals. Provide reminders and support to the students as necessary, but also encourage the students to work independently toward their personal goal.

> **CHECK:** How are my students doing?
> Do I need to make any adjustments for the next class?

See Appendix A for a list of questions to guide your self-reflection and refer to the Troubleshooting section (Appendix B) to address common problems or any challenges that may have arisen with the curriculum.

TOPIC 4.1: Developing a Personal Goal: Using Executive Function Skills in Our Real Lives

DAILY SELF-AWARENESS RATING: UNIT 4

NAME: _____

Executive Function Skills

Flexibility + Big Picture Thinking + Goals and Planning = POWER

Mark an X on the arrow to show how you feel today:

Are you using the flexibility and planning skills in your other classes?

Not Using Skills — Using Some Skills — Using Executive Function Skills Every Day

Are you using the flexibility and planning skills at home?

Not Using Skills — Using Some Skills — Using Executive Function Skills Every Day

Topic 4.1: Developing a Personal Goal: Using Executive Function Skills in Our Real Lives

HOME EXTENSION FOR TOPIC 4.1: DEVELOPING A PERSONAL GOAL: USING EXECUTIVE FUNCTION SKILLS IN OUR REAL LIVES

In today's class, each student selected a personal goal to accomplish over the next few classes. They also discussed how executive function skills are useful when used for completing homework, planning for the future, making friends, getting along with family members, and other real-life situations.

Key Vocabulary/skills:

Flexible Thinking   *Plan A/Plan B*   *Managing Frustration and Disappointment*

Setting a Goal   *Making a Plan*   *Compromise*

How to use the Key Vocabulary/skills:

- Ask your child to tell you about the personal goal they've chosen to work toward. Praise your child for setting the goal and discuss the kind of power that accomplishing the goal will provide them (e.g., the power to get a better grade, the power to work on making a friend, the power to help a neighbor in need).

- On the next page of this Home Extension handout is an Executive Function Skills List of all the Key Vocabulary and skills practiced in this program. Discuss with your child how you can help them use these skills every day at home and talk about how the rest of the family can use them, too. For example, you could post the list on a wall and have each family member share one example of how they used a particular word or skill during the day. Find fun and creative ways to use these words in daily life with your family.

Topic 4.1: Developing a Personal Goal: Using Executive Function Skills in Our Real Lives (continued)

EXECUTIVE FUNCTION SKILLS LIST

Flexible Thinking
"Thanks for being flexible!"
"Nice job being flexible."
"You were flexible and got what you wanted even faster. Nice job!"

Plan A/Plan B
"If Plan A doesn't work, then we'll try a Plan B."
"I'm feeling stuck—my Plan A didn't work. Can you help me come up with a Plan B?"
"Do you need a Plan B?"

Stuck/Unstuck
"How can I get unstuck?"
"Nice work. You were flexible and got unstuck."
"You noticed you were stuck and then got unstuck. That's how you boost your power!"

Goal-Why-Plan-Check
"What's the goal?"
"Why is the goal important?"
"What are the steps of the plan?"
"Let's check to see if we reached our goal."

Are We Focused on Our Big Picture Goal or Stuck on an Off-Topic Detail?
"What's our big picture goal?"
"Is this an off-topic detail?"
"Should we get stuck on this detail or get back to our big picture goal?"

Compromise
"Let's come up with a compromise."
"Compromising lets us both get some of what we want."
"Nice compromise! It's a win-win for both of you."
"You both let go of your Plan A so you both could get *some* of what you want. That is a winning compromise and helps you boost your power!"

Efficiency = Doing a Task Well and Fairly Quickly
"Keep your eyes on the prize—stay focused and excited about your goal!"
"Watch the clock—don't get stuck on off-topic details!"
"Great work. You were efficient. You didn't get stuck."

Managing Frustration and Disappointment
"Being disappointed is normal. How can we manage it?"
"When we're frustrated, there's always a Plan B!"

Topic 4.1: Developing a Personal Goal: Using Executive Function Skills in Our Real Lives

USING EXECUTIVE FUNCTION SKILLS IN MY DAY-TO-DAY LIFE

Flexible thinking

Getting unstuck

Plan A/Plan B

Goal-Why-Plan-Check

Putting your plan on trial
(checking your plan)

Eyes on the prize
(staying excited about a goal)

Focusing on the big picture goal

Managing disappointment

Figuring out, should I compromise?
Who cares more? You can't always be a 2!
- 0 = Little deal, no strong preference
- 1 = Care a bit, some preference
- 2 = Big deal, strong preference

How to compromise?
1. Each gets a part
2. Combine ideas
3. Take turns
4. Do something different you both like

Managing frustration

Efficiency
(Doing a task *well* and *fairly quickly*)

Eyes on the clock
(Planning quickly and carefully)

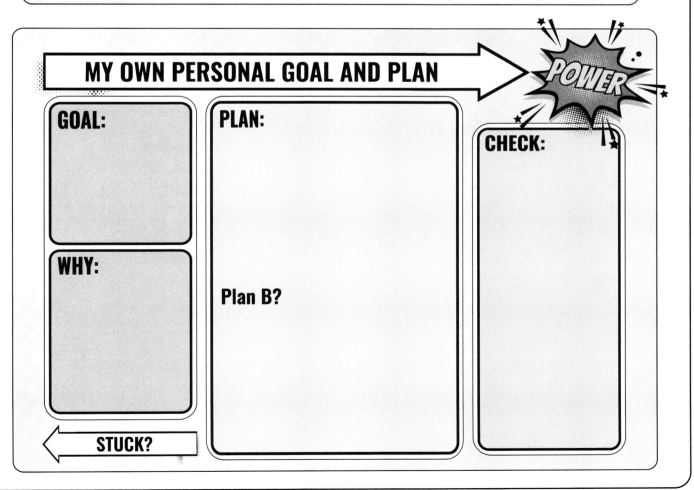

MY OWN PERSONAL GOAL AND PLAN

GOAL:

WHY:

PLAN:

Plan B?

CHECK:

STUCK?

Topic 4.1: Developing a Personal Goal: Using Executive Function Skills in Our Real Lives (continued)

EXECUTIVE FUNCTION SKILLS IMPORTANT FOR MY LIFE

Executive function skills important for my life

Executive function skill	Why will it be important in my life?
1.	
2.	
3.	

Advice for students in next year's class

1.

2.

3.

TOPIC 4.2   Using Executive Function Skills for Personal Goals

BIG PICTURE SUMMARY

This topic further encourages students to consider how to use the executive function skills taught in this curriculum in their lives outside of class. Students will also finalize the plans for their personal goals.

Key Things to Do Here are the two most important things to do in today's class:

1. **Use this Key Vocabulary often and in fun and playful ways:**

   ★ Executive Function Skills

   ★ Using Executive Function Skills in Day-to-Day Life (or the version of this phrase the students decided on in Topic 4.1)

   ★ Flexible Thinking

   ★ Getting Unstuck

   ★ Plan A/Plan B

   ★ Goal-Why-Plan-Check

   ★ Putting Your Plan on Trial (Checking Your Plan)

   ★ Managing Frustration and Disappointment

   ★ Should I Compromise?

   ★ How to Compromise:
      - Each Gets Part.
      - Combine Ideas.
      - Take Turns.
      - Do Something Different You Both Like.

   ★ Eyes on the Prize = Staying Excited About a Longer-Term Goal

   ★ Keeping Focused on the Big Picture Goal (Instead of Getting Stuck on Off-Topic Details)

   ★ Efficiency = Doing a Task Well and Fairly Quickly

   ★ Watch the Clock = Planning Quickly and Carefully

2. **Find ways to spontaneously model executive function skills (compromise, flexibility, and planning)** *at least once* **during class today.** Make this fun and engaging! Use compromise, flexibility, and planning skills with the students to solve challenges that come up naturally or challenges that you've invented. For example, you could say to the class: *"The cashier in the grocery store was having trouble scanning something. Finally, she decided to enter the code by hand. I looked at her and said, 'Good thing you have a Plan B!' These executive function skills work everywhere!"*

Special instructions for today: During this class, students will continue to develop their plans for their personal goals. They may need to follow through on parts of their personal plans outside of class. For example, if a student has the goal of making a plan with a friend to do something fun, one step of their plan might involve contacting the friend to ask about possible times to hang out. Students may need encouragement, support, and reminders to make progress on their goals during the week. This can be accomplished by checking in with the student, coordinating with parents and family members, and asking for support from other educators. Also, during today's class, be prepared to share your progress and challenges related to your personal goal. Make sure to have the Slide 2 Power Plan filled in with your goal and plan, listing any progress you've made (through checks in the Check column) and any Plan Bs you've used.

Materials

   ★   Unit 4 Daily Self-Awareness Rating (worksheets copied for each student or found in the Student Workbook)

   ★   PowerPoint for Topic 4.2, projected

★   Power Equation Poster, posted

   ★   Power Level card: Affix the card to the bottom of the Power Arrow on the Power Equation Poster.

★   The personal Power Plan and graduation PowerPoints or worksheets that each student began working on in Topic 4.1

EDUCATOR PLAN

Goal: Students will review their plans and the progress they've made toward their personal goals. They will also consider how they will use the executive function skills in their daily lives.

Why: Taking skills learned in one setting and applying them to another is challenging for many students with executive function difficulties. Getting students to generalize skills often requires intentional teaching and practice. It may not immediately occur to students to apply the skills learned in this curriculum to other classes and in their daily lives. Today's topic allows students to practice thinking about different ways executive function skills can help them in their day-to-day lives.

Plan: Do the following before class:

★   Post the Power Equation Poster and place the Power Level card at the bottom of the Power Arrow on the poster. Raise the Power Level card when students compromise, are flexible or kind, show planning skills, or successfully manage their frustration and disappointment.

★   Project the PowerPoint for Topic 4.2.

★   Each student's personal Power Plan and graduation documents from Topic 4.1 should be available to them during class. Students should already have a goal on their Power Plan, as well as part of the plan.

Topic 4.2: Using Executive Function Skills for Personal Goals

CLASS LESSON PLAN

Slide 1: Power Plan

1a. Ask students to fill out the Unit 4 Daily Self-Awareness Rating worksheet.

1b. Review the Power Plan for today.

Slide 2: Educator's Personal Goal: Sharing Progress and Challenges

2. **Share with the class the progress you've made toward your personal goal.** Also share any challenges you've faced and invite the class to help you come up with solutions (e.g., Plan Bs). Make sure to have the PowerPoint Power Plan filled in with your goal and plan. List any progress you've made (through checks in the Check column) and any Plan Bs you've used (in the bottom part of the Plan column).

Slide 3: Personal Power Plans

3a. **Working on personal goals and plans.** Have the students pull up their personal Power Plan and graduation documents from last class. Have students think through the steps of their plans for reaching their personal goal, encouraging them to use the skills they've learned in class: Plan A/Plan B, eyes on the prize, staying focused on the big picture goal, watching the clock, putting their plan on trial (checking their plan), and managing frustration and disappointment. Ask students to continue to fill in their plans on their personal Power Plan document, providing individual support when necessary.

3b. **Have each student share the steps of their plan with the class, including what they plan to do outside of class to work toward their goal.** Tell students that next class they will report back on how their planning is going, so that the students can help one another problem-solve and come up with Plan Bs.

 When a student shares their plan, remember to raise the Power Level card with a praising statement, such as, *"That was a great example of Plan A/Plan B thinking—so powerful!"*

3c. **Take a picture of, copy, or write down the completed personal Power Plans for each student** so that you can have a copy and the student can continue working on their plan outside of class.

Slide 4: Using Executive Function Skills in Everyday Life to Get More Power

4a. Review the using executive function skills in day-to-day life skill (whichever phrase the students picked last class to remember this important concept).

Start the discussion with this sample script, and then encourage student contributions:

"We've learned how to get more power in our lives by using flexibility and planning skills. But to get more power, we have to use these executive function skills outside

of this class. That's why we are learning and practicing this final skill: using executive function skills in day-to-day life [or whatever motto the class came up with in Topic 4.1]. A great way to practice the skills outside of class is by working toward personal goals."

4b. Students should consider how they can use the executive function skills taught in this class in their day-to-day lives. Tell the students that they'll be playing a game to earn a reward today (e.g., free time at the end of class), but that their biggest reward will be the power they get from using executive function skills outside of this class. Using student input, develop simple rules for the game. Say something like:

"The goal of this game is to think about which executive function skills you could use in different areas of your life. Each time you identify an executive function skill you plan to use in your daily life—and explain how you'll use that skill to improve your life—the class earns 10 seconds (or what the leader feels is appropriate) of free time at the end of the lesson."

Highlight or circle each skill as it is mentioned (each skill can be mentioned more than once). Consider adding the rule that all of the skills on the list must be mentioned at least once with an explanation of how they can be used in the real world.

Slide 5: Topic 4.2 Wrap-Up: Why Is It Important to Use Executive Function Skills Every Day?

5a. Ask the class, *"Why did we think about how to use executive function skills outside of class?"* Point to the Why section of the Power Plan. Students can fill in the answer or just discuss.

5b. Provide the end-of-class reward as discussed above.

5c. Send Home Extension for Topic 4.2 home with students or e-mail it to parents.

5d. Look for generalization opportunities in other classes and at home. During the week, students may need encouragement, support, and reminders to make progress on their personal goal. This could involve check-ins with the student, coordinating with parents and caregivers, and support from other educators.

> **CHECK:** How are my students doing?
> Do I need to make any adjustments for the next class?

See Appendix A for a list of questions to guide your self-reflection and refer to the Troubleshooting section (Appendix B) to address common problems or any challenges that may have arisen with the curriculum.

TOPIC 4.2: Using Executive Function Skills for Personal Goals

DAILY SELF-AWARENESS RATING: UNIT 4

NAME: _____

Executive Function Skills

Flexibility + Big Picture Thinking + Goals and Planning = POWER

Mark an X on the arrow to show how you feel today:

Are you using the flexibility and planning skills in your other classes?

Not Using Skills — Using Some Skills — Using Executive Function Skills Every Day

Are you using the flexibility and planning skills at home?

Not Using Skills — Using Some Skills — Using Executive Function Skills Every Day

TOPIC 4.2: Using Executive Function Skills for Personal Goals

HOME EXTENSION FOR TOPIC 4.2: USING EXECUTIVE FUNCTION SKILLS FOR PERSONAL GOALS

In today's class, the students reviewed all of the executive function skills taught in this program. They also discussed how the skills are powerful when they are used in real life for things like homework, planning for the future, and making friends. Each student continued to work on their plan for achieving their personal goal and began to follow through with the steps to complete it.

Key Vocabulary/skills:

Flexible Thinking   *Plan A/Plan B*   *Managing Frustration and Disappointment*

Setting a Goal   *Making a Plan*   *Compromise*

How to use the Key Vocabulary/skills:

- Ask your child how the planning is going for their personal goal and see if they need some help figuring out how to reach the goal. Praise your child for using the flexibility and planning skills.

- Discuss different types of short- and long-term goals with your child and family (for example, going to college, getting a job, learning how to do laundry, learning how to shop, learning how to save money). Consider writing down some of the goals and using the executive function skills list (on the next page of this Home Extension handout) to think with your child about what skills would be helpful in accomplishing these goals.

- Try to use all of the vocabulary on the executive function skills list in daily interactions with your entire family. Use these words in positive, fun, and affirming ways. Be careful not to use them in a critical or negative way, or your child might come to dislike them!

TOPIC 4.2: Using Executive Function Skills for Personal Goals (continued)

EXECUTIVE FUNCTION SKILLS LIST

Flexible Thinking
"Thanks for being flexible!"
"Nice job being flexible."
"You were flexible and got what you wanted even faster. Nice job!"

Plan A/Plan B
"If Plan A doesn't work, then we'll try a Plan B."
"I'm feeling stuck—my Plan A didn't work. Can you help me come up with a Plan B?"
"Do you need a Plan B?"

Stuck/Unstuck
"How can I get unstuck?"
"Nice work. You were flexible and got unstuck."
"You noticed you were stuck and then got unstuck. That's how you boost your power!"

Goal-Why-Plan-Check
"What's the goal?"
"Why is the goal important?"
"What are the steps of the plan?"
"Let's check to see if we reached our goal."

Are We Focused on Our Big Picture Goal or Stuck on an Off-Topic Detail?
"What's our big picture goal?"
"Is this an off-topic detail?"
"Should we get stuck on this detail or get back to our big picture goal?"

Compromise
"Let's come up with a compromise."
"Compromising lets us both get some of what we want."
"Nice compromise! It's a win-win for both of you."
"You both let go of your Plan A so you both could get *some* of what you want. That is a winning compromise and helps you boost your power!"

Efficiency = Doing a Task Well and Fairly Quickly
"Keep your eyes on the prize—stay focused and excited about your goal!"
"Watch the clock—don't get stuck on off-topic details!"
"Great work. You were efficient. You didn't get stuck."

Managing Frustration and Disappointment
"Being disappointed is normal. How can we manage it?"
"When we're frustrated, there's always a Plan B!"

TOPIC 4.3   Putting Personal Plans on Trial

BIG PICTURE SUMMARY

In this topic, students put their plans on trial and come up with Plan Bs to successfully reach their personal goal.

Key Things to Do Here are the two most important things to do in today's class:

1. **Use this Key Vocabulary often and in fun and playful ways:**
   - ★ Executive Function Skills
   - ★ Using Executive Function Skills in My Day-To-Day Life (or the version of this phrase the students decided on in Topic 4.1)
   - ★ Flexible Thinking
   - ★ Getting Unstuck
   - ★ Plan A/Plan B
   - ★ Goal-Why-Plan-Check
   - ★ Putting Your Plan on Trial (Checking Your Plan)
   - ★ Managing Frustration and Disappointment
   - ★ Should I Compromise?
   - ★ How to Compromise:
     - Each Gets Part.
     - Combine Ideas.
     - Take Turns.
     - Do Something Different You Both Like.
   - ★ Eyes on the Prize = Staying Excited About a Longer-Term Goal
   - ★ Keeping Focused on the Big Picture Goal (Instead of Getting Stuck on Off-Topic Details)
   - ★ Efficiency = Doing a Task Well and Fairly Quickly
   - ★ Watch the Clock—Planning Quickly and Carefully

2. **Find ways to spontaneously model executive function skills (compromise, flexibility, and planning)** *at least once* **during class today.** Make this fun and engaging! Use compromise, flexibility, and planning skills together to solve challenges that come up naturally or challenges that you've invented. For example, talk to the class about how you made a plan to do something, but it turned out to be a fiasco. You could say something like: *"I wanted to make my partner a birthday cake. So I went to the store, bought the ingredients, got home, and realized I didn't have any baking soda. No problem! My Plan*

Topic 4.3: Putting Personal Plans on Trial 197

B was to substitute yeast. I put that plan on trial—epic fail. There is no substitute for baking soda! I should have had a Plan C and asked my neighbor for some baking soda."

The goal is for the students to feel successful with their planning. It may be helpful to introduce the self-advocacy skill; if students need help, they can ask an educator, other students, or a family member for help with their plan.

Materials

 ★ Unit 4 Daily Self-Awareness Rating (worksheets copied for each student or found in the Student Workbook)

 ★ PowerPoint for Topic 4.3, projected

★ Power Equation Poster, posted

 ★ Power Level card: Affix the card to the bottom of the Power Arrow on the Power Equation Poster.

★ The personal Power Plan and graduation PowerPoints or worksheets that each student began working on in Topic 4.1

★ Optional: Courtroom imagery to get the students excited about putting plans on trial (a gavel, a judge's robe, images of popular courtroom TV shows)

EDUCATOR PLAN

Goal: Students will review their personal plans by thinking them through, checking them (i.e., putting them on trial), and making adjustments as necessary.

Why: Students with executive function challenges often need practice planning, thinking through their plan to make sure they're on track to meet their goal, and trying a different approach when necessary (i.e., Plan B).

Plan: Do the following before class:

★ Post the Power Equation Poster and place the Power Level card at the bottom of the Power Arrow on the poster. Raise the Power Level card when students compromise, are flexible or kind, show planning skills, or successfully manage their frustration and disappointment.

★ Project the PowerPoint for Topic 4.3.

★ Each student's personal Power Plan and graduation documents should be available to them during class. Students should already have the Goal section on their Power Plan filled in, as well as the Why and Plan sections.

CLASS LESSON PLAN

Slide 1: Power Plan

1a. Ask students to fill out the Unit 4 Daily Self-Awareness Rating worksheet.

1b. **Review the Power Plan for today and then discuss the progress students have made toward their personal goals.** What executive function skills did they use to make progress on their plan? If they did not make progress, what helpful skills could they have used (e.g., keep your eyes on the prize, watch the clock, stay focused on the big picture goal)?

Slide 2: Putting a Plan on Trial (Checking Your Plan)

2a. **Tell the class you're going talk about what makes a good plan versus what makes a not-so-good plan.** Referring to the Powerful Plan column of the PowerPoint, discuss with the students the qualities of a good plan:

- ★ A plan is powerful if we've checked each step.
- ★ A plan is powerful if it's not missing any important details.
- ★ And, finally, a plan is especially powerful if we come up with a Plan B in case the plan doesn't work exactly as we expected.

2b. **Referring to the Problem Plan column of the PowerPoint, discuss with the students the qualities of a not-so-good plan:**

- ★ A plan may have problems if we didn't check each step.
- ★ A plan will not work if we missed important details.
- ★ Sometimes our Plan A doesn't work, and that's normal. But we'll be stuck if we don't come up with a Plan B.

2c. **Briefly discuss with students how putting a plan on trial and checking it step-by-step lets us find problems in the plan and fix them.** Refer to the horizontal arrow at the bottom of the PowerPoint slide, "Can I fix the Problem Plan to make it a Powerful Plan?"

Explain to the class that you're going to check your personal plans by putting them on trial:

"Let's check our personal plans by putting them on trial. Will we reach our goals? Did we come up with a good plan for reaching our goal? While we're checking our plans, let's make sure to use flexibility and kindness skills, so everyone feels respected. Let's see if our plans work, or if there are any problems we need to fix."

Slide 3: Putting Our Personal Plans on Trial (Checking Our Plans)

3a. **Have the students take turns putting their personal plans on trial.** First, project and share your own personal goal and plan using the routine below. Then invite each student to share their personal goal and put their plan on trial. For each student's plan, pull up their Power Plan PowerPoint or quickly type it into the blank Power Plan template. Remember, if any changes (e.g., Plan Bs) are needed, make sure they are entered into the student's Power Plan so they won't be forgotten.

Create a courtroom feel with courtroom visuals and, if the class wants to, a judge and jury. Have the students go through each step of their plan and put a check in the Check column if the step is good or place an X next to any step that needs to be reworked. As the class evaluates each step of the plan, classroom volunteers can act out each step. Encourage the class to help each student come up with another idea for steps that need to be adjusted or improved. Some questions for discussion include the following:

- ★ Is there someone or something (e.g., educator, parent, friend, Google) that can help me accomplish this goal that I didn't think of before?
- ★ Do I need a Plan B?
- ★ Do I need to compromise?
- ★ Did I get stuck on an off-topic detail? How can I stay focused on my big picture goal?
- ★ Did I correctly estimate how long the plan will take? How can I remember to watch the clock?
- ★ How can I keep my eyes on the prize? Do I need the educator or a classmate to text or e-mail me outside of class to remind me to stick with my plan?

3b. **Come up with a Plan B if necessary.** If there is a problem with a step in a student's plan, make sure the student leaves class with a good Plan B for how to reach their personal goal. Emphasize the power of using a Plan B.

3c. **Take a picture of, copy, or write down the revised personal Power Plan for each student so you can have a copy and the student can continue working on their plan outside of class.** Tell the students that at the beginning of next class, they will report back on their progress following through with the steps of their plan. Students will need encouragement and support to follow through with the plans for their personal goals. Some students may have already made significant progress, whereas others may still need to get started. Enlisting the help of parents and caregivers if needed, provide as much support as possible so students can successfully complete the plan by next class. See below.

Slide 4: Topic 4.3 Wrap-Up: Why Are We Thinking Through Our Plans (Putting Them on Trial)?

4a. Ask the class, *"Why are we thinking through our plans and coming up with Plan Bs?"* How is this skill powerful? In what other parts of your life can you use the skill of thinking through a plan? Students can fill in the answer under the Why section or just discuss. Also discuss how the students will remember to keep working on their personal plans outside of class. Suggest that students use a reminder system (e.g., writing on your hand, programming a reminder in your calendar or phone, an e-mail from the educator, a reminder from a parent) so they will remember to complete the steps in their plan before next class.

4b. Send Home Extension for Topic 4.3 home with students or e-mail it to parents.

4c. Look for generalization opportunities in other classes. Coordinate with educators, school personnel, and parents and caregivers to help support the students' efforts to complete the steps in their plans before next class. Provide reminders and support to the students when necessary, but also encourage the students to be as independent as possible.

> **CHECK:** How are my students doing?
> Do I need to make any adjustments for the next class?

See Appendix A for a list of questions to guide your self-reflection and refer to the Troubleshooting section (Appendix B) to address common problems or any challenges that may have arisen with the curriculum.

TOPIC 4.3: Putting Personal Plans on Trial

DAILY SELF-AWARENESS RATING: UNIT 4

NAME: _____

Executive Function Skills

Flexibility + Big Picture Thinking + Goals and Planning = POWER

Mark an X on the arrow to show how you feel today:

Are you using the flexibility and planning skills in your other classes?

⟵───◯───────────◯───────────◯───⟶

Not Using skills   Using Some Skills   Using Executive Function Skills Every Day

Are you using the flexibility and planning skills at home?

⟵───◯───────────◯───────────◯───⟶

Not Using skills   Using Some Skills   Using Executive Function Skills Every Day

TOPIC 4.3: Putting Personal Plans on Trial

HOME EXTENSION FOR TOPIC 4.3: PUTTING PERSONAL PLANS ON TRIAL

For the last few classes, students have been working toward their personal goals. Today, the students worked on their plans to reach their goals, checking their plans to see if there are any problems or missing parts to their plans.

Key Vocabulary/skills:

Flexible Thinking *Plan A/Plan B* *Managing Frustration and Disappointment*

Setting a Goal *Making a Plan* *Compromise*

How to use the Key Vocabulary/skills:

- Ask your child how the planning is going for their personal goal and see if they need help with any part of the plan. Praise your child for using flexibility and planning skills. **We would like each student to have tried to complete the steps of their plan by the next class.**

- Discuss with your child their upcoming graduation from this class. Ask them what skills from the program (see the next page of this Home Extension handout) they want to keep using in their life.

TOPIC 4.3: Putting Personal Plans on Trial (continued)

EXECUTIVE FUNCTION SKILLS LIST

Flexible Thinking
"Thanks for being flexible!"
"Nice job being flexible."
"You were flexible and got what you wanted even faster. Nice job!"

Plan A/Plan B
"If Plan A doesn't work, then we'll try a Plan B."
"I'm feeling stuck—my Plan A didn't work. Can you help me come up with a Plan B?"
"Do you need a Plan B?"

Stuck/Unstuck
"How can I get unstuck?"
"Nice work. You were flexible and got unstuck."
"You noticed you were stuck and then got unstuck. That's how you boost your power!"

Goal-Why-Plan-Check
"What's the goal?"
"Why is the goal important?"
"What are the steps of the plan?"
"Let's check to see if we reached our goal."

Are We Focused on Our Big Picture Goal or Stuck on an Off-Topic Detail?
"What's our Big picture goal?"
"Is this an off-topic detail?"
"Should we get stuck on this detail or get back to our Big picture goal?"

Compromise
"Let's come up with a compromise."
"Compromising lets us both get some of what we want."
"Nice compromise! It's a win-win for both of you."
"You both let go of your Plan A so you both could get *some* of what you want. That is a winning compromise and helps you boost your power!"

Efficiency = Doing a Task Well and Fairly Quickly
"Keep your eyes on the prize—stay focused and excited about your goal!"
"Watch the clock—don't get stuck on off-topic details!"
"Great work. You were efficient. You didn't get stuck."

Managing Frustration and Disappointment
"Being disappointed is normal. How can we manage it?"
"When we're frustrated, there's always a Plan B!"

TOPIC 4.4 Preparing for Graduation: Celebrating Our Executive Function Skills

BIG PICTURE SUMMARY

In this topic, students reflect on what they have learned and practiced in this program and prepare for the upcoming graduation.

Key Things to Do Here are the two most important things to do in today's class:

1. **Use this Key Vocabulary often and in fun and playful ways:**
   - ★ Executive Function Skills
   - ★ Using Executive Function Skills in Day-to-Day Life (Making the Skills Work in My Life, or the version of this phrase the students decided on in Topic 4.1)
   - ★ Flexible Thinking
   - ★ Getting Unstuck
   - ★ Plan A/Plan B
   - ★ Goal-Why-Plan-Check
   - ★ Putting Your Plan on Trial (Thinking Through and Checking Your Plan)
   - ★ Managing Frustration and Disappointment
   - ★ Should I Compromise?
   - ★ How to Compromise:
     - Each Gets Part.
     - Combine Ideas.
     - Take Turns.
     - Do Something Different You Both Like.
   - ★ Eyes on the Prize = Staying Excited About a Longer-Term Goal
   - ★ Keeping Focused on the Big Picture Goal (Instead of Getting Stuck on Off-Topic Details)
   - ★ Efficiency = Doing a Task Well and Fairly Quickly
   - ★ Watch the Clock = Planning Quickly and Carefully

2. **Find ways to spontaneously model executive function skills (compromise, flexibility, and planning) *at least once* during class today.** Make this fun and engaging! Use compromise, flexibility, and planning skills with the students to solve challenges that come up naturally or challenges that you've invented.

Special instructions for today: This topic may take more than one class period to complete. Savor the insight that your students offer while preparing for their graduation.

During this topic, students will likely require individual support from you to finalize their ideas for their upcoming graduation presentations. They may also need support to finish their personal goals. In some cases, progress toward a personal goal may be sufficient for graduation, especially if the student can achieve some level of insight about their progress and next steps for the future in working toward their goal. There is no classroom PowerPoint for this lesson because students will be preparing for graduation independently using their personal PowerPoints or worksheets.

Materials

- Unit 4 Daily Self-Awareness Rating (worksheets copied for each student or found in the Student Workbook)

- Power Equation Poster, posted

- Power Level card: Affix the card to the bottom of the Power Arrow on the Power Equation Poster.

- The personal Power Plan and graduation PowerPoints or worksheets that each student began working on in Topic 4.1

EDUCATOR PLAN

Goal: Students will evaluate their progress in achieving their personal goal and prepare their presentation for graduation. They will consider which executive function skills are most important for their lives.

Why: It's important for students to reflect on and celebrate the progress they have made using executive function skills and making them relevant to their own lives. Preparing a presentation helps students organize information they have learned throughout the curriculum in a meaningful way and share their progress with others. It also provides them with visual reminders they can use to remember key skills in their daily lives.

Plan: Do the following before class:

- Post the Power Equation Poster and place the Power Level card at the bottom of the Power Arrow on the poster. Raise the Power Level card when students compromise, are flexible or kind, show planning skills, or successfully manage their frustration and disappointment.

- Each student's personal Power Plan and graduation documents from previous Unit 4 topics should be available to them during class.

CLASS LESSON PLAN

1. **Ask students to fill out the Unit 4 Daily Self-Awareness Rating worksheet and then discuss the progress they've made toward their personal goals.** What executive function skills did they use to make progress on their plans? Have students check off the

steps of their plans they have already completed. If they did not make progress, what helpful skills could they have used (keep your eyes on the prize, watch the clock, stay focused on the big picture goal, etc.)?

2. **Introduce the upcoming graduation as a time to celebrate everything the students have learned and practiced in this class. Build enthusiasm by mentioning that today's class is a preparation for graduation.** Here are a few key discussion points to cover with the class:

    ★ *"We have learned about how to get more power in our lives using flexibility and planning skills."*

    ★ *"You have been practicing using these skills outside of class to work toward your personal goal."*

    ★ *"Today, you're going to prepare your presentation for our graduation next class, where we'll celebrate all of your powerful new flexibility and planning skills."*

3. **Provide students with the materials they will need to create their PowerPoint or poster presentation.** Each presentation should be based on the following sections of the personal Power Plan and graduation PowerPoint or worksheets:

    ★ **Personal Power Plan.** Provide each student with a copy of their personal Power Plan for their personal goal. Have students finalize their personal Power Plans so they can present how their personal goal and plan went. What did they learn from working toward a personal goal?

    ★ **What three executive function skills are most important and helpful for your life and why?** Using the Executive Function Skills List in the PowerPoint or worksheets as a reminder, ask the students to consider which three executive function skills they find most useful. Have the students enter their answers in the PowerPoint or worksheet titled "Executive Function Skills Important for My Life." Ask them to describe why those three skills are most helpful to them. Discuss with each student individually or as a class, but make sure each student comes up with their own personalized list.

    ★ **What advice would you give to the next class?** In the "Advice for Students in Next Year's Class" PowerPoint or worksheet, ask students to record what advice they would give to the next group of students in this program. If a student provides a negative response, you could reframe by asking, *"What advice would you give the next group of students to make sure they don't feel the way you feel?"*

4. **Help students practice their PowerPoint presentations (if students don't have computer access, they can create posters that incorporate the worksheets and appropriate decorations).** If a student is anxious about presenting, model flexibility and ask them if they have a Plan B. You could say, *"I can certainly be flexible. Should we do the presentation together? Is there another Plan B?"* Celebrate any solutions the student comes up with or flexible thinking skills they use.

5. **Ask the class, "Why are executive function skills important in our lives?"**

6. **Ask students if they want to invite family members, other educators, or the principal or other school administrators to their graduation.**

7. Send Home Extension for Topic 4.4 home with students or e-mail it to parents.

8. **Look for generalization opportunities in other classes:** Coordinate with educators or other school personnel to build excitement for the students' upcoming graduation. Ask other educators to praise your students for their work learning executive function skills and ask which skills are most important to the presenting student.

> **CHECK:** How are my students doing?
> Do I need to make any adjustments for the next class?

See Appendix A for a list of questions to guide your self-reflection and refer to the Troubleshooting section (Appendix B) to address common problems or any challenges that may have arisen with the curriculum.

TOPIC 4.4: Preparing for Graduation: Celebrating Our Executive Function Skills

DAILY SELF-AWARENESS RATING: UNIT 4

NAME: _____

Executive Function Skills

Flexibility + Big Picture Thinking + Goals and Planning = POWER

Mark an X on the arrow to show how you feel today:

Are you using the flexibility and planning skills in your other classes?

Not Using skills — Using Some Skills — Using Executive Function Skills Every Day

Are you using the flexibility and planning skills at home?

Not Using skills — Using Some Skills — Using Executive Function Skills Every Day

TOPIC 4.4: Preparing for Graduation: Celebrating Our Executive Function Skills

HOME EXTENSION FOR TOPIC 4.4: PREPARING FOR GRADUATION: CELEBRATING OUR EXECUTIVE FUNCTION SKILLS

The students have prepared for their graduation presentations. Next class, they will present a summary of how the planning for their personal goal went, discuss which executive function skills from the class they find most helpful, and provide big picture feedback about the program.

Key Vocabulary/skills:

Flexible Thinking   *Plan A/Plan B*   *Managing Frustration and Disappointment*

Setting a Goal   *Making a Plan*   *Compromise*

How to use the Key Vocabulary: By now, the Key Vocabulary and skills (on the next page of this Home Extension handout) should be very familiar to your child. Continue to integrate the Key Vocabulary and skills into the life of your family by posting the list in your home and using the words every day. Praise your child's use of the skills and encourage family members to talk about how they use executive function skills in daily life. Here are a few examples:

- *"I felt stuck today when my boss told me to redo a project I've been working on. First, I had to get over the disappointment—I was flexible and let go of it. Then I had to come up with a Plan B for how to do the project. I did that, and then my power and reputation went up with my boss. It wasn't easy, but being flexible saved my day."*

- *"I'm getting stuck on details with this project. I need to stay focused on the big picture so that I can get it done efficiently and not have to work on it all night."*

- *"I really wanted to go to the store today, but I ran out of time. I'll have to do Plan B and go to the store tomorrow."*

- *"It's clear that we want to do different things. Is it important to both of us? Should we compromise?"*

- *"I need to watch the clock. I'm getting distracted here. Let me focus on the big picture goal so I can get it done."*

TOPIC 4.4: Preparing for Graduation: Celebrating Our Executive Function Skills (continued)

EXECUTIVE FUNCTION SKILLS LIST

Flexible Thinking
"Thanks for being flexible!"
"Nice job being flexible."
"You were flexible and got what you wanted even faster. Nice job!"

Plan A/Plan B
"If Plan A doesn't work, then we'll try a Plan B."
"I'm feeling stuck—my Plan A didn't work. Can you help me come up with a Plan B?"
"Do you need a Plan B?"

Stuck/Unstuck
"How can I get unstuck?"
"Nice work. You were flexible and got unstuck."
"You noticed you were stuck and then got unstuck. That's how you boost your power!"

Goal-Why-Plan-Check
"What's the goal?"
"Why is the goal important?"
"What are the steps of the plan?"
"Let's check to see if we reached our goal."

Are We Focused on Our Big Picture Goal or Stuck on an Off-Topic Detail?
"What's our big picture goal?"
"Is this an off-topic detail?"
"Should we get stuck on this detail or get back to our big picture goal?"

Compromise
"Let's come up with a compromise."
"Compromising lets us both get some of what we want."
"Nice compromise! It's a win-win for both of you."
"You both let go of your Plan A so you both could get *some* of what you want. That is a winning compromise and helps you boost your power!"

Efficiency = Doing a Task Well and Fairly Quickly
"Keep your eyes on the prize—stay focused and excited about your goal!"
"Watch the clock—don't get stuck on off-topic details!"
"Great work. You were efficient. You didn't get stuck."

Managing Frustration and Disappointment
"Being disappointed is normal. How can we manage it?"
"When we're frustrated, there's always a Plan B!"

TOPIC 4.5 Graduation

BIG PICTURE SUMMARY

The focus of the last topic is celebrating the students' participation and accomplishments throughout the program, while giving them a chance to reflect on the executive function skills they have learned and will take with them in the future.

Key Things to Do Here are the two most important things to do in today's class:

1. **Use this Key Vocabulary often and in fun and playful ways:**
   - Executive Function Skills
   - Using Executive Function Skills in My Day-to-Day Life (or the version of this phrase the students decided in Topic 4.1)
   - Flexible Thinking
   - Getting Unstuck
   - Plan A/Plan B
   - Goal-Why-Plan-Check
   - Putting Your Plan on Trial (Checking Your Plan)
   - Managing Frustration and Disappointment
   - Should I Compromise?
   - How to Compromise:
     - Each Gets Part.
     - Combine Ideas.
     - Take Turns.
     - Do Something Different You Both Like.
   - Eyes on the Prize = Staying Excited About a Longer-Term Goal
   - Focusing on the Big Picture Goal
   - Efficiency = Doing a Task Well and Fairly Quickly
   - Watch The Clock = Planning Quickly and Carefully

2. **Find ways to spontaneously model executive function skills (compromise, flexibility, and planning)** *at least once* **during class today.** Make this fun and engaging! Today is a great opportunity to reflect on and share with the students your own growth during the class. You can do your own presentation, or you could just mention some of the changes you've noticed in yourself (e.g., being more flexible, planning more, setting more long-term goals). This is a great way to model lifelong learning for your students.

Special instructions for today: Make sure to invite families or other educators to the celebration if you haven't already. Some students may feel uncomfortable presenting in front of a large group. If this is the case, consider demonstrating Plan B and compromise skills by making the presentation together or having the student present only a portion of their presentation in a way that feels comfortable.

Materials

- Unit 4 Daily Self-Awareness Rating (worksheets copied for each student or found in Student Workbook)
- Power Equation Poster, posted

- Power Level card: Affix the Power Level card to the bottom of the Power Arrow on the Power Equation Poster.
- The personal Power Plan and graduation PowerPoints or worksheets on posters that each student will use for their graduation presentation
- Supplies for a graduation party

EDUCATOR PLAN

Goal: Students will share their presentations in class and celebrate their accomplishments.

Why: Having students reflect on and celebrate everything they've learned during the class will help support their use of executive function skills in the future.

Plan: Do the following before class:

- Post the Power Equation Poster and place the Power Level card at the bottom of the arrow on the poster.
- Each student's completed personal Power Plan and graduation documents should be available to them during class for their presentations.

CLASS LESSON PLAN

1. **Ask students to fill out the Unit 4 Daily Self-Awareness Rating worksheet.** If there are invited guests in class, make sure to provide them with copies of the Unit 4 Daily Self-Awareness Rating worksheet. Ask one of the students in the class to teach the guests how to fill out the worksheet.

2. **Discuss with the students how the executive function skills learned in this class can help them get what they want and need in life.** Praise students for their hard work during class and tell them today is all about celebrating their accomplishments and growth. Discuss how much power they've gained learning about and using executive function skills. Ask students for examples of how they've used the skills in this class, in

other classes, and at home (e.g., completing homework, making friends, solving conflicts that come up).

3. **Help get students motivated for their graduation presentations by reviewing the purpose of the presentation.** Here is a sample script you can use:

    "Today's presentations are an opportunity to celebrate all of the important executive function skills that you have learned. But remember, as powerful as flexibility, goal-setting, planning, checking, and compromise are, these skills can only help you if you keep using them! After the presentations today, each of you will be given copies of the executive function skills list and your Power Plans to take with you so you can put them up in places where you'll see them every day."

4. **Have each student stand and give their presentation to the group.** If necessary, provide support for the student by helping them think through the steps of their presentation. For example, you could say:

    "The goal is for you to share your presentation. The plan is to first talk through your personal goal, the steps you took, and how it turned out. Then you can share the three executive function skills that are most important to you and why."

    If a student continues to struggle, use Key Vocabulary to help them problem solve. For example:

    "Our Plan A was for you to give your presentation standing in front of the class. But we can also be flexible and think about a Plan B if that isn't going to work. What would be a good Plan B? Is there a compromise?"

5. At the end of each presentation, solicit praise from the class and guests about each student's successes using the executive function skills. Then ask each student which visual might be helpful to post in an important place (e.g., in their bedroom, on the refrigerator, on the front of their notebook, on the screen of a computer or phone) as a reminder to use their skills. The reminder could be the Executive Function Skills List, the Power Plan visual, or the "Executive function skills are important for my life" page from their presentation. Explain to the class:

    "There's so much power that we get from these executive function skills, but we don't want you to forget them and lose all of that power in your life. One way to remember them is to have a printed copy of the skills on your wall, or make it a screen saver on your computer or phone. What would help you remember?"

    Work with each student to make a plan for posting the reminder and help support them by checking in later to see if they followed through.

    Finally, some educators choose to give out awards to each student: the most changed, the Gumby award for being the most flexible, the most encouraging of other students, champion compromiser, and so forth. Make sure that each student gets their own award.

6. **Celebrate the graduation with a party.**

7. **Ask the class, *"Why did we spend this time learning about flexibility, goal setting, planning, and compromise?"*** Why are executive function skills important? Discuss with the class and their guests.

8. **Send Home Extension for Topic 4.5 home with students or e-mail it to parents.**

9. **Look for generalization opportunities in other classes.** Encourage other educators to continue to use the Power Plan and the Key Vocabulary from the curriculum.

> **CHECK:** Did students feel celebrated, successful, and empowered?

It is very important to end this group on a positive note!

TOPIC 4.5: Graduation

DAILY SELF-AWARENESS RATING: UNIT 4

NAME: _____

Executive Function Skills

Flexibility + Big Picture Thinking + Goals and Planning = POWER

Mark an X on the arrow to show how you feel today:

Are you using the flexibility and planning skills in your other classes?

Not Using Skills — Using Some Skills — Using Executive Function Skills Every Day

Are you using the flexibility and planning skills at home?

Not Using Skills — Using Some Skills — Using Executive Function Skills Every Day

TOPIC 4.5: Graduation

HOME EXTENSION FOR TOPIC 4.5: GRADUATION

The class celebrated their work with a graduation ceremony in which they presented the plans for achieving their personal goals and considered the executive function skills they learned in the program. If you didn't attend the graduation, ask your child if they want to share their presentation with you.

Key Vocabulary/skills:

Flexible Thinking   *Plan A/Plan B*   *Managing Frustration and Disappointment*

Setting a Goal   *Making a Plan*   *Compromise*

How to use the Key Vocabulary/skills: At this point, the most important thing is to make sure that your child doesn't forget the skills taught and practiced in this program. Continue to make the Key Vocabulary and skills a central part of your family's routines. The executive function skills taught in this program (see the next page of this Home Extension handout) are useful not only for your child, but also for everyone in their daily lives. If you practice the skills daily and post visual reminders in your house, at work, and in the car, you can model them for your family and help make them stick. Make it obvious when you're using the skills by thinking out loud and then celebrating your successes with your whole family.

TOPIC 4.5: Graduation (continued)

EXECUTIVE FUNCTION SKILLS LIST

Flexible Thinking
"Thanks for being flexible!"
"Nice job being flexible."
"You were flexible and got what you wanted even faster. Nice job!"

Plan A/Plan B
"If Plan A doesn't work, then we'll try a Plan B."
"I'm feeling stuck—my Plan A didn't work. Can you help me come up with a Plan B?"
"Do you need a Plan B?"

Stuck/Unstuck
"How can I get unstuck?"
"Nice work. You were flexible and got unstuck."
"You noticed you were stuck and then got unstuck. That's how you boost your power!"

Goal-Why-Plan-Check
"What's the goal?"
"Why is the goal important?"
"What are the steps of the plan?"
"Let's check to see if we reached our goal."

Are We Focused on Our Big Picture Goal or Stuck on an Off-Topic Detail?
"What's our big picture goal?"
"Is this an off-topic detail?"
"Should we get stuck on this detail or get back to our big picture goal?"

Compromise
"Let's come up with a compromise."
"Compromising lets us both get some of what we want."
"Nice compromise! It's a win-win for both of you."
"You both let go of your Plan A so you both could get *some* of what you want. That is a winning compromise and helps you boost your power!"

Efficiency = Doing a Task Well and Fairly Quickly
"Keep your eyes on the prize—stay focused and excited about your goal!"
"Watch the clock—don't get stuck on off-topic details!"
"Great work. You were efficient. You didn't get stuck."

Managing Frustration and Disappointment
"Being disappointed is normal. How can we manage it?"
"When we're frustrated, there's always a Plan B!"

APPENDIX A

Questions for Reflection

CHECK: How are my students doing?
Do I need to make any adjustments for the next class?

- Were students engaged?
- It is critical to give the students praise much more often than commands/corrections. Did I maintain a 4:1 praise-to-correction ratio?
- Did I reinforce the Key Vocabulary during class?
- How can I help my students use the Key Vocabulary and skills in their everyday lives?
- Are there specific words or activities that students do not like? If so, can I come up with alternatives?
- Was this topic too hard?
- Did I get into a power struggle with a student?
- Am I having trouble telling the difference between willful behavior and executive function problems?

APPENDIX B

Troubleshooting FAQs: When Challenges Come Up

Q: I'm having a hard time keeping my students engaged. What should I do?

A: First, think about how you can personalize the lesson content. We are all inherently more interested in a topic of personal interest and/or relevance to us. Although the lessons in this curriculum were created to have broad applicability, the information and strategies will be more meaningful if you can add scenarios or examples from your students' lives. For example, if your students are interested in certain video games or movies, weave their characters and themes into your examples. If you know students gravitate toward certain activities or topics during free time or in the lunchroom, integrate those into your examples.

Second, consider highlighting the "why"—that is, the motivation or reward value for your students learning the skills and activities. Because the skills taught throughout this intervention don't come automatically or easily to many young people with executive function difficulties, your students may not immediately see how the activities and skills will make a difference in their lives. You can help your students authentically connect with the material and learn by making the power, importance, and relevance of the skills and activities explicit to your students. Highlight why the skill you are teaching is and should be meaningful to them—and be sure to think like a young teen when you do this. A teen may not care that using kind language is what educators want, but they may care that using kind language could help convince people to be more flexible with them, which could help the student get more of what they want.

Third, monitor the pace of the lessons and student engagement. Keep the curriculum moving and be mindful not to lecture. The activities are designed to be hands-on, and throughout the course of the intervention, you'll discover which activities your students like best. Feel free to alter the presentation of an activity to cater to their preferences (e.g., your students may especially love role plays, games, or deep conversations). As we'll explore in the next section, it's also important to praise and acknowledge your students' efforts during each activity. We all improve our effort when that effort is acknowledged and explicitly connected to outcomes that matter to us.

 Positive feelings and actions from you will create more positive feelings in your students.

Q: I feel like I am constantly nagging and redirecting the students. What should I do?

A: Keep it positive! This may be the single most powerful suggestion in this book. Just as you teach your students that their behavior has both positive and negative consequences, remember that your mood and behavior both have consequences, too. Happiness, sadness, anxiety, and frustration are all contagious. Negative feelings and actions from you (expressed in critiques, yelling, and punishing) will increase negative feelings and behaviors in your students, which will create a negative cycle. Positive feelings and actions from you will create more positive feelings in your students.

One key positive action you can take is to praise students *four times more often* than you give commands or corrections (4:1). Recognize how hard your students are working to live in a neurotypical world and be sure to celebrate every effort and sign of progress rather than only praising success. Research shows that this strategy is effective at reducing behavioral problems and improving social skills. Keeping up this 4:1 praise-to-correction ratio also trains you to pay more attention to the things that are going well than to things that need improvement.

Keep in mind that if you give vague praise (e.g., *"You are doing great"*) or praise that isn't true (e.g., *"You are the smartest kid in the world!"*), your students will quickly learn to disregard it. Deliver specific and true praise, which is often based on observations of the effort needed to achieve something rather than on successful completion. Be sure to validate what the students are experiencing and their efforts to be more flexible and organized. Here are some examples of specific and true praise:

- *"That's creative and flexible thinking that will help us get unstuck!"*
- *"I see that you're working hard to be flexible. That is how you get unstuck."*
- *"I like the way you came up with a plan to solve that problem on your own!"*
- *"You kept working really hard on that math problem, and you solved a challenging problem!"*
- *"Great job staying flexible and open to others' ideas."*
- *"I know it can be hard work to compromise. Keep going, so that each of you can get some of what you want."*
- *"I'm impressed by how hard you're trying to stay flexible. Keep at it!"*

Q: How can I help my students use the Key Vocabulary and skills in their everyday lives, both in and out of school?

A: Research tells us that in order for a skill to become automatic or routine, we need at least 12 exposures or practice opportunities. As with any skill your students learn (reading, writing, athletics, social skills, etc.), the more opportunities they have to practice and try the skill in multiple settings, the more likely they are to use the skills and strategies independently and effectively. That's why we've created ready-to-share documents that help make sharing information and strategies as quick and easy as possible.

To help students generalize these skills, we need to share the Key Vocabulary and strategies with as many people as possible. If all of the individuals who support your students—including school staff, other educators, parents, coaches, grandparents, and therapists—are aware of and understand the Key Vocabulary, they can all help students use them and prompt for them when necessary. Casting this wide net of support can be as easy as drafting a quick e-mail or document defining the Key Vocabulary and giving brief examples of how and when to use the skills and words. Establish an e-mail chain with people who interact with and support your students. As you introduce new skills/Key Vocabulary, send off an e-mail with a description of the new skills/vocabulary and a brief suggestion for how they can be used. Here is a sample e-mail:

> We just learned about compromise. We think about compromise as a way for everyone to get part of what they want. When the opportunity presents itself, help Alex think about which compromising strategies they'd like to use. Here are four possible strategies for compromise:
>
> 1. Each person gets part of what they want.
>   OR
> 2. They combine their ideas in some way.
>   OR
> 3. They take turns doing what they want.
>   OR
> 4. They choose a different idea that both of them agree on.
>
> Celebrate when Alex compromises and reflect on the fact that each person got part of what they want. Students in class really responded when we framed compromise

positively: *"Wow, it looks like you both have something you want to do. Let's figure out a compromise, so both of you can get part of what you want."* You can try this at home, too!

Please shoot me an e-mail if you notice or have any experience helping Alex come up with a compromise. We will be sure to celebrate it in class!

Throughout the manual, we've provided several documents for you to disseminate to people who can help your students practice using the skills and Key Vocabulary. We encourage you to customize these documents and add information about when and where the skills/Key Vocabulary have been helpful. Also, be sure to let students know you are sharing this information with the people in their world. It may be comforting to know that others will be supporting them in using the skills and Key Vocabulary and that they can anticipate a predictable and routine approach to working on the skills that are most difficult for them.

Q: Some of the Key Vocabulary terms and phrases seem to greatly annoy one of my students. How important is it for me to stick to the Key Vocabulary?

A: It's important to pay attention to the students' reaction to the Key Vocabulary and activities because they are an integral component of this intervention. Students may react negatively to a word or phrase if they have learned to associate it with a negative experience or outcome. For example, a student may "become allergic" to the term flexible if it has been used negatively (e.g., *"Stop throwing a tantrum—you need to be more flexible!"* or *"Why can't you just be more flexible? You're making this hard for everyone!"*). If a student has a negative reaction to a word or phrase, you can choose another word to use in its place that conveys a similar meaning. Be sure that the chosen word or phrase is used positively and consistently and that it is shared with other educators, school staff, and parents so they can use it with the students as well.

Q: What do I do if my students don't like an activity?

A: First, determine whether the activity is too hard or if your students don't understand it. If you determine that your students could more effectively and enjoyably learn a key concept and/or strategy through a different activity, please trust your assessment and experience and change the activity to better engage your students.

Q: My students are finding some of the concepts in these lessons too hard. How do I help them understand?

A: Each lesson comes with a big picture summary and a goal, which underscore the key components of the intervention. Using these key components as your guide, you can adapt lessons and activities based on the individual skill sets of your students. To make the materials relevant to your learners, you may want to consider whether they have the foundational competencies necessary to understand a concept. For example, if a student is having difficulty understanding why it's important to compromise on choosing an activity, check to see whether that student understands that their friends may have a different opinion on what constitutes a fun activity. If not, you may need to teach this foundational concept to make the lesson more accessible. The following strategies may also be helpful:

- **Visuals:** Some students, particularly those who have difficulty with language comprehension, benefit greatly from the use of added visuals to illustrate ambiguous concepts. Use pictures, movies, or acting to illustrate concepts and engage students.

- **Role-plays:** When teaching new concepts, using role-plays can get students engaged For example, students with executive function challenges may have difficulty translating learned concepts into skills they use on a daily basis. Using role-plays can help teens generalize their skills to other settings and make abstract concepts more concrete. You may wish to role-play a concept with another educator or student to illustrate a real-world example or encourage students to create role-play scenarios themselves. Be mindful that some students may be shy at first, but they may begin to participate the more they are exposed to role-play scenarios.

- **Relevant examples:** Consider using current events, pop culture, and topics that appeal to your students to illustrate concepts. For example, if students are studying a famous world leader in history or tracking an upcoming election, you could make a Power Level card for that figure and track their trajectory of power gains or losses over time by moving their Power Level card up or down on the Power Equation Poster (along with the group's Power Level card, which will only move up).
- **Special interests:** Students have a more positive self-image when engaged in activities associated with their special interests. For example, if a student has a particular interest in video games, you might incorporate this interest into developing Plan B scenarios (e.g., *"You invite a friend over, but they don't want to play the same video game as you do. How can you be flexible and come up with a Plan B?"*).

Q: How do I avoid power struggles?

A: Start by modeling flexibility for your students. When you see a student getting upset, use your own coping strategies to stay calm and available to support them. Remember, you can increase the likelihood that your student will use a coping strategy when you can cue them with your own clear and calm example. If everyone gets overwhelmed, coping strategies become less accessible.

Building the habit of using coping strategies takes persistence and patience. Bring in Key Vocabulary as needed, discussing key concepts like flexibility and coming up with a Plan A/Plan B. Once you have covered compromise in Unit 2, you can use some of those strategies to address power struggles. You might say to your students, *"It seems like you and I are having difficulties with flexibility today. But I'm going to work to be flexible and meet you halfway."* Or, if a student is struggling significantly, you might say, *"It seems like you might not have a lot of energy to be flexible today, so I can be flexible and do it your way this time."*

Be cognizant of demands that might cause students to become overloaded and shut down. In those situations, it's especially important to match your expectations for what students should do to their actual capabilities and skill sets. As their competencies improve, you can gradually increase the frequency and/or complexity of opportunities to be flexible.

Q: Sometimes I can't tell what is willful misbehavior and what is an executive function difficulty. How can I make that distinction?

A: It's important to work extra hard to understand the perspectives of students with executive function difficulties because their perspectives and experiences are so easily misunderstood. For example, sometimes the gifts of neurodivergence—such as an expansive vocabulary or a remarkable memory—can increase the risk of misinterpretation: *How can a student who knows so much about physics not realize he's being rude when he says something about my body shape?* If you try to understand the world from the perspective of a child who is neurodivergent, you can recognize that this student believes they are only stating a fact; they are not trying to be rude or hurtful at all.

Effective teaching and interventions to expand skills can only happen when there is clarity about why a student is doing or saying what's been observed. You can use your understanding of neurodivergence to get curious and be a detective to figure out the why. A critical question to start with is this: *Is it "can't yet" or a "won't" for your student?* For example, consider a student who is standing at a cafeteria table telling another student to get out of "my seat." Rather than think of them as rude and unkind, ask yourself, "Why did that happen? Is there a 'can't yet' or something that's difficult for them?" You wouldn't get mad at a student for not being able to read without their glasses. Instead, you'd remember their needs and ensure they have glasses to read. Similarly, you can support your neurodivergent students by remembering their brain-based differences like misreading social cues or having trouble being flexible about where to sit in the cafeteria.

In short: If a student is not doing something as expected, try to think of *why* they are having difficulty. Often, you'll find that what looks like a defiant "won't" is actually a "can't yet." (See Table B.1 for more examples.)

Table B.1. Reasons for Unexpected Behaviors

What looks like *won't*...	May actually be *can't yet*
"Oppositional, stubborn"	• Cognitive inflexibility • Protective effort to avoid overload
"Can do it when they want to"	• Difficulty shifting from one thing to another • Trouble paying attention to what other people think is important • Subtle changes in demands can drastically impact performance
"Self-centered"; "Doesn't care what others think"	• Impaired social problem solving • Trouble understanding subtle social cues
"Doesn't try"	• Difficulty getting started (initiation) • Impaired planning and trouble generating new ideas
"Won't put good ideas on paper"	• Poor fine motor skills • Trouble organizing thoughts in a way that makes sense to a reader
"Sloppy, erratic"	• Problems monitoring/checking • Overload • Impaired impulse control
"Won't control outbursts"	• Overload • Impaired inhibition or impulse control
"Prefers to be alone"	• Impaired social understanding • Needs a break from processing complex social information • Social system just works differently (i.e., less socially motivated)
"Doesn't care about what is important"	• Natural ability to focus on details, but has a harder time relating to the big picture/main idea or other people's priorities

As important as it is to support students with executive function challenges, be careful not to create limitations or "can't" situations by *over-supporting* a student. When you're eager to reduce overload and help students move through a task, it's easy to get caught up in "do it for them" mode. Although this may be helpful in the moment, you may also be preventing the student from becoming a more independent problem solver.

Use the Socratic method, a method of teaching that involves asking questions to stimulate independent and critical thinking. You may have to pause for a long time while waiting for a student to come up with a response or a solution, but it's worth waiting in the long run if you can resist jumping in. It's also essential to withdraw your coaching gradually over time in order for the student to develop and demonstrate independence with a skill. Otherwise, you could be creating a "can't" situation by doing too much for the student and making them more dependent on you.

Index

Page numbers followed by *t* and *b* indicate tables and boxes, respectively.

Anxiety, xi, 221
Attention-deficit/hyperactivity disorder (ADHD), xi

Blank Power Plan, 114*b*
   slides, 67, 79–80, 115–118, 123, 143–144, 145–146, 160–161
   worksheets, 141, 149, 157, 164, 170
Building a Powerful Plan slide, 182

Can't, not won't, xiv, 224
Celebration Day! The Plan B Party topic, 77–82
Class size, xi, xii
Comparing Short-Term and Longer-Term Goals slide, 134
Compromise
   strategies for, 222
   topics, 84–130
Compromise Competition and Scenarios slide, 88–90
Compromise Detective—Figuring Out When to Compromise slide, 99
Compromise Detective—Use the Listen, Think, and Talk It Through Steps to Figure Out How Much the Other Person Cares slide, 99–100
Compromise Skill slide, 86
Compromise Video slide, 87
"Compromiser" game rules slide, 108–109
"Compromiser" game slide, 109
Compromising Is a Win-Win topic, 84–95
Concepts, examples for illustrating, 224
Continue Planning for the Big Event/Project slide, 153–154
Coping strategies, 44*b*, 45*b*
Coping Strategies Experiment Log slide, 46, 47*b*
Coping Strategies Experiment Log worksheet, 53
Coping Strategies to Feel Better and Get Unstuck When Overwhelmed, Stressed, Frustrated, or Disappointed topic, 40–53
Coping Strategies to Get Unstuck slide, 45–46
Curriculum
   implementation of, xii
   key techniques used in, xii–xiii
   teachers of, xi

Daily Self-Awareness Rating worksheets
   Unit 1, 11, 25, 38, 48, 63, 74, 81
   Unit 2, 93, 103, 110, 119, 124, 130
   Unit 3, 139, 147, 155, 162, 168, 175
   Unit 4, 184, 193, 201, 208, 215
Dealing With Frustration and Disappointment slide, 56–57

Deciding on an Important Longer-Term Goal Using Compromise Skills slide, 136–137
Developing a Personal Goal: Using Executive Function Skills in Our Real Lives topic, 178–188
Doing over knowing, xiv

Educators of curriculum, xi, xii
Educator's Personal Goal: Sharing Progress and Challenges slide, 191
Educator's Personal Goal slide, 181
Efficiency and Watching the Clock slide, 152
Efficient planning topics, 132–176
Efficient Planning—Staying Focused on the Big Picture Goal topic, 142–149
Efficient Planning—Watching the Clock topic, 150–157
Executive function
   component to improving, xii–xiv
   definition of, xi
   examples of, xi–xii
   skills topics, 178–217
   teaching, importance of, xii
   willful misbehavior *vs.*, 224
Executive Function Skills List worksheets
   Developing a Personal Goal: Using Executive Function Skills in Our Real Lives, 186
   Executive Function Skills Important for My Life, 188
   Flexible Thinking, 14
   Graduation, 217
   Preparing for Graduation: Celebrating Our Executive Function Skills, 209–210
   Putting Personal Plans on Trial, 202–203
   Using Executive Function Skills for Personal Goals, 194–195
   Using Executive Function Skills in My Day-To-Day Life, 187
Eyes on the Prize, Big Picture Thinking, and Efficiency slide, 160

4:1 praise-to-correction ratio, xiii, 221–222
Feelings, avoid invalidating, 41*b*
Feelings Target visual
   worksheet, 50–52
   slide, 42–43
Finalizing the Goal for the Longer-Term Event/Project slide, 137
Flexibility
   definition of, xi
   modeling, xiii, 206
   topics, 2–82

Flexibility = Power slide, 22–23
Flexibility (the First Part of the Power Equation) slide, 5–6
Flexibility Videos: Flexibility Is Stronger slide, 6–7
Flexible thinking strategies, 54
Flexible Thinking topic, 2–14
Flexible Thinking Trick 1: How Long Should I Be Stuck on Being Frustrated or Disappointed? slide, 58–59
Flexible Thinking Trick 2: How Can I Refocus on My Big Picture Goal? slide, 59–60
Flexible Thinking Trick 3: There's Always a Plan B slide, 60–61
Flexible Thinking—Accepting and Letting Go of Frustration and Disappointment topic, 54–64
Flexible–Rigid Table slide, 6

Generalization, xiii
Getting (and Staying) Excited About a Future Goal topic, 132–141
Goal-Why-Plan-Check, xiv
Graduation topic, 211–217
Graphic of the Four Ways to Compromise slide, 88

Health education policies, 100b
Home Extension worksheets
   The Long-term Event/Project—Efficient Planning = Power!, 169
   The Special Event, 125
   Celebration Day! The Plan B Party, 82
   Compromising Is a Win-Win, 94–95
   Coping Strategies, 49
   Developing A Personal Goal: Using Executive Function Skills in Our Real Lives, 185
   Efficient Planning— Staying Focused on The Big Picture Goal, 148
   Efficient Planning—Watching the Clock, 156
   Flexible Feelings—Accepting and Letting Go of Frustration and Disappointment, 64
   Flexible Thinking, 13
   Getting (And Staying) Excited About a Future Goal, 140
   Graduation, 216
   How To Increase Your Power to Help Yourself and The World, 39
   Plan Another Special Event Together Using Compromise Skills, 120
   Plan A/Plan B = More Power, 28
   Preparing For Graduation: Celebrating Our Executive Function Skills, 209
   Pulling It All Together—Using All the Key Vocabulary/skills To Finalize the Plan, 163
   Putting A Plan on Trial (Checking Your Plan Before Trying It Out), 75–76
   Putting Personal Plans on Trial, 202
   Reviewing The Long-Term Event/project: Learning from Our Successes and Challenges, 176
   Should I Compromise?, 104
   Try Out Your Compromise Skills, 111–112
   Using Executive Function Skills for Personal Goals, 194
Home Extensions, vii
   see also Worksheets
How the Brain and Body Experience and React to Overwhelming Feelings slide, 44–45
How the Brain Handles Frustration and Disappointment slide, 57
How To Boost Our Power Level: Reminder List worksheet, 12
How to Boost Your Power and Get More of What You Want and Need slide, 4–5
How to Compromise slide, 87–88
How to Increase Your Power to Help Yourself and the World topic, 29–39
Humor, for engaging students, xiv

Important Times Not to Compromise slide, 100
Inhibition, definition of, xi
Initiation, definition of, xi

Keeping Your Eyes on the Prize: A Phrase to Stay Focused on Our Goal slide, 135
Key Vocabulary, xii–xiii, 2b, 54b, 84b, 132b, 178b
   incorporating into curriculum, xii–xiii
   negative reactions to, 223
   teaching, 19b
   using in everyday life, 222–223

Learning How to Plan by Planning a Good Party (the Plan B Party) slide, 70–72
Learning How to Plan by Planning a Ridiculously Bad Party slide, 69–70
Lesson PowerPoint files, vii
Longer-Term Event/Project Is Celebrated Today slide, 166–167
Longer-Term Event/Project—Efficient Planning = Power! topic, 165–170

Motivational techniques, xiii–xiv

Neurodivergence, 224

Obstacle Course: Flexible Is Faster slide, 7
Online materials, vii
Organization, definition of, xi

Parent Workbook, vii
Personal Power Plans
   worksheet, 187
   slide, 191
Personal safety policies, 100b
Plan Another Special Event Together Using Compromise Skills topic, 113–120
Plan A/Plan B = More Power topic, 15–28
Plan A/Plan B = Power slide, 18
Plan A/Plan B Video slide, 18–19
Planning
   definition of, xii
   efficient planning topics, 132–176
Planning a Party and Putting the Plan on Trial slide, 68–69
Playfulness, xiv
Playing Group Planning Games While Keeping Track of Our Power slide, 35

Index

Positivity, xiii, 221*b*, 221–222
Power Arrow, 33*b*
Power Boost and Power Loss: What Makes Our Power Go Up or Down? slide, 33
Power Boosters: How to Boost Your Power and Get More of What You Want and Need slide, 16–17
Power Equation Poster, vii
Power Equation Review slide, 41, 56, 67–68
Power Equation slide, 5, 17–18, 31, 123
Power Equation: The Compromise Skill slide, 86
Power for Self and the World: Power Level slide, 31–33
Power Game
   options, 19–20*b*
   printable, 27
Power Game Level 1 Scenarios slide, 21–22
Power Game Level 2 Scenarios slide, 22
Power Game slide, 19–21
Power Level, 31–33, 32–33*b*, 41*b*, 56*b*, 97*b*, 107*b*
Power Level Cards, 68*b*, 78*b*, 85*b*, 143*b*, 152*b*
Power Plan, xiv, 3*b*
Power Plan slide, 3–4, 16, 30–31, 41, 56, 86, 97, 107, 127, 134, 152, 172, 180, 191, 198
Power struggles, 224
PowerPoints (accompanying online materials), vii, xiii
Practice the Self-Monitoring System (Example 1) slide, 144
Practice the Self-Monitoring System (Example 2) slide, 144
Practice Using the Power Level System: Story 1 slide, 33–34
Practice Using the Power Level System: Story 2 slide, 34
Praise, xiii, 85*b*, 222
Preparing for Graduation: Celebrating Our Executive Function Skills topic, 204–210
Preparing for Unit 3: Beginning to Think About a Longer-Term Group Goal slide, 128
Preparing for Unit 4: Beginning to Think About Your Personal Goal in This Class slide, 173
Pulling It All Together—Using All the Key Vocabulary/Skills to Finalize the Plan topic, 158–164
Putting a Plan on Trial (Checking Your Plan) slide, 198
Putting a Plan on Trial (Checking Your Plan Before Trying It Out) topic, 65–76
Putting Our Personal Plans on Trial (Checking Our Plans) slide, 198–199
Putting Personal Plans on Trial topic, 196–203

Questions
   Questions for Reflection, 219
   troubleshooting FAQs, 221–225, 225*t*
Questions for Reflection, 219
Quick Rewards Versus Long-Term Payoff slide, 136

Ready-to-share documents, 222
   see also Worksheets
Realistic–Unrealistic Power List slide, 17
Realistic–unrealistic Power List worksheet, 26
Recognizing When You're Getting Off Target slide, 45
Remember, and Stay Excited About, the Goal (a Strategy to Keep Our Eyes on the Prize) slide, 138
Review the Graphic of the Four Ways to Compromise slide, 107, 108*b*
Review the How to Compromise visual slide, 107
Review the "Should I Compromise?" Formula slide, 107

Review the Special Event slide, 128
Review the Special Event/Project slide, 173
Reviewing The Special Event topic, 126–130
Reviewing the Longer-Term Event/Project: Learning from Our Successes and Challenges topic, 171–176
Revisiting the Pink Panther: How Does He Deal with Frustration and Disappointment? slide, 61
Role-play, 7–8, 99–100, 106, 223

Self-advocacy skill, 197*b*
Self-monitoring, definition of, xii
Setting Students' Personal Goals slide, 181–182
"Should I Compromise?" Formula slide, 98
Should I Compromise? topic, 96–104
"Should They Compromise?" Lightning Round Scenarios slide, 100–101
Skills We'll Practice in This Group slide, 4
Slides
   "The Compromiser" game, 109
   "The Compromiser" game rules, 108–109
   The Power Game, 19–21
   The Power Game Level 1 Scenarios, 21–22
   The Power Game Level 2 Scenarios, 22
   Blank Power Plan, 67, 79–80, 115–118, 123, 143–144, 145–146, 160–161
   Building a Powerful Plan, 182
   Comparing Short-Term and Longer-Term Goals, 134
   Compromise Competition and Scenarios, 88–90
   Compromise Detective—Figuring Out When to Compromise, 99
   Compromise Detective—Use the Listen, Think, and Talk It Through Steps to Figure Out How Much the Other Person Cares, 99–100
   Compromise Skill, 86
   Compromise Video, 87
   Continue Planning for the Big Event/Project, 153–154
   Coping Strategies Experiment Log, 46, 47*b*
   Coping Strategies to Get Unstuck, 45–46
   Dealing With Frustration and Disappointment, 56–57
   Deciding on an Important Longer-Term Goal Using Compromise Skills, 136–137
   Educator's Personal Goal, 181
   Educator's Personal Goal: Sharing Progress and Challenges, 191
   Efficiency and Watching the Clock, 152
   Eyes on the Prize, Big Picture Thinking, and Efficiency, 160
   Feelings Target visual, 42–43
   Finalizing the Goal for the Longer-Term Event/Project, 137
   Flexibility (the First Part of the Power Equation), 5–6
   Flexibility = Power, 22–23
   Flexibility Videos: Flexibility Is Stronger, 6–7
   Flexible Thinking Trick 1: How Long Should I Be Stuck on Being Frustrated or Disappointed?, 58–59
   Flexible Thinking Trick 2: How Can I Refocus on My Big Picture Goal?, 59–60
   Flexible Thinking Trick 3: There's Always a Plan B, 60–61
   Flexible–Rigid Table, 6
   Graphic of the Four Ways to Compromise, 88
   How the Brain and Body Experience and React to Overwhelming Feelings, 44–45
   How the Brain Handles Frustration and Disappointment, 57

Slides—*continued*
  How to Boost Your Power and Get More of What You Want and Need, 4–5
  How to Compromise, 87–88
  Important Times Not to Compromise, 100
  Keeping Your Eyes on the Prize: A Phrase to Stay Focused on Our Goal, 135
  Learning How to Plan by Planning a Good Party (the Plan B Party), 70–72
  Learning How to Plan by Planning a Ridiculously Bad Party, 69–70
  Longer-Term Event/Project Is Celebrated Today, 166–167
  Obstacle Course: Flexible Is Faster, 7
  Personal Power Plans, 191
  Plan A/Plan B = Power, 18
  Plan A/Plan B Video, 18–19
  Planning a Party and Putting the Plan on Trial, 68–69
  Playing Group Planning Games While Keeping Track of Our Power, 35
  Power Boost and Power Loss: What Makes Our Power Go Up or Down?, 33
  Power Boosters: How to Boost Your Power and Get More of What You Want and Need, 16–17
  Power Equation, 5, 17–18, 31, 123
  Power Equation Review, 41, 56, 67–68
  Power Equation: The Compromise Skill, 86
  Power for Self and the World: Power Level, 31–33
  Power Plan, 3–4, 16, 30–31, 41, 56, 86, 97, 107, 127, 134, 152, 172, 180, 191, 198
  Practice the Self-Monitoring System (Example 1), 144
  Practice the Self-Monitoring System (Example 2), 144
  Practice Using the Power Level System: Story 1, 33–34
  Practice Using the Power Level System: Story 2, 34
  Preparing for Unit 3: Beginning to Think About a Longer-Term Group Goal, 128
  Preparing for Unit 4: Beginning to Think About Your Personal Goal in This Class, 173
  Putting a Plan on Trial (Checking Your Plan), 198
  Putting Our Personal Plans on Trial (Checking Our Plans), 198–199
  Quick Rewards Versus Long-Term Payoff, 136
  Realistic–Unrealistic Power List, 17
  Recognizing When You're Getting Off Target, 45
  Remember, and Stay Excited About, the Goal (a Strategy to Keep Our Eyes on the Prize), 138
  Review the Graphic of the Four Ways to Compromise, 107, 108*b*
  Review the How to Compromise visual, 107
  Review the "Should I Compromise?" Formula, 107
  Review the Special Event, 128
  Review the Special Event/Project, 173
  Revisiting the Pink Panther: How Does He Deal with Frustration and Disappointment?, 61
  Setting Students' Personal Goals, 181–182
  "Should I Compromise?" Formula, 98
  "Should They Compromise?" Lightning Round Scenarios, 100–101
  Skills We'll Practice in This Group, 4
  Stress, Frustration, and Disappointment and Strategies to Feel Better, 42
  Stuck on a Detail Versus Big Picture Thinking, 7–9
  Three Flexible Thinking Tricks to Deal with Frustration and Disappointment, 57–58
  Tracking the Power Level for Our Group, 34–35
  Using Executive Function Skills in Everyday Life to Get More Power, 191–192
  Using the Executive Function Skills in Our Day-to-Day Lives, 180–181
  Web Quest: Feelings in the World, 43
  What's Your Clue That You're Getting Off Target?, 43–44
  What's Your Strategy?, 46
  see also Wrap-Up slides
Special Event topic, 121–125
Special interests, 224
Specific praise, 85*b*, 222
Stress, Frustration, and Disappointment and Strategies to Feel Better slide, 42
Stuck on a Detail routine, 8*b*, 89*b*, 115*b*
Stuck on a Detail Versus Big Picture Thinking slide, 7–9
Student engagement, xiii–xiv, 221
Student Workbook, vii

Three Flexible Thinking Tricks to Deal with Frustration and Disappointment slide, 57–58
Topics
  The Longer-Term Event/Project—Efficient Planning = Power!, 165–170
  The Special Event, 121–125
  Celebration Day! The Plan B Party, 77–82
  Compromising Is a Win-Win, 84–95
  Coping Strategies to Feel Better and Get Unstuck When Overwhelmed, Stressed, Frustrated, or Disappointed, 40–53
  Developing a Personal Goal: Using Executive Function Skills in Our Real Lives, 178–188
  Efficient Planning—Staying Focused on the Big Picture Goal, 142–149
  Efficient Planning—Watching the Clock, 150–157
  Flexible Thinking, 2–14
  Flexible Thinking—Accepting and Letting Go of Frustration and Disappointment, 54–64
  Getting (and Staying) Excited About a Future Goal, 132–141
  Graduation, 211–217
  How to Increase Your Power to Help Yourself and the World, 29–39
  Plan Another Special Event Together Using Compromise Skills, 113–120
  Plan A/Plan B = More Power, 15–28
  Preparing for Graduation: Celebrating Our Executive Function Skills, 204–210
  Pulling It All Together—Using All the Key Vocabulary/Skills to Finalize the Plan, 158–164
  Putting a Plan on Trial (Checking Your Plan Before Trying It Out), 65–76
  Putting Personal Plans on Trial, 196–203
  Reviewing The Special Event, 126–130
  Reviewing the Longer-Term Event/Project: Learning from Our Successes and Challenges, 171–176
  Should I Compromise?, 96–104
  Try Out Your Compromise Skills, 105–112
  Using Executive Function Skills for Personal Goals, 189–195
Tracking the Power Level for Our Group slide, 34–35
Troubleshooting FAQs, 221–225, 225*t*
Try Out Your Compromise Skills topic, 105–112

Index

Unexpected behaviors, reasons for, xv*t*, 225*t*
Using Executive Function Skills for Personal Goals topic, 189–195
Using Executive Function Skills in Everyday Life to Get More Power slide, 191–192
Using the Executive Function Skills in Our Day-to-Day Lives slide, 180–181

Visuals, xiii, xiv, 223
    Feelings Target, 42–43, 50–52
    How to Compromise visual, 107

Web Quest: Feelings in the World slide, 43
What's Your Clue That You're Getting Off Target? slide, 43–44
What's Your Strategy? slide, 46
Why Are We Learning How to Gain More Power? wrap-up slide, 36
Why Are We Practicing Compromise? wrap-up slide, 109
Why Are We Practicing Goal Setting and Planning? wrap-up slide wrap-up slide, 128–129
Why Are We Thinking Through Our Plans (Putting Them on Trial)? wrap-up slide, 199–200
"Why," focusing on, xiv, 221
Why Is Compromise Powerful? wrap-up slide, 91–92
Why Is It Important to Know When to Compromise? wrap-up slide, 101–102
Why Is It Important to Use Executive Function Skills Every Day? wrap-up slide, 192
Why Learn Coping Strategies? wrap-up slide, 47
Why Learn to Keep Our Eyes on the Prize for Longer-Term Goals? wrap-up slide, 138
Why Practice Coming Up with Plan Bs? wrap-up slide, 23–24
Why Practice Flexibility? wrap-up slide, 9
Why Practice Managing Frustration and Disappointment? wrap-up slide, 62
Why Review the Special Event or Project? wrap-up slide, 174
Why Work Toward Personal Goals? wrap-up slide, 183
Words/ideas, students struggling to accept, 23*b*
Working memory, definition of, xi
Worksheets, vii
    Unit 1, 11–14, 25–28, 38–39, 48–53, 63–64, 74–76, 81–82
    Unit 2, 93–95, 103–104, 110–112, 119–120, 124–125, 130
    Unit 3, 139–141, 147–149, 155–157, 162–164, 168–170, 175–176
    Unit 4, 184–188, 193–195, 201–203, 208–210, 215–217
Wrap-Up slides
    Why Are We Learning How to Gain More Power?, 36
    Why Are We Practicing Compromise?, 109
    Why Are We Practicing Goal Setting and Planning?, 128–129
    Why Are We Thinking Through Our Plans (Putting Them on Trial)?, 199–200
    Why Is Compromise Powerful?, 91–92
    Why Is It Important to Know When to Compromise?, 101–102
    Why Is It Important to Use Executive Function Skills Every Day?, 192
    Why Learn Coping Strategies?, 47
    Why Learn to Keep Our Eyes on the Prize for Longer-Term Goals?, 138
    Why Practice Coming Up with Plan Bs?, 23–24
    Why Practice Flexibility?, 9
    Why Practice Managing Frustration and Disappointment?, 62
    Why Review the Special Event or Project?, 174
    Why Work Toward Personal Goals?, 183